A Glorious Disaster

A Glorious Disaster

BARRY GOLDWATER'S
Presidential Campaign and the
Origins of the Conservative Movement

J. William Middendorf II

A Member of the Perseus Books Group
New York

Books published by Basic Books are available at special discounts for bulk
purchases in the United States by corporations, institutions, and other
organizations. For more information, please contact the Special Markets
Department at the Perseus Books Group, 11 Cambridge Center, Cambridge
MA 02142, or call (617) 252-5298 or (800) 255-1514, or e-mail
special.markets@perseusbooks.com.

Designed by Brent Wilcox
Set in 11 point New Baskerville

Library of Congress Cataloging-in-Publication Data
Middendorf, John William, 1924–
    A glorious disaster : Barry Goldwater's presidential campaign and the origins
of the conservative movement / J. William Middendorf II.
        p.   cm.
    Includes bibliographical references and index.
    ISBN-13: 978-0-465-04573-0
    ISBN-10: 0-465-04573-1
    1. Presidents—United States—Election—1964.   2. Goldwater, Barry M.
(Barry Morris), 1909–1998.   3. Presidential candidates—United States—
Biography.   4. Legislators—United States—Biography.   5. Middendorf, John
William, 1924–   6. Political consultants—United States—Biography.
7. Goldwater, Barry M. (Barry Morris), 1909–1998—Friends and associates.
8. Political campaigns—United States—History—20th century.
9. Conservatism—United States—History—20th century.   10. United States—
Politics and government—1963–1969.   I. Title.
    E850.M53   2006
    324.973'0923—dc22
                                                                    2006020246

10 9 8 7 6 5 4 3 2 1

To Jerry Milbank, my mentor;

Peter O'Donnell, my hero;

*and Ed Feulner, who helped guide
the conservative movement
from fledgling to eagle*

Goldwater won the election of 1964. It just took 16 years to count the votes.

GEORGE WILL

Contents

Preface

SHORTLY AFTER SENATOR Barry Goldwater was trounced in the presidential election of 1964, Robert Novak wrote, in *The Agony of the G.O.P. 1964,* that "this debacle . . . was the inevitable outcome of the Goldwater nomination." "How, then," Novak asked, "did this nomination—one that violated every precept of American politics—come about? And will the damage it caused—damage threatening the very existence of the two-party system—prove irreparable?"

The short answer to the second question is no. Whatever damage the campaign may have caused—a media fixation at the time—it did not prevent the Republicans from winning five of the next six presidential elections. Winning, perhaps, not in spite of the Goldwater nomination, but because of it.

And though there is no short answer to Bob Novak's first question, the long answer is a fascinating story—and one that I may be uniquely positioned to tell, as I was one of the small group of men and women who, convinced that the most popular conservative of the day was the best choice to bring rationality to the federal government, persuaded him to make the run. The story has been told before, often by authors copying earlier authors, but it has never been fully explained. We did not violate *every* precept of American politics, but we did create some new moves that are now essential strategies for any Republican campaign. Barry Goldwater became, for a time, the most vilified man in American politics, and he remains to this day one of the most misunderstood. But his 1964 campaign represented nothing less than a political revolution. Understanding the true scope of that revolution is vital to understanding what came after.

The story begins with a clandestine effort involving only a few dozen people, a small group of "revolutionaries" who organized what has been described as the first true presidential draft in history. While Goldwater was indeed publicly reluctant, he was privately somewhat encouraging, and even though we were organized as the "Draft Goldwater Committee," I would say he was not "drafted" into the contest so much as nudged. To sweeten the nudge, we began, years ahead of time, to develop a true grassroots campaign, quietly filling vacant Republican Party posts with supporters at every level—precinct, district, and state. The candidate went to the 1964 Republican Convention with the winning votes in his pocket.

And came out of it having already lost the election. We just didn't know it at the time.

Goldwater did not lose the race because he was an "extremist" or a captive of the radical right. Despite what is claimed in many—if not most—published accounts, he did not advocate using nuclear weapons in Vietnam, did not call for the elimination of Social Security, and was not an opponent of civil rights. Those were charges laid on him by Republican opponents before the nomination, carried on by the Democrats in the fall campaign, and kept alive to this day by the ongoing mythology surrounding Goldwater's place in American politics.

He lost for a combination of reasons: He was sabotaged by Republican competitors, advised poorly by a well-meaning but inexperienced and headstrong campaign staff of longtime cronies, and damaged by the illegal and unethical actions of his opponent, President Lyndon Johnson. He was often an inept campaigner, irritable and impatient. Because he so much wanted to get his message across in an unvarnished way, "shooting from the lip" was practically a campaign theme. The Senator Barry Morris Goldwater who seemed so bold, the leading conservative elected official in America who excited so much passionate support, was not always the Goldwater who showed up on the campaign trail. The former had the power of myth; the latter could have feet of clay.

Nevertheless, he changed American politics forever. The Goldwater campaign was established and run by men and women far younger than most elected officials. Our half-million volunteers were drawn from such conservative incubators as the Young Republican National Federation and Young Americans for Freedom. The Goldwater "revolution" pioneered the use of small-dollar donations and generated some 1.5 million contributions for the primaries and the campaign, an astonishing increase over the 50,000 supporters who had contributed to the 1960 Nixon campaign. Every one of those donors, no matter how small their contribution, became a committed supporter helping to lay the foundation for the growth of the conservative movement. We also submitted the first fully audited report of presidential campaign financing in U.S. history. Political fund-raising has never been the same.

The Goldwater campaign gave many of today's conservative politicians their first national hearing. By replacing the conventional wisdom of the Republican Party leaders in the Northeast (a "me, too" imitation of Democratic policies) with a refreshing conservative logic ("The government does not have an unlimited claim on the earnings of individuals"), we brought about a marked shift in Republican philosophy and geography—from liberal to conservative, and from the Northeast to the South and West. We created the conditions that put conservative Republicans back in power after more than thirty years of domination by the liberal eastern establishment—the so-called "Country Club" Republicans, exemplified by governors Thomas E. Dewey, Nelson A. Rockefeller, William Scranton, and the 1960 vice-presidential candidate, Henry Cabot Lodge. Mostly wealthy, mostly old money. You may recall the ditty:

Here's to the city of Boston,
The land of the bean and the cod,

Where the Lowells speak only to Cabots,
And the Cabots speak only to God.

It wasn't a joke. This inbred crew grew more and more like the Democrats with every passing year (perhaps they were suffering from the Stockholm syndrome), but they argued that the public should elect Republicans instead. They would do exactly what the Democrats were doing but more efficiently—because so many of them had gone to the Harvard Business School.

The organization that we created to win the Republican nomination for Barry Goldwater—state by state, county by county, precinct by precinct—and the conservative vision that attracted so many supporters came to represent a new baseline for the Republican Party. The defeat in 1964 left behind a cadre of millions of true believers, a loyal base of future convention delegates and activists. In the very next election, the 1966 midterm, the "destroyed" Republican Party gained 700 seats in state legislatures, 8 governorships, 47 seats in the House, and 3 in the Senate. Nixon was nominated in 1968 with the decisive support of the Draft Goldwater leaders and delegates. I believe it is safe to say that without Goldwater, there would have been no Reagan or Bush administrations—nor even, perhaps, the centrist administration of Bill Clinton. Our efforts to elect Barry Goldwater gave muscle to the embryonic conservative movement, which, indeed, had been our basic goal all along.

I joined the Goldwater Draft in 1962 as a thirty-seven-year-old investment banker with a growing interest in politics. I served as Barry's campaign treasurer through the primaries and then as treasurer of the Republican National Committee (RNC) for the election, staying on in that position through the Nixon campaign of 1968, after which I was appointed ambassador to the Netherlands. I was a member of Goldwater's inner circle from the start and remained part of it throughout the campaign—coordinating finances, arranging TV and speaker schedules, going on the road with the candidate, taking notes, recording conversations, saving documents (at my own expense, I hired a photographer to follow Barry everywhere), and creating the extensive personal archive—perhaps the most complete of any presidential campaign—from which this narrative is drawn.

In this, I would be remiss if I did not acknowledge the assistance of two retired naval officers, members of my personal staff when I was secretary of the Navy (1974–1977); some years later, Eric Berryman helped me assemble and catalogue my archives, and Brayton Harris—a brilliant compiler—assisted in winnowing down to the more useful material. And I must offer a public appreciation for my editor, William Frucht, whose guiding hand ensured that this narrative was not just a collection of anecdotes but actually had a beginning, a middle, and an end.

The thoughts, observations, recollections, opinions—and errors, if any—are, however, my own.

PART I

Goldwater, in some imperceptible investiture, had been crowned king of the nation's conservatives.

TIME, AUGUST 8, 1960

CHAPTER 1

The Secret Meeting

O N NOVEMBER 10, 1962, F. Clifton White, a New York–based public relations counselor and political consultant, sent me a brief note offering kind comments on my work as treasurer for a losing congressional campaign in Connecticut. "Congratulations on the tremendous run," he wrote. "I'm sure you feel as I do that it was a very important vote."

My profession was investment banking; my partner, Austen Colgate—a member of the family that was famous for toothpaste and for being instrumental in the founding of Colgate University—and I had recently set up our own business, Middendorf, Colgate & Company. We bought a seat on the New York Stock Exchange for $155,000; the price soon dropped to $90,000; we took that as bad timing, not an omen. Within a few years we would have offices in Boston, Baltimore, San Francisco, and New York.

But my personal interests were gravitating toward public policy and politics. I served as a Republican block captain for the 9th District of Manhattan in the 1948 election (along with almost everyone else, I predicted that New York Governor Thomas Dewey would win over President Harry Truman). A few years later, after moving to Connecticut, I became a member of the Greenwich Representative Town Meeting. Fellow member Jeremiah Milbank, Jr., became my mentor— five years older and wiser, he had solid political experience. Jerry's day job was running the Milbank Memorial Fund, which focused on issues of health policy. His great-grandfather had financed inventor Gail Borden's development of canned milk and made a fortune providing the product to the Union Army during the Civil War.

My next-door neighbor in Greenwich was Prescott Bush—the U.S. senator and father of George H.W. Bush. At that time, George (whom everyone called "Poppy") was just getting started in the oil business in Texas, but he already had an interest in politics and spent a lot of time in Connecticut. Some evenings, when this old Yale University clan had gathered, I could sit on my back porch, Scotch in hand, and hear the sounds of the "Whiffenpoof Song" drifting across the lawn. The senator and his sons—Poppy, Prescott (Jr.), and Johnny—made a pretty good quartet.

Jerry and I frequently teamed up with Pres Bush, Jr., on local campaigns—we learned the ropes on the financial side, with winning candidates for local offices, the state legislature, and the U.S. Congress. At the Representative Town Meetings I learned a couple of other lessons. One had to do with a phenomenon of local politics that I call the "stoplight" mentality. Most people cannot get their arms around a really large civic project and thus pay it little attention, but if the project is small, everyone will not only understand it but have a lot to say. Greenwich wanted to put a stoplight out on one of the back roads and had a contractor's estimate of $24,000. That sparked a debate that continued for weeks. Was $24,000 the right cost, or should it be $17,000 or $28,000? Should the yellow light be set to a 30- or a 45-second cycle? Meanwhile, a proposal for a new $15 million high school sailed through in a couple of days.

Another thing I learned at the town meetings was that few residents knew the party affiliation, let alone the names, of most local political leaders—but everyone seemed to have a complaint or an opinion on the major issues of the day.

Clif's letter invited me to a meeting on Sunday, December 2, at the Essex Inn in downtown Chicago. "This is *the* important one," he wrote. He didn't have to mention the purpose—I was well aware of his quiet efforts to set up a "Goldwater for President" movement, and John M. Lupton, our losing congressional candidate, was already a member. Jerry and I had been involved, too, but on the fringes. Clif's fund-raising was anemic, and we had helped underwrite the rent on his modest two-room office in Midtown Manhattan. As part of the effort to avoid attention, the sign on the door said only "3505," although Clif's printed stationery identified the tenant as "F. Clifton White & Associates, Inc."

Clif's invitation began my transformation from Wall Street to a life of public service.

The seeds of the 1964 Goldwater candidacy were planted in 1960, when his name was placed in nomination at the Republican National Convention. Goldwater's supporters harbored no illusions but hoped that a good showing would put him on the short list for vice president. At the proper moment, Goldwater took the podium to announce his withdrawal and threw his support to Nixon. Nixon chose Henry Cabot Lodge as his running mate, and loyalist Goldwater hit the road on their behalf, making some 177 speeches. No matter: As we all know, Nixon and Lodge lost the election to John F. Kennedy and Lyndon B. Johnson by only 118,550 out of some 68 million votes cast. Nixon, after some brief soul-searching, decided not to challenge the result, even though there was compelling evidence of vote fraud in Illinois and, possibly, Texas.

The night he pledged support to Nixon, Goldwater said something else from the podium: "Let's grow up, conservatives!" he challenged. "If we want to take this party back, and I think we can someday, let's get to work." *Time* magazine reported: "Goldwater, in some imperceptible investiture, had been crowned king of the nation's conservatives."

Two months later, inspired by that ringing call—or, perhaps, by their own inner demons—a group of conservative firebrands met at the home of intellectual provocateur William F. Buckley, Jr., and launched Young Americans for Freedom (YAF). Though perhaps more philosophical than practical, they helped set the stage for what was to come.

Buckley first made a name for himself with the publication of his devastating 1951 book *God and Man at Yale,* which indicted the university—accurately, to my mind—as a bastion of official atheism and collectivism. In 1955, with a group of like-minded friends and relatives, he launched the *National Review*—in support of which, for many years, I wrote the occasional check. Thanks to Bill Buckley, conservative politics in America has never been the same since.

On September 11, 1960, YAF issued the seminal "Sharon Statement" (written by M. Stanton Evans and named after the town in which Buckley was living), which began, "In this time of moral and political crises, it is the responsibility of the youth of America to affirm certain eternal truths."

Such as:

> That liberty is indivisible, and political freedom cannot long exist without economic freedom;
> That the purpose of government is to protect those freedoms through the preservation of internal order, the provision of national defense, and the administration of justice;
> That when government ventures beyond these rightful functions, it accumulates power, which tends to diminish order and liberty.

An editorial in the *New York Sunday News* gave a more man-in-the-street explanation:

> In recent weeks, an organization called Young Americans for Freedom has been curdling the blood of any number of radicals and "liberals."
> Roughly, its philosophy agrees with that of Sen. Barry Goldwater (R-Ariz.), but it is not tied to the political chariot of Sen. Gold-

water or anybody else. Its members are out to annoy, contradict and harass "liberals," radicals and Communists in every lawful way they can, and to convert as many of their fellow Americans to conservatism as the good Lord will let them.

They are fed up with professors who preach socialistic welfare statism and Keynesian spend-and-spendism, in season and out. Many are fed up with hearing New Deal philosophy at home, from parents who have not had a new political or economic thought since about 1935. They insist on thinking for themselves and disputing such stock liberal ideas as "the idea that the government should do more and more for people while people do less and less for themselves."

Here's a tip to practical politicians of both parties. . . . Better keep a sharp eye on the young conservatives, gentlemen, because it is eminently possible that they are riding the "wave of the future" in this country.

That prediction was validated just a year later, in 1961, when YAF demonstrated remarkable skill in staging a conservative spectacle in the heart of liberal New York City: a full-house rally at Madison Square Garden. Some 18,000 cheering spectators wouldn't let Barry speak—for almost an hour, by some accounts, but more likely for about twenty minutes—so great was their enthusiasm. Eighteen thousand voices chanted "We want Barry!" When Barry, who had been introduced as "the conservatives'" choice for president, finally got their attention, he said, "Well, if you'll shut up, you'll get him." With tickets priced from $1 to $25, the rally added a reported $80,000 to the YAF treasury.

The *Sunday News* had put a finger on the pulse of a generation, dissatisfied and disaffected conservatives. I was most definitely one of them, although a Johnny-come-lately to the cause. My early political and economic thinking had been conditioned in the quasi-Marxist world of eastern prep schools and Harvard; when I entered the university in

1943, I was an unfocused and mildly irresponsible student. Released from the strict prep-school environment, I discovered that partying was more interesting than studying.

A cautionary tale: At six foot four, I was, technically speaking, a "Big Man on Campus," but frankly, I was pretty much an outsider. I was awkward, with a compromised complexion, and shy to a fault. Imagine my surprise and pleasure, my first week at school, at being overwhelmed by a team of absolutely stunning girls wearing some sort of Eastern European peasant garb. They wanted me to join their club and perhaps thereby enjoy their friendship. The club was the John Reed Society. At the time, the name meant no more to me than the Sons of the American Revolution. I was tempted—the girls were vivacious—but the membership fee was $10, so I declined. It was only later that I learned that John Reed had been a Harvard graduate of the class of 1910, a radical journalist and a certified Communist. Had I accepted their offer to join this Communist club, you most likely would not be holding this book today. I certainly wouldn't have made it past the confirmation hearings for the presidential appointments that grew out of the tale that unfolds below.

Three things soon happened that would change my life. First, I was accepted into a World War II naval officer training program, which enforced discipline. Second, I became a disciple of the Austrian libertarian school of economics, having studied under Joseph Schumpeter (an odd-man-out at Harvard, later named by the *Wall Street Journal* as the most important economist of the twentieth century) and Ludwig Von Mises (at New York University). Schumpeter and Von Mises saw entrepreneurship as a major driving force in economic development, considered private property—protected by an independent judiciary—essential to the efficient use of resources, and held that government interference in market processes was usually counterproductive.

Third, I read Friedrich Hayek's 1944 *The Road to Serfdom*, which had been described on the cover as "A classic warning against the

dangers to freedom inherent in social planning." Hayek wrote of en-
croachments on liberty and human dignity, on the abuse of government power, and on the danger of policies created to further social
goals. He warned that social planning could eventually destroy all individual freedom—political no less than economic—as it already had
in Germany and Russia.

The Austrians helped me create a frame of reference: People with
whom I disagree believe that the government is a working tool that
should be used to shape society; I believe that society is shaped by individuals. People with whom I disagree believe that earning a profit
means abusing workers and that employing hundreds of people is a
form of exploitation. The demonization of all business owners, of
course, makes no sense: They provide the jobs whereby most Americans earn a living. Demonizing big business just because it's big
makes even less sense, especially in a global economy where American firms may already be at a disadvantage. But planning every aspect
of the lives of those "abused" workers—economic and otherwise—is
seen by some as a holy calling. More people with whom I disagree.

I had discovered a new world—the world of economic conservatism—and, because of this, found myself drawn to the political
process. Politics provided a way of taking these ideas, in which we so fervently believed, beyond theory and into practical application. For a
time, Barry Goldwater became the figure at the center of that world.

Right after the 1960 elections, a number of Goldwater's friends
tried to talk him into making a serious run for 1964. He would have
none of it, but his popularity continued to grow apace.

Goldwater was charismatic, a born salesman. In the one year he
spent at Phoenix Union High School in Arizona, he got abysmal
grades—and was elected class president. His father sent him off to
Staunton Military Academy in the hope that the school might instill
some sense of discipline in his wayward son; the academy kept asking
his father to take him back, but in four years he became captain of
the football team and the outstanding cadet in his class. He was offered

an appointment to the U.S. Military Academy at West Point, but his
father's poor health led him to decline.

Barry was a solid citizen. After his father's death in 1929, he helped
transform the family-owned department store in Phoenix from middle-
grade middle class to an upscale equivalent of Neiman Marcus. Four
months before the Japanese attack on Pearl Harbor, he talked his way
into a desk job with the U.S. Air Force—though he was overage and
not physically fit (his knees were damaged from playing semi-pro bas-
ketball). Since he already had a private pilot's license, he soon had
his wings. He ferried P-47 fighters to the Mediterranean and saw action in the China-Burma-India theater, came out of the war a lieutenant colonel, and organized the Arizona Air National Guard. By
1962, he was a major general in the reserves with a logbook listing
pilot hours in seventy-five different types of aircraft.

He was elected to the nonpartisan Phoenix City Council in 1949,
and to the U.S. Senate in 1952 and 1958. While in the Senate, he
served twice as chairman of the Republican Senatorial Campaign Committee, a job that took him all over the country to raise money and
speak in support of Republican candidates, conservative and liberal
alike. He offered blunt descriptions of what was wrong with America
and challenged the conventional wisdom that the government was the
solution to all ills—that only the government had enough money to
tackle all the problems of society and the collective wisdom to make the
right decisions. He charged that the government was engaged in activities in which it had no legitimate business, that the government was reluctant to pursue victory over "the tyrannical forces" of international
communism, that "powerful" union officials were taking advantage of
the working man, and that high taxes removed money from the mar-
ketplace where it belonged. One paragraph from his 1960 book, *The
Conscience of a Conservative,* supplies an apt summary of his views:

I have little interest in streamlining government or in making it
more efficient, for I mean to reduce its size. I do not undertake to

promote welfare, for I propose to extend freedom. My aim is not to pass laws, but to repeal them. It is not to inaugurate new programs, but to cancel old ones that do violence to the Constitution, or that have failed in their purpose, or that impose on the people an unwarranted financial burden. I will not attempt to discover whether legislation is "needed" before I have first determined whether it is constitutionally permissible. And if I should later be attacked for neglecting my constituents' interests, I shall reply that I was informed their main interest is liberty and that in that cause, I am doing the very best I can.

The senator found a willing audience: conservatives who felt locked out of the political process, and who responded with an enthusiasm that at times slipped into adulation. By the summer of 1961, Goldwater was getting 200 invitations a month for personal appearances, and his mail was running to 800 letters a day. He and a ghost (his senatorial campaign manager, Stephen Shadegg) wrote a widely syndicated newspaper column, and *The Conscience of a Conservative,* a collection of his speeches assembled and edited by Brent Bozell, was selling at the rate of 50,000 copies a month. Total sales through 1964 would reach 3.5 million; a second book, *Why Not Victory?,* dealt with the rise of communism and was published in 1962. At one point in 1961, thirteen national magazines were simultaneously working on cover stories about Goldwater, including *Popular Mechanics,* whose editors liked the fact that he was an inveterate tinkerer. A *Time* article published on June 23 was not the predictable "Arizona cowboy goes to Washington" story but took as its focus "the hottest political figure this side of Jack Kennedy." The fifty-two-year-old Goldwater, *Time* said, was "traveling tirelessly about the land to champion the cause of the Republican Party, U.S. conservatism and his own variety of rugged individualism." His "unabashed, unapologetic conservatism has struck a responsive note in a nation wondering if there is some clear-cut alternative to an ever-expanding welfare state," the article said.

When *Time* asked Goldwater if he hoped to make a run for the presidency, he replied, "I have no plans for it. I have no staff for it, no program for it, and no ambition for it." Then, this grandson of a Jewish peddler (raised as an Episcopalian) added with a grin: "Besides, I've got a Jewish name. . . . I don't know if the country is ready for me."

Perhaps encouraged by *Time*—or feeling it was an idea whose time had come—a close-knit group of political conservatives, to several of whom Goldwater had already said "not interested," began nevertheless to construct the movement that would make him the Republican candidate for president in 1964.

The effort began on July 10, 1961, when Ohio Republican Congressman John Ashbrook (freshman class of 1960) and *National Review* publisher William Rusher had lunch together. They met to discuss a troublesome change in the leadership of the Young Republican National Federation (YRNF), a thirty-year-old social-political organization that was then (and remains today) an incubator for conservative leadership. Ashbrook had started his political career as president of YRNF in the biannual election of 1957, with the backing of longtime YRNF string-pullers Rusher and Clif White. But Rusher and Clif moved away to pursue other interests, and the incoming 1961 YRNF president was, for the first time in a long time, not a conservative but of the eastern tilt. The congressman and the publisher were concerned.

The conversation drifted to what they saw as a leadership vacuum in the Republican Party—gentrification at the top, superannuated officials out of touch with the present, let alone the future. But at the same time, there was a cadre of young (and conservative) Republicans who could be brought forward with the right encouragement. Rusher noted, "If we held a meeting of our old Young Republican group, it would probably comprise about the third or fourth largest faction in the Republican Party." After lunch, Ashbrook showed Rusher a file cabinet full of YRNF contact information, and the wheels started turning.

Three days later, Rusher had lunch with Clif and carried on the discussion. Clif volunteered that he had his own files, not just YRNF contacts but many others. Perhaps, he mused, they could combine the files and launch a nationwide organization committed to nominating a conservative candidate for president—or, at the least, to influencing the 1964 platform. After a few more conversations among themselves, Ashbrook, Rusher, White, and some others determined to move forward, with Clif taking the lead.

Thus began what Robert Novak would call "one of the most remarkable clandestine operations in American political history." A writer for the *Harvard Crimson* would describe Goldwater's eventual nomination as the result of "a secret decision" by "the White Machine." Secret, yes. Machine? A bit over the top.

Rusher, Ashbrook, and White began with a few dozen carefully selected friends who held compatible philosophies, were interested in participating, and could be expected to keep a secret. The early meetings focused on broad concepts: Could the conservatives take control of the party and nominate a conservative—Goldwater was frequently mentioned—and if so, how could this best be accomplished? Their resources included boundless enthusiasm and a passionate belief in conservative government.

The "how" part, they decided, was a given. Working with local, district, and state organizations, they would have to ensure, wherever possible, that committed conservatives became delegates to the next Republican National Convention. Only sixteen states held primary elections, selecting 541 delegates; 767 were selected by caucus—the good old-fashioned smoke-filled room. Six hundred and fifty-five votes were needed to win the nomination. A candidate might lose every primary or enter none, but by controlling each caucus, could still walk into the convention with the winning votes in hand.

The mechanics of delegate selection varied from state to state, but some portion of the party machinery always came into play. Precinct committeemen—down at the level where people worried about stoplights, where they felt their voice could make a difference—were often the most influential players, and precinct committeemen were selected two years before the presidential nominating convention. Ergo, it would be essential to start early. It was no small task: They would have to get organized; have a thorough understanding of the often arcane local statutes, bylaws, and customs of each precinct; identify solid conservative leaders; motivate conservatives to become involved and stand for election to various positions; and fill empty slots in the party organization. Indeed, at that time, as many as half of the state, county, and local GOP committee posts were vacant, and no one seemed to care. The plan was to quietly put conservatives into those jobs, without fanfare, so as not to alert the other side, and create a pipeline for sending sympathetic delegates to the 1964 Republican National Convention. Although this was not exactly a "machine," Clif White most certainly was the driver.

By the time of the December 2 gathering in Chicago—which Jerry and I attended—the White-Ashbrook-Rusher group had expanded to fifty-five members and was ready for action. We later would be dubbed "a bunch of amateurs" by Bob Novak and electoral historian Theodore White—even, at times, by Goldwater himself. If by that they meant "unpaid," most of us qualified (Clif was drawing a modest salary). If they meant "inexperienced," I think the term applied to none of us. I may have been an idealistic thirty-seven-year-old soon to be caught up in the glamour of presidential politics, but I had been walking a lot of political streets. Other attendees included members of Congress, current and former Republican state chairpersons, and an assortment of elected and appointed state and federal officials. Leaders of our movement would say that the "amateur" label could more aptly have been applied to a few individuals who came along later in the process, took command of the campaign, and botched the job. They were not part of our movement.

More to the point, Clif White was the consummate professional politician. Average voters (even, I believe, most candidates) think of politics in terms of media exposure, headline-grabbing rallies, and demonstrations. The professional's lexicon includes petitions, county chairmen, precinct captains, phone banks, convention tactics, *Robert's Rules of Order,* voter registration, poll watchers, and fund-raising. Clif White was a professional.

Clif opened our meeting with an announcement: "We're going to take over the Republican Party." Those words were later to be widely quoted, and the citation was accurate—as far as it went. The media usually left out the second half of Clif's statement: "and make it the conservative instrument in American politics."

Clif reported that he had met several times with Goldwater, and in explaining the purpose of the group, he said it would set out to encourage support and raise funds for conservative candidates, with Barry Goldwater as first choice. The senator, Clif said, thought raising money was a good idea, but expecting him to run for president was not. He had not agreed to endorse the effort, but neither had he asked Clif to cease and desist. Our goal was to coax him aboard.

We needed 655 winning votes; Clif believed that Barry could easily get 451 from southern and western states, with the balance coming from states we felt were sympathetic to the cause. He also handicapped the Electoral College, adding up the states where Nixon had won in 1960 and those that barely gave a majority to Kennedy and were possibly winnable in 1964. Clif believed that Goldwater could carry the necessary 270 electoral votes.

Clif submitted a budget for the eighteen months leading up to the convention: We would need $3.2 million (pushing $25 million in 2006 dollars; use a general factor of 7.5 in making conversions). About half would finance entry in the primaries; the rest was for rent, the convention, and staff salaries—a campaign director, a public relations manager, a research director, three financial and fund-raising experts, five field men, an office manager, and six secretaries. For 1964, we should add two more public relations men, four additional researchers, five field men, and four secretaries.

With the stage thus set, it was time for us to get to work. We organized a public relations committee, a survey committee to work with polling firms, and a research committee to identify issues of greatest concern to the public. There was to be a women's division as well, and the chairs of the various committees and the head of the women's division would form a strategy committee.

We created a checklist. In December, we would organize the financial operation. During January 1963, we'd establish our group in proper legal fashion, and in February, after Congress returned from the winter recess, we'd meet with Goldwater, show him that we were serious, and seek, if not his blessing, at least a sustained interest. We hoped to make a public announcement in March or April, and from April through June, we would mount petition drives ("Sign here to encourage Senator Goldwater to run for president") and set up state-by-state affiliated committees. October would be the time to review what we had accomplished so far and make needed adjustments. By November, we could focus on selected local elections to test the effectiveness of efforts to that date.

At one point, someone asked, "Who wants to be finance chairman?" I didn't see any hands raised. Most of the men were politicians or industrialists, not financiers. I volunteered to be treasurer. I was not well enough connected with the national organization to take on the job of finance chairman, but my Wall Street background and campaign experience in Connecticut gave me the confidence that I could keep track of spending, establish controls, and maintain an impeccable audit trail. Chicago entrepreneur (Fannie May Candies) and philanthropist J.D. Stetson ("Stets") Coleman, Jerry Milbank, and I became "trustees" of the finance committee, pending appointment of a real chairman.

We briefly agonized over the challenge of raising $3 million, but Stets got things moving when he declared, "Look, everybody's been talking about how we need all this money, but who's going to put some up? I pledge $25,000." I added $10,000 of my own, and within an hour, we all had pledged, to a total of $285,000. A few days later, Fred LaRue was among the first to honor his pledge with a $25,000 cashier's check, from "Republicans in Mississippi, the poorest state in the nation."

I like to think of December 2 as a watershed, the beginning of a practical modern conservative political movement. It was our symbolic "St. Crispin's Day," on a fictitious version of which Shakespeare's Henry V told his inner circle, "From now until the end of the world, we . . . shall be remembered. We few, we band of brothers."

We were in business.

CHAPTER 2

The Brush-Off

BARRY GOLDWATER AND I were acquaintances before the December meeting, but not close. A few years earlier, I had attended some fund-raisers at which he was the star attraction, and, like any good politician who knows how to mind his manners, Barry had acknowledged my contributions with brief notes. They were friendly, but impersonal, as befitting our relationship at that time.

Later, Milbank and I had taken on a special challenge for the National Republican Senatorial Committee to raise funds for six key 1962 senatorial races. The premise was that incumbents did not always have a free ride to reelection—especially those who might have to travel great distances, fighting the schedule in the Senate, to meet with voters at home. Some Republican senators had been defeated by margins of less than 1 percent by opponents who could campaign at home all year round. These incumbents might benefit from funds to assist with "voter education"—a transparent fiction, but it meant that the contributions were not reportable campaign funds. Around the nation, committees were set up to help. One of our candidates, New Hampshire Senator Norris Cotton, had three committees working on his behalf at the same time. He was challenged by an opponent just before the election for not having revealed the "contributions." The opponent wanted him declared ineligible. Senator Cotton won on the merits—as spelled out in the law, but not necessarily as they might have been decided by common sense.

We explained to potential contributors that all donations would be deposited directly: Nothing would be siphoned off for overhead. If any candidate should drop out, his share would be distributed to the others. To establish our credibility, we informed them that "Senator Barry Goldwater, who, as Chairman of the Senate Republican Campaign Committee, is directly responsible for successful Republican Senate campaigns next year, has given his approval to our effort."

By August 1962, I was a member of the New York Advisory Committee to the National Republican Senatorial Committee and was asked to take on a new task. This would mirror the earlier efforts, but this time, instead of helping Republican incumbents, we would be raising funds for Republican challengers in races with Democratic incumbents. Our efforts were successful, and the thank-you notes I received from Barry grew more personal.

Building Republican coalitions was then in fashion. Two weeks before our December 2 meeting, the *New York Herald-Tribune* reported that New Jersey Republican Senator Clifford P. Case was seeking "a cooperative arrangement among the party's moderate and liberal officials." These included governors Nelson Rockefeller of New York, William Scranton of Pennsylvania, and George Romney of Michigan—all of whom had just been elected (or reelected). Senator Case and friends were not accused of having any nefarious purpose. But our group, also working toward a "cooperative arrangement," was soon to be raked over the coals for "splintering" the party.

The Case meeting had been announced to the press; our Essex gathering, like the earlier sessions, was held in secret. There were three simple reasons for this: We didn't want to alert the "establishment" to the effort; we didn't want to force Barry into a corner; and we wanted the opportunity to lay some groundwork, build an organization, and establish an agenda before we had to start answering questions.

Our secrecy lasted less than a day. There was, it seemed, a spy in our midst—with an agenda of his own and a hidden tape recorder. Or maybe there was just a hidden tape recorder, planted by an informed outsider—we never found out. However it was engineered, a synopsis of what we talked about and a list of attendees ended up in the hands of a reporter with the Associated Press, who had a story on the wire by the afternoon of December 3. Less than two hours later, the CBS *Evening News with Walter Cronkite* featured a Chicago-bureau reporter and some hastily grabbed footage of a room at the Essex, where, he noted, a group of prominent Republicans had met to plot a presidential campaign for Barry Goldwater. The CBS footage was of the wrong suite in the hotel—Stets Coleman's room, I believe, which was not nearly large enough to hold the group—but the essence of the story was correct.

As for the print media, the story that made headlines on December 4 was also accurate in the main, although we preferred the *San Francisco Examiner*'s version—"Secret Move to Push Goldwater in 1964"—to the *New York Herald-Tribune*'s "Move to Block Rocky." The *New York Times* said we were "splintering" the Republican Party. The *Times* also reported Barry's reaction to the news: "I don't know a thing about it. I don't know who the group was, where they met or what it's all about. I did see or hear something about it today, but don't know a thing." This was a bit disingenuous. He had heard about it because Clif had called and warned him to expect inquiries from reporters.

We also could have done without the *Herald-Tribune*'s editorial of December 5, "The Folly of Factionalism, or, How to Fail Without Even Trying." It said: "The latest Republican drama, that somewhat secret meeting of conservatives in Chicago, should be appropriately titled, 'How to Fail in Politics Without Even Trying.' Neither the plotting to promote Sen. Goldwater for the Presidential candidacy nor the conspiracy to block Gov. Rockefeller contributes to the health or harmony of the party. . . . Whatever the exact details, the conservatives are guilty of bad timing, narrow motives and poor politics."

A few lines further on, however, the editor made a prescient point: "We don't blame the conservatives for dreaming of Barry Goldwater for President. The Rockefeller people are working with understandable zeal for their man, and the same can be said for supporters of Michigan's Romney and Pennsylvania's Scranton. But the point is, none of these men will have a chance and all their preparations will be purely academic if every faction pursues its own fractious way and the main goal of a party victory is submerged by the lesser goals of personal victory."

At a regular meeting of the Republican National Committee (RNC) later in the week, the news sparked some lively but not particularly argumentative conversation. Some party leaders were irritated to learn that we had raised a reported $250,000 for our purposes, while the party was struggling with a $400,000 deficit from the recent midterm elections.

The "move to block Rocky" theme was frequently and vigorously encouraged by the Rockefeller forces, which were hoping to create an impression that the governor was the underdog and in need of protection from a conservative juggernaut. This stance was undermined when James L. Wick, executive publisher of *Human Events,* reported that "the President's Inner Circle leaks to visitors that the only G.O.P. candidate causing loss of sleep in the White House is the New York governor." Wick assumed the leaks were a tactic to panic the Republicans into nominating Rockefeller—and he was right.

Meanwhile, Bobby Kennedy told "a senior Democratic Senator from the Deep South" that the First Family feared Goldwater far more than they feared Rockefeller. And the *Chicago Tribune* (March 26, 1963) ran a headline that read, "Kennedys Fear One Man in 1964 Election—Goldwater." As that issue was hitting the streets, delegates to the 1960 Republican National Convention were being asked by *Congressional Quarterly* who was most likely to get the 1964 nomination, Rockefeller or Goldwater. Better than 2 to 1 said "Rockefeller."

When asked which man they would prefer, the count was about 4 to 3 for Goldwater.

Some reports that came out later said we didn't pick a name for our group right away; others claimed we called ourselves "Draft Goldwater" right from the start—both are incorrect. My notes of the meeting clearly state, "Goldwater for President Committee." On December 11, 1962, Clif, Stets, Jerry, and I set up a "Goldwater for President" account with the First National Bank in Dallas. On December 19, I sent Barry a copy of a letter that I had just sent to state finance chairmen urging them to action. In my note to Barry, I wrote, "We have been amazed at the speed with which the money has come in." Below my signature appeared "Treasurer, Goldwater for President." There was no ambiguity in our minds, either about the name of our committee or its purpose.

Barry's true position, however, was unclear. We weren't sure whether he was interested in running for president, willing to tolerate but not participate in the effort, or totally opposed to it. The record is rife with confusing statements, contradictory remarks to the media, and conflicting "insider" accounts. I think the truth is that for a long time he was ambivalent about leaving the Senate but open to suggestion. Soon after the Chicago meeting, Barry asked Steve Shadegg if he would manage his 1964 campaign. Shadegg asked him if it would be for the Senate or the presidency? Barry said: "I still haven't made up my mind." They agreed to assume, for the time being, that the campaign would be for the Senate. "If I change my mind," Barry said, "you can change your plans."

On December 27, when Barry met with a group of friends in Phoenix, they told him that winning the nomination was "within the realm of reasonable possibility." There were issues, however. It would be very difficult to beat Kennedy, and if Goldwater ran and lost, he could lose any influence he might have had in the future. Sufficient funds could probably be raised for a national campaign, and a campaign organization could likely be put together. But it would not be wise, they said, for Barry to run for the Senate and the presidency at the same time. (In 1960, LBJ made a run for the Senate and the vice-presidency at the same time; he won both races, but could accept only one office. In a special election held in May 1961, John Tower became the first Republican since Reconstruction to be elected to the Senate from Texas.)

All in all, this was not very encouraging, and the situation was made even less so by a mid-December Gallup poll on Republican "presidential possibilities." Rockefeller came in at 41 percent; Nixon, 21 percent; Romney, 15 percent; Illinois Senator Everett Dirksen, 11 percent; and Goldwater, 4 percent. Goldwater must have questioned whether there was much interest in his candidacy, after all.

These thoughts were no doubt on his mind on January 14, 1963, when Clif visited him to report details of the December meeting and discuss progress to date and our plans for the future. Clif expected a friendly welcome, but instead he found an angry and personally distant man. Goldwater's reason for being angry was clear enough: Some of his colleagues from the eastern establishment had just maneuvered him off the Senate Policy Committee. The reason that he was distant didn't become apparent until later, when we realized that he didn't understand Clif's motives. Barry had been told (perhaps by the same person who had leaked the details of the Chicago meeting) that Clif was only in the game for a big salary and an enhanced reputation, and that he was looking for a big boost to his political consulting business. When I heard this, I thought, Clif? Clif was perhaps the most self-effacing man I'd ever known, and his salary from the movement was so modest that he had to draw from his children's college account to get by.

As Clif described the encounter, he was about to run through some details with Barry—focusing on funding, delegate predictions, and the like—when Goldwater stopped him and said he had no intention of running for president. Clif said, "Well, we thought we might have to draft you." At this Goldwater became incensed, replying, "Draft nothin', I told you I'm not going to run. And I'm telling you now, don't paint me into a corner. It's my political neck and I intend to have something to say about what happens to it."

Later that day, I stopped by Room 3505, expecting to find a happy man, fresh from the field of victory. Instead, I found Clif, his secretary, and a couple of other members of our group so depressed that they could have been holding a wake. As a morale-boosting contribution, I took everyone out to dinner.

At almost the same moment—give or take a couple of days—Barry was complaining to a writer for *Business Week* about the public image of the Republican Party. Back in 1961, as the Kennedy administration was about to take over, Republicans in Congress had hit upon a clever way to carry the party's message to the people—they created a weekly press conference starring the floor leaders, Senator Everett Dirksen and Congressman Charles Halleck. However, the so-called "Ev and Charlie Show" suffered from comparison with John F. Kennedy's witty press conferences and created the impression that the Republican Party was being led by a pair of behind-the-times warhorses. Commenting on these press conferences, one GOP congressman said: "There's Dirksen with his fuzzy hair and Halleck with his big red nose." Goldwater spoke for many of us when he said, "The image is wrong now. . . . They should give the American people a picture of Republicanism that is something other than two elderly men who have had a hard life and look it."

He seemed to agree that it was time for the Republican Party to put on a younger face. We just had to get him to agree with us about whose face it should be.

CHAPTER 3

The Draft

WORD OF THE BRUSH-OFF traveled fast. The newsletter of the
Republican National Committee, *Battle Line,* reported on January 16, 1963: "Senator Barry Goldwater urges his backers to give him
the rest of the year to decide about running for president in 1964, . . .
says present intention is to run for re-election to Senate in '64 'but I'd
rather stay in a fluid position for the rest of this year and then see
how the situation looks.'"

Of course, "fluid position" is not quite "I'm not going to run";
and "see how the situation looks" translates into finding demonstrated support and tangible finances. Whatever his true feelings,
however, his public disclaimers were not helpful; they dampened
our ability to raise money, and by fostering the impression that he
was not interested in running, they created a vacuum into which
Rockefeller moved. That standard-bearer for the liberal wing of the
Republican Party was getting his electoral ducks in a row. He assembled a personal staff of researchers, speechwriters, and political experts, and his field operatives were roaming the country lining up
supporters.

Rockefeller started with two big advantages over us. He had money
and passionate ambition. He could easily hire a talented campaign
team. Clif White's efforts, in contrast, were supported by handouts
from a few friends. He operated with a staff of two—himself and a

secretary—in support of a candidate who did not seem to want the nomination or to believe he could get it.

On January 23, I sent Barry a copy of a letter from Georgia businessman Howard ("Bo") Callaway. He had heard of our effort and had begun raising funds on behalf of the movement, especially from Democrats. Jerry Milbank met with Barry at his Senate office on January 24 to discuss fund-raising; Barry responded to my letter, "Thank you very much for your encouraging letter of January 23 which was on my desk when Jerry came in for a visit." And Barry accepted my invitation to address a dinner meeting in Greenwich, set for mid-spring.

Also on January 24, Bill Rusher sent me page proofs of an article he had prepared for the February 12 edition of *National Review* entitled "Crossroads for the G.O.P." He wrote that the "tea-leaf readers," studying the results of the 1962 midterm elections, opined that the GOP had "an astonishingly good chance" of taking most of the 165 electoral votes of the southern and border states in 1964—and that the man with the best chance of carrying those states was Barry Goldwater.

Rusher offered other musings: "Whether Senator Goldwater is willing to shoulder the burden of a campaign of this sort—first against Nelson Rockefeller's millions, and then against John Kennedy and the massed batteries of the American left—is presently not known." But, he said, the Republicans should nominate a candidate "who—win or lose—will galvanize the party in a vast new area, carry fresh scores and perhaps hundreds of Southern Republicans to unprecedented local victories, and lay the foundations for a truly national Republican Party, ready to fight and win in 1968 and all the years beyond."

The man was not only brilliant but psychic.

Jerry and I were moving ahead, not at all discouraged, but Clif was despondent. He sent a "confidential memo" to key members of the movement on February 1: "As you know from the newspaper publicity, the Senator has urged his friends to do nothing in his behalf in 1963. This requires us to make some serious decisions as to what we, as a group, should do." He scheduled a meeting for "a small, select number of our total group" for February 17. "This will enable us," he wrote, "to make collectively, the essential judgments as to our future course of action."

Bill Rusher wrote to Barry urging him to reconsider. He was told, "At no time have I committed myself to anyone that I would seek the nomination, nor have I indicated that I would stand still for a draft. . . . Any overt action at this time could do me irreparable damage, because I plan to run for the Senate in 1964 and do not want anything like this to happen. Clif is coming down sometime in the immediate future and you can iron out the areas of misunderstanding."

"Sometime" was February 4, for a meeting held at the urging of Charles R. Barr of Chicago, a key member of our group and one of those who had been encouraging Barry to run for president since 1960. In his published description of that visit, Clif White did not mention that I had tagged along to handle any funding questions that might arise. My impressions of the meeting were quite different from Clif's.

This was to be my first up-close and personal meeting with Barry, and I was in awe from the moment I stepped into the lobby of the classic Senate Office Building—monumental architecture is one thing the Depression-era federal government did really well. Barry's outer office was impressive in a more personal way, the walls covered with spectacular photos of Arizona (taken by the senator), every flat surface supporting wood carvings of cowboys, Indians, part of his vast collection of Indian kachina dolls, and models of planes he had flown.

And then we were ushered into the inner sanctum. "In awe" became, well, star-struck. To me, he signified the last of a breed—independent, unbending, a bit unreal in the middle of the twentieth century, when most Americans had adopted "luxury" as the standard and replaced self-reliance with convenience.

Barry was in a better mood than he had been the last time Clif had met with him, having been restored to the Policy Committee, and, I suppose, because the meeting included two people he knew better than he knew Clif White—me and Charles Barr. The tone was cordial, and the results, to my mind, constructive. In essence, Barry didn't give us a definite yes, but he definitely didn't say no, either. Rather than impose opinion on possibly faulty memory, I present verbatim the notes I set down immediately after the meeting:

1. BG expressed the definite wish that our committee should continue and be expanded. He is impressed by the number of political pros and the states that have been coordinated to date.
2. Fund-raising also should be continued. "Money for conservative causes is sorely needed and never available when you need it most. Don't send it back if you don't have to." . . . However, he brightened up and said that "we'll need a lot of money in the convention." He pointed out that he has an assistant who is "doing research on my potential opponents" which doesn't cost a great deal. I interpreted this to mean the convention opponents, not his local Arizona picture.
3. He said he wants the flexibility of being able to watch his strength grow, but reserves the right to withdraw throughout, without committing himself now. He continues to say "I am not now a candidate." Charley Barr feels that this means that he won't go unless he thinks:
   A. He can have sufficient strength for the nomination, both political and cash, and
   B. Events develop that Kennedy slips enough so he can be beaten and BG would have a fair chance. BG doesn't want to cut his bridges and lose out on Arizona, where four candidates will declare overnight if he declares for the Presidency now.
4. BG expressed the wish that our movement not be expressly to make him President, but to expand and foster the conservative movement in U.S. through the Republican Party. This, he said, would permit conservatives to take control of the Repub-

lican Party, which, of course, must be done. Even if we fail, he
feels we'll have a great influence on the 1964 Republican platform and selection of candidates, if for any reason he decides
not to run.

5. I expressed thought that we win either way if he goes for it.

   A. If he loses in convention, at least he'll be sufficiently strong
   to dictate important platform and party policy. Then, when
   Rocky loses to JFK, Goldwater picks up all the marbles for
   his group.

   B. If Goldwater wins the nomination, for three months, the
   American public, through the legitimacy of a presidential
   campaign, will be exposed for the first time since 1932 to a
   clear conservative choice, and 20 million or more will be
   convinced and will form a hard core, which will mean that
   JFK cannot go all the way to Socialism.

6. BG said he will go into states to help conservatives but is sick
   and tired of bailing out the liberals and their deficits.

I saw what I think Goldwater wanted us to see: encouragement
without commitment. Clif White interpreted Barry's comments in
quite a different light: He heard "I am not a candidate" and that our
only goal should be "to expand and foster the conservative movement." He saw the campaign door clanging shut, the key to victory
out of reach.

When Clif gave his version to core members of the group on February 17, his despair was evident. I had another engagement, but had
I been able to attend, I think I could have kept things in perspective.
As it was, Clif's report set the tone for the meeting and generated perhaps more heat than light. As reported in Clif's memoir, Bob Hughes
finally stood up and said, "There's only one thing we can do. Let's
draft the son-of-a-bitch."

Someone said, "What if he won't let us?"

Hughes answered, "We'll draft him anyway. I mean *really* draft him."

On that somewhat combative note, the group officially became the National Draft Goldwater Committee, and Peter O'Donnell, head of the Texas Republican Party, was appointed chairman. Clif soon took the first step in shifting operations from New York to Washington by renting a D.C. postal box with a most symbolic number: 1964.

When feedback from that February 17 meeting reached Bo Callaway, he put his Georgia fund-raising efforts in limbo. He sent letters to his key people advising them to "hold tight" until Clif was able either to provide encouragement or pull the plug—at which point Callaway would return the money he had raised. His friends were not as interested in supporting "conservatism" as they were in supporting a Goldwater presidential candidacy.

I met with Barry on February 19 to report on our financial condition. I gave my report—we were encouraged by the early returns, and some top-rate people were coming aboard as state finance chairmen. He said, "That's great, really a good start. For whoever will be our candidate." But he emphasized that it was only a start. "A campaign is like a stool with three legs," he explained, "a good message, a good candidate, and someone to pay for it. Most campaigns do well on the first two. Without the third, the cash, the stool falls over." Then he asked me about the art and science of fund-raising. "You guys on Wall Street, how do you do it?"

I don't know if he was testing me, if he really wanted to know, or if he was just being sociable, but thus encouraged, I launched into a brief tutorial. First, make your own contribution, then invite close personal friends of the candidate, well-known supporters, and influential celebrities to serve on the executive committee or as a director of some organization, perhaps newly created for the purpose. Issue press releases to local news organizations, with the names of the campaign team prominently noted. These names should also appear on the organization letterhead, to be mailed far and wide as part of a funding solicitation. Enlist these supporters as "sponsors" for some event—a dinner, a rally, or a private audience with the candidate—and mail personal invitations, over their signatures, to lists of potential attendees they had provided. The invitations should mention that the sender has already contributed to the cause.

Always, of course, ensure follow-up and feedback, sending thank-you notes for each contribution. Cash checks. Repeat. Invite newly found major donors to serve in the cause. Create a new letterhead. "Letterheads," I offered, "may be the single most powerful fund-raising tool ever invented." And Barry laughed.

On that visit, I also delivered some newspaper clippings sent to me by my brother-in-law, F. Ward Paine. In the upcoming election for president of the California Young Republicans, it seemed that the conservative candidate, Bob Gaston, was one of the most dangerous men in the world, right up there with Khrushchev and Castro. His sins had something to do with the California-based John Birch Society, a far-right anti-Communist group about which, to that point, I had heard very little. Gaston was described by one newspaper as an arch-conservative, Bircher-supported candidate, and self-described as a Goldwater Republican. Ergo, Goldwater must be connected with the Birchers.

I didn't understand—then, or later—why Birchers were deemed to be such a threat to democracy. Yes, it was a militantly anti-Communist group that had some pretty far-out ideas; for example, the founder, Robert Welch, suspected Eisenhower of being either a "mere stooge" or a willing participant in the "communist conspiracy." But the society did not advocate bomb-throwing or the violent overthrow of the government. In retrospect, I can say that the John Birch Society had minimal influence on the Goldwater campaign—or, for that matter, on life or politics in America. But at the time, Barry's opponents and the media did try to create connections that didn't exist, and we responded with slightly paranoid efforts to avoid a close association.

At the beginning of March, reporters asked Barry about the "Draft Goldwater" committee. He said that he had done everything he could "to convince these people that I am not their man." He stressed that he had no ongoing contact with the committee. I guess he didn't consider Jerry and me to be of "the committee."

Our Draft movement did not have an exclusive franchise, and so great was the enthusiasm for Barry that a number of "Goldwater for President" organizations were popping up like spring flowers. They operated under similar names, but with little coordination—and, in some instances, not much cooperation. They held petition drives (to the effect of "Tell Barry you want him to run"), raised funds, and did their own local advertising and promotion. Their dedication offset their isolation from our efforts. I don't recall any serious conflicts.

However, one of the more significant was a group in Barry's hometown, Phoenix, which might easily become viewed as the "official" Goldwater for President committee. The first week of April, I flew out to do damage control. Or, more to the point, to make a gentle pre-emptive strike. I found the Phoenix group to be wonderfully enthusiastic, full of energy, albeit a bit naive about such minutiae as building voter support and controlling delegate selection. We could use their energy; they could use our expertise, and they were willing to work with us. With a few phone calls, I brokered a tentative agreement between Clif and their leadership. Clif soon learned, however, that some of the dreaded Birchers were active in the group and damage control was, indeed, appropriate. When he warned them that public identification with the John Birch Society "could do irreparable harm" to Goldwater's candidacy, they trimmed the rolls.

We did, by the way, have some broader competition in the "draft" business. A group in North Hollywood—describing itself as "the national grassroots movement to draft loyal Americans for America"—launched "Draft J. Edgar Hoover for President," complete with petitions and a fund-raising effort. It sank without a trace, although one of my correspondents suggested a Goldwater-Hoover ticket.

I spent a few days socializing in Phoenix, starting with a meeting with Barry and his family at the Goldwater home in the nearby suburb of

Scottsdale. It was spectacular—the house, the setting, the view, the music of the backyard waterfall (picked up by a microphone and piped throughout the house), the flag that automatically unfurled at sunrise and rolled back up at sunset. It was a large contemporary home, the home of a wealthy and secure man, filled with tokens and totems of the West—some hanging on the walls, some inset in floor tiles, kachina dolls everywhere.

The morning had been cool, but by the time I reached his home, the temperature was pushing 80, and I was overdressed in a blue blazer and dress shirt; Barry was relaxed in a dark green polo shirt. His son Barry, Jr., took some photos to memorialize the occasion and then drifted off to his own pursuits. Barry, his wife, Peggy, and I sat around a huge coffee table in the living room, just getting acquainted.

Well, Barry and I got acquainted. Peggy was quiet, unassuming, happy to be floating on the fringes of the conversation—a position she graciously occupied every time I was to see her as our enterprise went forward. Barry probed me a bit—again, I thought he might be testing me. What was my background? Why should he trust his future to my ability to create financial magic, if he ever decided to run? My story was easy to tell. Harvard, Navy at the end of the war, first job in a bank, then partner in a large investment firm, now in my own company with a seat on the Stock Exchange. I reminded him that I had already done some work in political fund-raising. "And," I emphasized, "it's not just me working 'financial magic,' it's Jerry Milbank and a team of experts from all over the country dedicated to the cause. And a lot of people willing to contribute."

For his part, Barry put his feet up on the coffee table—rather, he put his magnificent hand-tooled cowboy boots on the table—and gave me a casual rundown on major political figures of the day, the competition, if you will. I don't remember all the details, but key comments stand out. JFK: good friend, poor president. LBJ: a "son of a bitch" (Peggy winced, but I'm sure it was not the first time she'd heard that particular phrase applied to the sitting vice president), a wheeler-dealer without scruples. Nixon: hard worker, insecure. Rockefeller: good friend, big spender of other folks' money. Scranton: good friend, member of Barry's Air Force Reserve unit in D.C., entered the Pennsylvania governor's race at Barry's urging. Romney: didn't know him very well, and didn't know much about him. Hubert Humphrey: salt of the earth, stand-up guy, you could always trust him to keep his word, a truly nice fellow but way too liberal.

I told him that the committee would be going public in a few days with a press conference in Washington. He gave me a look—perhaps of surprise, perhaps one of those inscrutable expressions that could mean anything you wanted it to mean—but then he made sure that I understood his position: "I'm not a candidate at this time and won't become one unless I'm convinced that I have widespread support . . . and the backing of a strong, well-financed organization." No surprises there.

Later, I spent some time with Barry's friends, supporters, and the proverbial man in the street. In his hometown, at least, Barry's popularity was assured. This was quite a contrast to what I was used to in New York, where people seemed more cynical about their elected officials: I don't think I ever met anyone who admitted to voting for New York City Mayor Robert Wagner, and few people had anything particularly good to say about our governor. I was so impressed that I created a slogan—corny, to be sure, but rehearsed to good effect at several cocktail parties—"Arizona lends Goldwater to the nation so that our country can be returned to us."

I passed all of that along to Barry in my post-visit thank-you note and added that Clif, Peter O'Donnell, Ione Harrington, and a host of others had been working hard on the Draft project. "It is simply amazing," I wrote, "the enthusiasm that is now spreading throughout the country for you." I enclosed a check for $1,000, which was for a forthcoming Republican Senatorial Dinner. I sent it to Barry because I had misplaced the invitation with the "send to" address. Or perhaps I sent it to Barry so he would notice the donation. In his response,

Barry wrote, "I am greatly flattered by what you say in your letter. I only hope that half of it is true."

On April 8, 1963, at a press conference at Washington's Mayflower Hotel, Peter announced the formation of the National Draft Goldwater Committee. Its purpose, he said, was "to mobilize the tremendous, spontaneous enthusiasm for Senator Goldwater that is sweeping the country . . . and to encourage and channel the efforts of all volunteers who want to help Senator Goldwater."

At a committee meeting following the announcement, Clif reported on his progress in tracking down every influential Goldwater supporter and potential delegate, state by state. There were now Draft Goldwater chairs in thirty-three states, each with an active committee. Collectively, they had lines of communication into a majority of the nation's cities and towns.

But we had a more immediate concern, and the suspense was palpable: How would Goldwater react to the public announcement? That afternoon, some reporters tracked him down and pressed for a comment. He said, "I'm not taking any position on this draft movement. It's their time and their money. But they are going to have to get along without any help from me." A week later, we were able to relax somewhat when he told the *New York Times:* "I don't want the nomination. I'm not looking for it. I haven't authorized anybody to look at it for me. But who can tell what will happen a year from now? A man would be a damn fool to predict with finality what he would do in this unpredictable world." I heard a strong echo of what I'd written in my notes about Goldwater's reaction at our February 4 meeting: "He wants the flexibility of being able to watch his strength grow, but reserves the right to withdraw throughout, without committing himself now."

The first public outing of the National Draft Goldwater Committee came at the Republican Women's Conference in Washington, D.C. during the last week of April. Judy Fernald and Rita Bree organized a hospitality suite, and over the three-day conference, 1,080 women signed the guestbook. They also dropped enough money into a gold-painted bucket, strategically placed by the door, to more than cover the event's expenses.

A Gallup poll taken at the same time had Rockefeller leading among Republican voters with 43 percent; Goldwater had come up sharply, to 26 percent. Michigan governor George Romney stood at 13 percent, and Pennsylvania governor William Scranton at 7 percent. Richard Nixon was not included in the poll, although he was still considered a potential candidate.

However, three things happened during the first week of May that changed the Republican landscape. Richard Nixon announced that he was moving from California to New York, thus abandoning whatever political base he still had. George Romney's nascent presidential aspirations were dashed by Michigan's largest newspaper, the *Detroit News*. "Come home, George," the editor wrote, "and let's get on with the chores." And Nelson Rockefeller got married.

When Rockefeller divorced his wife of thirty-one years, the mother of his five children, late in 1961, most political insiders gave it little significance. But when the fifty-four-year-old Rockefeller was remarried May 4, 1963, to a thirty-six-year-old woman, whose own divorce had just become final—and who appeared to be abandoning four children in the process—things changed. Long-standing rumors of "another woman" were now confirmed. There were rumblings in the press: In the eyes of many church leaders, the new Mrs. Rockefeller should have waited for at least a year. In the eyes of many mothers, Rockefeller was a home wrecker. Even the moderate Prescott Bush, Sr., made a moral issue of the affair. "Have we come to the point in our life as a nation," he told the graduating class of an upper-class prep school for young women, "where the Governor of a great state—one who perhaps aspires to the nomination for President of the United States—can desert a good wife, mother of his grown children, divorce her, then persuade a young mother of four youngsters to abandon her husband and their four children and marry the Governor? Have we come to the point where one of the two great political parties will confer upon such a one its highest honor and greatest responsibility? I venture to hope not."

Rockefeller's Gallup poll standing dropped to 29 percent almost overnight. Barry's rose from 26 to 40 percent. Bill Rusher put it in perspective: "Rockefeller is the only candidate who has turned motherhood into a liability," he said.

At this point, Stets Coleman suggested that we pull back. "Goldwater is now way out in front by a wide margin. Therefore the necessity for a Draft Goldwater Movement has certainly been lessened if not done away with entirely. . . . I don't think we should dissolve the project but that we should make it inactive with a skeleton crew." Stets stood almost alone. But when he told Barry that he was trying to slow things down, Barry said, "God, I hope so!"

CHAPTER 4

The Quiet Revolt

O N JUNE 12, 1963, a former employee of Middendorf, Colgate, who had read "both of the Senator's books" and had once been "wholeheartedly enthusiastic" about his candidacy, sent me the following:

> I became disenchanted with the senator when I learned several things that were contrary to the ideals of a Conservatist:
> 1. Membership in the NAACP (since resigned)
> 2. His vote for Thurgood Marshall, after knowing all about the pro-Communist background of this man
> 3. His being Regional Vice President of the National Municipal League
> 4. His refusing to share the platform at Madison Square Garden in 1962 with General Walker—a proven American of high stature.

Major General Edwin Walker, commanding the 24th Infantry Division in Germany in 1961, had been caught distributing John Birch Society propaganda among the troops. He was relieved of command, then had resigned from the Army in protest. An invitation to appear as an honored guest at a March 1962 Young Americans for Freedom rally at Madison Square Garden was withdrawn at the urging of Goldwater, Senator John Tower, and others.

My correspondent was especially disturbed that the senator "didn't see fit to answer" her interrogatory letter "per questions 1 thru 4 above." The National Municipal League, she warned, "is attempting to destroy representative government. . . . It is part of the organization of the internationalists seeking to subvert the sovereignty of the U.S. itself to World Government." She was incensed by Barry's apparent willingness to support "any Republican" should he not get the nomination. "Does this sound like a true Conservatist?" she wrote. "Doesn't he KNOW that both political parties are controlled by the internationalists of the Council of Foreign Relations?" Well, the Goldwater tent was large, but perhaps not large enough for every "conservatist."

On the same day that letter was drafted, Dick Nixon told reporters that "among professional politicians, Senator Goldwater has the lead, and they have more influence on nominations than anyone else." Three days later, a headline in the *New York Times* proclaimed, "Goldwater Gaining in Northeast, Republican State Chairmen Say." The *Washington Star* reported that among a group of eastern Republican Party workers, "A surprising number—considering the scarcity of strong conservatives in the group—indicated a willingness, if not an eagerness, to see the nomination go to Senator Goldwater." That week's edition of *Time* noted, "If the Republican national convention were to be held today, Goldwater would almost certainly be its presidential nominee."

And, from the Rowland Evans–Robert Novak newspaper column of June 24:

> The fact that Senator Barry Goldwater is so far in front for the Republican Presidential nomination is proof of a little-understood transformation in the party's power structure.
>
> This transformation . . . is nothing less than a quiet revolt. The aggressive post-war club of conservative young Republicans from the small states of the West and South are seizing power, displacing the Eastern party chiefs who have dictated Republican policy and candidates for a generation.

I guess that meant we were winning. But where did our candidate stand? Actually, about where we wanted him. He told *Time* it was "too early" for a decision, saying, "There are a lot of things I have to consider." And on June 17 he told a man from United Press International: "I don't want this nomination. But it may be forced on me. If I'm put in the position where I have to take it, I won't be a reluctant tiger. I'll get out and fight."

The next milestone on the road to the nomination was to regain conservative control of the Young Republicans, an assignment given to Clif White and me at the December 2, 1962, meeting. In the 1961 biannual election for chairman, Goldwater supporter Robert E. Hughes had lost out to Leonard Nadasdy, who was friendly to the Rockefeller wing. Hughes became one of the original members of the Draft group (he's the one who had stood up and said, "Draft the son of a bitch").

At the 1963 YRNF convention, Nadasdy was determined to pass the baton to a candidate of his choosing. To us—and to Nadasdy's supporters—this was not a power struggle in some obscure club. The symbolism was palpable: To which camp do the Republican leaders of tomorrow belong? We were prepared for a fight. But the fight that ensued was not quite what we had in mind.

Goldwater, Rockefeller, Scranton, and Romney had been invited to address the convention; Goldwater was the only one who came, and he gave a fighting conservative speech. "The old, respectable, sometimes noble liberalism of fifty years ago is gone for good," he said. Don't be fooled, he warned, by the phony liberals "with corrupt big-city machines whose job it is to deliver the bloc votes in the big Northern cities." He called modern liberalism "only a form of rigor mortis" and said the liberal Democrats had not "had a new idea in thirty years."

A preconvention survey showed 75 percent of the 1,400 delegates and alternates leaning toward Goldwater, and therefore probably ready to support a sympathetic candidate for chairman. However, our efforts to post and elect a pro-Goldwater slate were blocked by a visibly

spooked Nadasdy, who hired a team of private security guards to enforce order and rigged switches at the podium from which he could
control all floor microphones.

The ruckus began when some of our delegates tried to protest an
unfair ruling from the chair and were physically blocked from reaching the microphones; the few who managed to grab a mike found
that it was dead. This led to a bit—well, a lot—of pushing and shov-
ing. The brilliant columnist Bob Novak was up in the balcony covering the convention—I think one of the delegates found out he was
with the media and punched him. Novak was really upset. In his post-
convention narrative, he wrote of "hard-faced, implacable young men
with crew cuts and buttoned-down collars, shrieking into floor microphones and chanting and stamping their feet in unison in a system-
atic effort to disrupt the convention."

I have never had a crew cut, and I don't think of myself as hard-
faced, although I have on occasion worn a buttoned-down collar. From
my perspective, people were shouting because the microphones had
been switched off, and they were stamping to show their disapproval.

There were other unparliamentary maneuvers, and when the winner of the election had been determined—our candidate, Donald E.
("Buz") Lukens—the chairman wouldn't allow the national secretary
to announce the tally; he shoved her away from the podium so hard
that she fell down. Frustration displaced both good manners and
good judgment on both sides.

Some in the news media had great sport with us. Outgoing chairman Nadasdy told the *St. Paul Pioneer Press* on July 6 that we "were using
the exact same techniques used by the Communists," and he predicted
that "the radical right" would be "running a slate of delegates for Senator Barry Goldwater for president." He told the *Minneapolis Sunday
Tribune* the next day that Goldwater's speech was like pouring "gasoline
on the flames." Other papers took a more accurate "Goldwater Takes
Control of Young Republicans" approach—a theme we welcomed.
Rockefeller did not.

CHAPTER 5

Rocky Declares War

The DRAFT GOLDWATER COMMITTEE added to its momentum with a July 4 Goldwater rally in Washington, which turned out to be one of the largest events ever held at the District of Columbia National Guard Armory. Our candidate was not there—we did not expect him, as he was riding a horse in an Arizona parade—but an overflow crowd of 9,000 supporters came in from far and wide. The program included Senator John Tower of Texas, Congressman John Ashbrook, and Governor Paul Fannin of Arizona (who traded the pleasure of riding a horse back home to promote the interests of the man who was), along with actors Walter Brennan, William Lundigan, Chill Wills, and Efrem Zimbalist, Jr. Clif White offered a tutorial on grassroots campaigning and the electoral process, which echoed the material in our just-developed operations manual for state and local committee chairmen.

Clif reminded his audience, "This is not a general election campaign—you are participating in a drive for the Republican presidential nomination. Your primary responsibility is to build an organization in your state that will translate grassroots support into delegate strength for Goldwater."

The manual included a statement of objectives of the Draft Goldwater Committee and tips on creating an organization, raising money, handling the media, supporting grassroots activities, and

starting local Goldwater Clubs. Our Communications Advisory
Committee developed a companion public relations plan for Draft
Goldwater. The twenty-five-member committee included my friend
Frank Shakespeare, a senior executive with CBS who had to work
with us in secret because his job at that most anti-Goldwater of networks might otherwise have been endangered. (Frank survived and
served in a variety of significant jobs in the Nixon, Ford, Reagan,
and Bush administrations, and then as chairman of the Heritage
Foundation.)

Rockefeller, unwilling or unable to see his drop in standing as the
consequence of his own actions, fumed at what he saw as a conservative vendetta. On July 14, he lashed out with a bitter condemnation.
There was "real danger," he said, from "extremist elements" trying to
take over the Republican Party. He recited a litany of charges:
"threatening letters, smear and hate literature, strong-arm and goon
tactics, bomb threats and bombings, infiltration and takeover of established political organizations by Communist and Nazi methods."
At the Young Republican convention, he charged, "Birchers and others of the radical right lunatic fringe" had resorted to the "tactics of
totalitarianism."

"Every objective observer," he said, "has reported that the proceedings there were dominated by extremist groups, carefully organized, well-financed and operated through the tactics of ruthless,
rough-shod intimidation. [Those] who successfully engineered this
disgraceful subversion of a great and responsible auxiliary of the Republican Party are the same people who are now moving to subvert
the Republican Party itself."

The headlines were predictable: "Rocky Declares War on Goldwater," said the *New York Journal-American*. But Rockefeller's strategy, if
that is what it was, soon backfired. *Time* suggested that the outburst
was a reaction to two things: his precipitous drop in the polls, and
embarrassment over Barry's "well-publicized personal triumph" at

The Hartford Times

**"LET US ALL GO OUT NOW AND REKINDLE
THE FLAME OF CONSERVATISM"**

the Young Republicans election. Mississippi Republican State Chairman Wirt Yeager called it "the scream of a drowning man going down for the third time." On the floor of the Senate, Nebraska's Carl

Curtis offered, "It is my considered judgment that a man who would take such desperate and destructive measures against his own party in a gamble to gain some temporary personal advantage has already forfeited any claim to loyalty from any part of the party organization." Evans and Novak wrote that Rockefeller "seems to have failed to accomplish what many thought to be [his] major purpose: pumping new life into the Rockefeller Presidential candidacy, which has been in a state of near-death since the Governor's marriage two months ago."

Rockefeller kept up the attack: A few days later, he suggested that Barry himself was likely to become a "captive" of the radical right. Barry was puzzled and hurt by this—he thought that they were friends. Rockefeller even had called to tell Barry about his marriage to Happy a few hours after the ceremony, before it was common knowledge. On policy matters, Rockefeller, whose state budgets far exceeded those of his predecessors, had agreed with Barry that some federal spending ought to be curbed.

But having staked out a claim, the governor was going to mine it for all it was worth, not just now, but for the next twelve months. He refused to believe that he was no longer a viable candidate. A mid-August Gallup presidential preference poll had Goldwater at 39 percent, Rockefeller at 22 percent, and Romney at 21 percent. Goldwater was receiving as many as a thousand letters a day urging him to run for president.

Through it all, Goldwater had been holding the committee at arm's length—but the arm wasn't very stiff. He still hadn't said no, but he wouldn't commit, either. The committee sailed on, Peter O'Donnell at the helm. Clif and others worked the field, adding a precinct committeeman here, a probable delegate there, making slow, steady progress. However, to the best of my recollection, for whatever reason, Clif and Barry did not speak to each other even once from the end of the February 5 meeting until October.

I think the "distance" was by tacit consent. Barry still believed that Clif was an opportunist trying to latch on to a big meal ticket. Clif was determined to finish the job he had started, but he sensed he was not fully welcome, so he stepped back. Jerry Milbank and I—two members of the committee with an established relationship with Barry—stepped into the communications gap.

When we felt that sufficient delegate strength had been lined up to make a decent showing, Jerry and I went down to Washington and asked for his commitment. Barry was very gracious but not yet ready to say yes. He reminded me of his three-legged stool analogy—message, candidate, and cash. In other words, the delegate count was interesting, but "show me the money."

Up to this point, our fund-raising had provided money for day-to-day operations but did not create any surplus; to earn Barry's approval, we were going to need a lot more. He did try to be helpful. He said, "I have a buddy out in Washington who said he'd give me half a million dollars, and I have another friend who can raise a million bucks, but I'm not going to go unless I see a big chunk of change in the kitty and ready to go."

So I called Barry's half-million-dollar buddy out in Washington—no dice, he said, he would contribute maybe $12,000. The million-dollar guy was astonished: "I don't know how Barry got that idea!" We kept plugging away and eventually built a respectable treasury. A few months later, we went back to Barry with the numbers, and he said all right, he would declare. Sometime.

In midsummer, Goldwater asked an Arizona associate, Denison Kitchel, to test the waters in Washington as a campaign manager-in-waiting. Ostensibly, the "campaign" would be for the Senate, but no one was fooled. This move gave us some reassurance that Barry was seriously considering entering the presidential race.

Kitchel—a lawyer with no background in politics and no political contacts—seemed a curious choice. As it would turn out, Barry believed that his former campaign manager, Steve Shadegg, had become too embroiled in a publicly contentious Arizona water project. He told Shadegg that he was sorry but would have to dissociate from him, saying, "I don't think I can afford to have you connected with my campaign." He turned to Kitchel, a friend of almost thirty years.

When Kitchel first walked into the Draft headquarters, he was hit with a barrage of suggestions. Barry had no schedule—he just seemed to "poop along" (one of Goldwater's favorite expressions), visiting this place, making a speech in that. There was no plan, no correlation, and a lot of wasted opportunity. We were anxious to get organized. Denny seemed to listen, but without comment. I later realized that he had a hearing deficit and hadn't heard half of what we were saying. During the campaign I found that his hearing problem caused strangers to perceive him as cold, distant, and even disinterested. Among friends—and I counted myself as one, despite ongoing disagreements with his management of the campaign—he was a truly sweet person, albeit somewhat out of his depth in the grinding world of national politics.

But he hit the ground running. By the end of October 1963, he had pretty much dropped the pretense of "Senate race" and expanded operations. All of Barry's speeches were being put on an "electronic memory device" that could cough forth exact quotations on every subject he had ever discussed. I'm not sure if it was ever used to any appreciable effect, for the good reason that Barry too often addressed the same subject in different terms.

Kitchel hooked up with a local Goldwater associate, William J. Baroody, president of the Washington think tank American Enterprise Institute. (As a footnote to this bit of history, my father had been a member of the board of the American Enterprise Association—the original name—when Bill was hired in 1954.) Baroody had worked with Goldwater since the election of 1958 as sort of an intellectual mentor.

Baroody saw his role in the campaign as more, however, than just a mentor. "Intellectual" was his turf: He needed no help and wanted no interference in this realm. *National Review* editors Bill Buckley and Brent Bozell proposed to assemble a team of well-known educators and other credentialed experts to add some credibility to the campaign, and they sat down to present their ideas to Kitchel, Baroody, and another staffer, David Kelley. Each suggestion they offered was turned aside by Baroody. The meeting ended with some ideas left hanging, and nothing decided.

The meeting *really* ended a few days later, when the *New York Times* reported that the "Goldwater for President ship has just repelled a boarding party from the forces who supposedly occupy the narrow territory to the right of the Arizona Senator." The "boarding party," represented by Buckley and Bozell, apparently had attempted to worm its way into the campaign at a high policy-planning level. "Feeling that what their candidate needs least is more support from the far right," the *Times* reported, "Goldwater advisers used an old political dodge. They played dumb."

Dumb, or stupid. That the story was wrong is one thing; that the details of a private conversation among five men made it into the *Times* is another. Who leaked the story and embroidered the facts? It certainly wasn't Buckley or Bozell. Kitchel and Kelley pled innocent. Baroody suggested that a bug must have been planted in the hotel room where the meeting took place. Barry, who became aware of the situation too late to mend the damage, came to the sad determination that the culprit was Baroody.

If Baroody suffered any consequence from this selfish blunder, I didn't hear about it. But Buckley, Bozell, and *National Review* publisher Bill Rusher—three of the most influential conservatives in the country—were effectively shut out of the campaign. Rusher continued to attend some of our meetings, but without much enthusiasm. Their exclusion must have been especially galling since Rusher had been one of the originators of the Draft Goldwater movement, and Bozell was the behind-the-scenes author of *Conscience of a Conservative.*

In the meantime, the Draft Goldwater steering committee was moving ahead. We engaged the Opinion Research Corporation of Princeton (which had the slogan "Market, Attitude and Motivation Research") to run surveys to determine where the "Goldwater image" stood with voters, Republican and Democrat alike. The results were interesting: Barry was viewed as warm, candid, and a man of strong convictions, and was not thought to be connected with the "radical right." His position on cutting government spending was warmly applauded. On the downside, he seemed to be "always against something," and if he had any programs to offer, they were unknown.

CHAPTER 6

An Out-of-Town Tryout

I THOUGHT IT MIGHT BE useful for Barry to make a foray into the liberal fortress of the Northeast, and through my insurance-industry contacts in Hartford, I arranged for him to be guest of honor and dinner speaker at a convention of insurance agents on October 24, 1963. A good-sized crowd of supporters—including my wife, Isabelle, and me, up from Greenwich—was on hand at the airport arrival to greet Barry, Peggy, and three staff members. The crowd could have been a great deal larger, but Denny Kitchel had asked me to ensure that the arrival would not "look like a rally." This was a puzzling request because we were going to have a full-bore rally later that evening. In any event, the unavoidable press contingent was waiting, and reporters pulled the senator immediately into conversation. When asked whether the purpose of his visit was "political or to give a speech," Barry replied, "I'm here to address the Insurance Agents convention . . . but I'm never out of politics." After a few unremarkable questions, I ended the session—not out of any animus for the press but because we had a schedule that included an official press conference later in the afternoon—and we headed off downtown.

First on the schedule was lunch with Connecticut Republican leaders and a handful of Draft Goldwater folks at the Hartford Club. There was another group of reporters waiting (or maybe the same group just drove faster than I had), but we didn't pause for a chat.

There also was a small, welcoming crowd of people, probably on their lunch break, eager to shake Barry's hand. Inside, Barry—a passionate amateur radio operator—split off to make a phone call to the local Ham Radio Operator's Club, but there was no answer.

Lunch was quite congenial, with the local Republican leaders pretty much dominating—but in a friendly, good-humored way. Barry offered some of his views: The United States should get out of the United Nations if Communist China was allowed in; the graduated income tax (with marginal rates as high as 91 percent) stifled initiative; however, if we could control government spending, taxes should go down. When asked about civil rights, Barry said, "I'd have to sit up all night to find a man whose vote I wouldn't be happy to have on election day."

I may have introduced an off-note when I mentioned that local political leaders were most interested in presidential candidates who were best able to help candidates in local races. Barry nodded but gave me a sour look.

The state Republican leaders urged him to put some credentialed foreign affairs experts on his team. This would be a great help in a liberal state like Connecticut, they said, where opinion was heavily influenced by the professors at Yale and Trinity. He was also invited to return to the state for a fund-raising dinner in April. Barry agreed— a good move, because it effectively kept the state leaders neutral for about six months.

After the lunch, I tried to gauge the impression Barry had made upon our hosts. Most offered such comments as "impressed," "enthusiastic for Barry," "marvelous," or "I've always liked Barry." One was neutral. But whether for good or ill, I know we made an impression on the Hartford Club: The manager told me that this was "the first time in ninety-three years" that women had been allowed inside.

While Isabelle took Peggy out for a visit to the Wadsworth Atheneum, Barry and I went on to the 3:30 press conference, where some forty to fifty reporters stood ready, many from the national media. Barry was his usual candid—often too candid—self. When asked what he thought of the competition from Rockefeller for the Republican nomination, he answered, "I'm not sure he's a Republican."

Right about then it began to dawn on me that the straight talk and blunt descriptions for which Goldwater was so admired might be handicaps in a presidential campaign. He had, I think, a constitutional inability to not answer a question, no matter how controversial the subject or unprepared his response. Candor had always been his hallmark; it served him well in the Senate and when addressing adoring crowds of conservative supporters, but it was a disaster with reporters, who could—and often did—emphasize the sensational or take his comments out of context. Too late, he learned that such openness was an unaffordable luxury at the level of national politics. I later learned that, while discussing a possible Goldwater campaign, John Kennedy told journalist Ben Bradlee, "People will start asking him questions, and he's so damn quick on the trigger that he will answer them. And when he does, it will be all over."

A few questions after the Rockefeller gibe, Barry set up what became one of the most contentious issues of the campaign. He was asked by a *Washington Post* reporter for a reaction to Eisenhower's recent suggestion that the six American divisions stationed in Europe could be cut to one. Goldwater said he did not fully agree but suggested that the number could indeed be cut perhaps by one-third as long as North Atlantic Treaty Organization (NATO) commanders in Europe had the power to use tactical nuclear weapons on their own authority in an emergency. He meant, *the* commander of NATO should *continue* to have the authority—which was the practice in the Eisenhower and Kennedy administrations—but did not explain.

The NATO–nuclear weapons comment made the front page of the *Washington Post* the next day, October 25, although not in any particular context. The context—and the controversy—would come later, when Barry had announced his candidacy and all remarks became subject to close and critical scrutiny. This comment then would be twisted to suggest that, as president, he would empower any mid-level officer to start a nuclear war. The twisting was courtesy of Nelson Rockefeller and Lyndon Johnson, both of whom saw a golden opportunity to paint Barry as some sort of nuclear maniac. But that takes us ahead of the story.

Otherwise, press coverage of the Hartford visit was generally helpful, reinforcing the positive impression that Barry had left with the state Republican leaders. The visit even generated an encouraging headline: "Goldwater Tells G.O.P. He's Willing—Says in Hartford That He Would Accept Nomination." In answer to a reporter's question, Barry had said, "Any man would be a damned liar if he said he wouldn't." By way of amplification, he said that Nixon also would accept the nomination, if offered. "Any man would," he continued. "There are only varying degrees of reluctance."

What about *actively* seeking the nomination? "I'm a poker player," he said, "and I'm sitting with a pair and I don't know what the draw will be. If it's a good one, I'll say yes."

After the press conference, we had thirty minutes in private with committee members Jerry Milbank, Gordon Reed, and Gerrish Milliken. Barry pronounced himself pleased with the "amateurish" ring of the campaign, which he believed was helping build grassroots momentum. We allowed the truth in that—as far as it went—but suggested that it was now time to get serious. The night before, Jerry had had dinner with the old pro Len Hall—a seven-term congressman, Nixon's 1960 campaign manager, and former chairman of the Republican National Committee. "Get some professionals," Len urged, "up to New Hampshire, quick." Even though Barry was not yet a declared candidate, he was beginning to look like one, and Republican donors in the state with the nation's first primary election would very soon be wondering which horse to back in this race. Goldwater's New

Hampshire supporters, who probably didn't know any better, were doing nothing to encourage donors, while Rockefeller's men were already at work. Barry listened but did not seem concerned. Something positive did come out of the meeting, though. Barry affirmed that he would declare his candidacy, and he set the timing: mid-December or early January.

We had arranged for Barry to deliver a speech at the Hartford Statler Hotel that evening, and our local organizer was to have his people—our "rally"—ready to go at precisely 6:05. And at precisely 6:05 we drove up to a placard-waving throng. Some were attending the convention, and some were office workers on their way home who had stopped by out of curiosity, but most were from the Young Republicans. Barry shook hands with as many as he could, called out a "thanks" to the crowd ("Nice to see so many young people here"), and went in for a reception and dinner with 800 insurance agents.

His speech was an unremarkable discussion of administration fiscal policy. He had already been upstaged when everyone in the audience discovered a Kennedy campaign gimmick hidden under the napkins: a "J.F.K. Vigah" candy bar. Barry was not amused. I was embarrassed. The audience was delighted. *Time* reported: "The chuckles were heard all the way to the White House, where President Kennedy was still letting it be known that he could hardly wait for next year's elections—particularly if his opponent is Goldwater. In fact, the President now thinks that Goldwater is his most likely opponent and is indulging in the tried and true tactic of making fun of a serious threat—the earlier the better."

An AP poll of GOP state and county leaders, released November 2, asked, in essence, who would be the strongest candidate against Kennedy. More than 85 percent said Goldwater. Rockefeller came in at just under 4 percent. Nixon—always hanging around, like a lone wolf out on the political horizon—had about 3 percent. This did not deter Rockefeller from formally announcing his candidacy on November 6.

On November 15, Jerry and I flew down to Washington to report that we had followed through on the Hartford recommendation and arranged for some foreign-affairs experts to join the team. We lined up General Lucius D. Clay, hero of the Berlin Airlift, as our expert for Europe, and former medical missionary and ten-term congressman Walter Judd for the Far East. Judd would be paid, and his salary would be covered by an executive at *Reader's Digest*. These appointments were fine with Barry, although he suggested that Clay be assigned to advise on European *military* affairs.

Barry also reiterated what he had told us in Hartford: He would announce his candidacy in mid-December or early January. Our short meeting was held in the Senate cloakroom; a vote on foreign aid was in progress, and Barry came off the floor just long enough for our conversation.

The next day—November 16, 1963—not quite one year from the election, five months from the first primary, and nine months from the Republican National Convention—the National Draft Goldwater Committee, including all state committee chairs, met in Washington for an all-day session. We assessed our chances and plotted our strategy.

Clif announced that formal "Draft" organizations were now in place in thirty-two states, and that legions of Goldwater volunteers were out gathering signatures, soliciting donations, and seeking support. (By the end of the campaign, the volunteers would number 500,000.) The tentative delegate count had reached 425; he wanted to arrive at the convention with 700 in pocket.

Clif emphasized that, once selected, delegates would be under tremendous pressure to change their allegiance wherever legally possible. "And don't ignore the alternates," he added. "If the delegate can't make the convention, the alternate has the vote." Clif asked each chairperson to prepare a report defining the Republican political structure in his or her state, listing names of major contributors and rules for delegate selection, and making a best guess as to who the delegates-at-large might be, along with contact information. In addition, he wanted them to describe the activity of other candidates in their state and identify who was working on their behalf, supply a list of important newspapers as well as radio and television stations, and note the names of the managers of these outlets and their big advertisers. The professional, at work.

We talked a lot about money that day. We were going up against two of the richest men in America—Rockefeller and Kennedy, either of whom could buy and sell us in one afternoon and never notice the transaction. Rockefeller had a seventy-person staff but no finance chairman. He didn't need a finance chairman.

Frank Kovac, of the Republican National Committee Finance Office, estimated that the cost of the whole presidential campaign for both parties and at all levels would exceed $200 million. He recommended that we have $1.1 million in the kitty the day Barry announced. We had $600,000 on hand and $150,000 pledged, so we needed to raise $350,000 over the next two months. Someone said, "Money that comes in after the nomination is best spent to buy flowers for the funeral." My immediate job was to send a letter to the first major contributors along the lines of "As treasurer . . . I have turned over to the senator the names of the first contributors of $100 and over. . . . Your name was number 36 on this list. You can imagine how grateful the senator is to you specifically for this early support of his candidacy."

We also discussed whether Barry should enter any primaries. In eleven of the sixteen primaries, the results were not binding on the delegates, and the overwhelming majority of delegates would be chosen at state conventions under the guidance of precinct committee and county chairpersons, many of whom might have been charmed by Barry as he went around the country supporting Republicans, or influenced by Clif's grassroots effort. It would therefore be possible to lose every primary and still win the nomination. If he didn't have to, we thought, why should Barry enter any? Primaries are battlegrounds splattered with the blood of victors and vanquished alike.

Perhaps he should seek the grand prize—California, with eighty-two delegates, as insurance—but take a pass on the others. The decision didn't need to be made until after the first of the year, and first up would be New Hampshire, March 10. With only fourteen delegates, it seemed a small prize for all the hoopla, but it could be critical for media exposure and momentum. A typically heavy vote in rural areas would work to our advantage; however, a sweepstakes issue on the ballot might bring out more city voters, to our disadvantage. We expected to have the media edge, with the state's largest paper, Bill Loeb's *Manchester Union Leader,* supporting Goldwater. The seven afternoon dailies might not support us, but neither would they endorse Rockefeller. There was a myth that Rockefeller "owned" New Hampshire because he had gone to Dartmouth, but Goldwater was running 3 to 1 among the voters. And we knew that when people in New Hampshire made a pledge, they stuck by it. Rocky was busy gathering pledges. It was important that Barry spend more time up there, since support usually goes to the first hand to be shaken.

Rockefeller really knew how to play the political game: The moment he announced his candidacy, every female delegate to previous conventions was sent a telegram and a bunch of red roses. The advance man making arrangements for a visit to St. Louis went in three weeks early and hired two local assistants. At the airport, they built a platform so that Rocky could wave to the crowds. They arranged for buses to haul children to the airport rally, timed for after school.

When told of this, Barry was not much impressed; it was not his style. He was to tell us—more than once—that he would not be packaged "by some Madison Avenue agency." He would later tell the brilliant campaign PR man Lee Edwards that if Edwards tried to create any "puff pieces" about hobbies and habits, he would be out of a job.

Nothing about ham radio. Nothing about his tinkering with automobiles, or his photography. By trying to force the campaign to stick with the issues, Goldwater the politician shut the public off from Goldwater the man.

As for other potential candidates, someone reported that Nixon had "his feelers" out, perhaps positioning himself to be the savior in case of a convention deadlock. We did not view him as a serious threat. Romney was minding his chores in Michigan. Nixon's 1960 running mate, the New England patrician Henry Cabot Lodge, might have been a challenger, but he had accepted JFK's offer of the post of ambassador to South Vietnam. Things were not going well there: On November 1, president Ngo Dinh Diem had been murdered in a military coup.

Regarding Scranton, John Tower reported that the governor had told him directly that he "did not seek" the office. This was more or less confirmed in a column by Robert S. Allen and Paul Scott, in which Scranton sought to refute rumors that he was "closely associated" with Rockefeller's drive to block Goldwater. "There is absolutely no truth to that story," Scranton asserted. "I have never been a party to a stop-Goldwater movement, and I don't intend to be. . . . I personally believe that if Senator Goldwater decides to run, he would make a powerful standard-bearer."

Approaching the end of one full year of operations, we had collected about $683,000—of which almost $80,000 came from the petition drives conducted under our umbrella; signers were asked to pay a dollar for the privilege. I suspect that the multitude of petitions being circulated by companion organizations produced a great deal more revenue, which went to the sponsors for their own purposes. Adding the $50,000 raised in 1961–1962 and income through December, we had raised more than $800,000, which I am sure was the largest fund ever publicly raised before a candidate's announcement.

We knew that Barry was looking forward to challenging Kennedy on the issues; the two men had even discussed engaging in a series of

Lincoln-Douglas type debates along the campaign trail. But Barry decided that he would hold off from making a formal declaration until January; otherwise, media coverage would disappear into the deep well of holiday indifference. Still, in an interview published in *Time* magazine—the edition of November 22, 1963—Barry said, "God knows I haven't sought this position. I'm still wishing that something would happen to get me out of all this. It's all a little frightening."

CHAPTER 7

World Turned
Upside-Down

As President John F. Kennedy and his vice president were
leaving their hotel the morning of November 22, 1963,
Kennedy—musing over the same election tea leaves that had
prompted Goldwater to agree to the race—jokingly said, "Well, Lyndon, I guess we can carry Massachusetts and Texas." That afternoon,
everything changed.

I knew the young Jack Kennedy in the early 1950s through several
mutual friends from Newport, Rhode Island. I attended his wedding
reception and once dated Jackie Kennedy's sister, Lee Bouvier. But
our paths diverged, and I didn't see Jack at all after he became president. News of the shooting came over the stock ticker in my office—
the clanging bell signaled "Bulletin, read immediately," but the shock
was so great I had to read it three times, thinking I was misinterpret-
ing some simple item.

It was a shock for the whole nation. For a time, the Kennedy assassination was blamed on the "radical right"; even some on Goldwater's staff suspected as much. Death threats forced us to close the
Draft Goldwater office in Washington—where PR man Lee Edwards was having his first day on the job—and caused John Tower's
family to move into a hotel. Even the discovery of assassin Lee Harvey

Oswald's connections to the Soviets and Cubans did not entirely quell the suspicions.

Walter Cronkite reported that Barry had not joined the outpouring of sympathy and would be "unable" to attend Kennedy's wake and funeral because he was off giving a political speech in Indiana. In fact, Goldwater had sent a telegram of condolence to the White House and was in Indiana helping to bury his mother-in-law. Barry, trying to determine the source of this erroneous story, asked Cronkite (whom he regarded as one of his true friends in the media), who said that someone had handed him "a slip of paper." A CBS spokesman cited "something from United Press," but no one had made any effort to verify the information.

It seemed as if, ultimately, Goldwater was also to be a victim as the effects of the tragedy rippled outward. As Robert Novak wrote, "It became the great cliché of Washington to say that the bullet that killed Jack Kennedy also struck Barry Goldwater." Any advantage in the South was now lost because Barry could not compete against "the first citizen of a Confederate state to occupy the White House since Andrew Johnson." In the Northeast, the gauche Texan Lyndon Johnson was deemed open to challenge by a "Republican Kennedy"—a "moderately liberal, handsome sophisticate." Many Republicans who had been neutral to a Goldwater candidacy felt relief. Now they could find someone else to support. A Gallup poll had Goldwater's approval rating down sixteen points.

Barry's immediate reaction was to give up before even declaring. He confided to us that he wasn't interested in competing with a man he knew to be "a dirty fighter." As he noted in his 1988 autobiography, a campaign with Lyndon Johnson "would involve a lot of innuendo and lies. Johnson was a wheeler-dealer . . . and treacherous to boot. He'd slap you on the back today and stab you in the back tomorrow."

He agonized and hedged, calling for a voluntary moratorium on public campaign activities to coincide with the official mourning period that ended at 1:30 P.M. on December 22. This was not a totally selfless gesture of respect: He later told me, "I asked for that moratorium because I wanted a certain governor to pay attention to his knitting and stay out of New Hampshire when I couldn't get up there."

On Sunday, December 8, Senator Norris Cotton of New Hampshire, former California Senator Bill Knowland, John Tower, Peter O'Donnell, and Barry's advisers Kitchel and Baroody twisted his arm—hard. The matter had gone too far; it was too late to quit. Barry gave them all of the reasons why he shouldn't run: No Republican could win, the country wasn't ready for three presidents in just over a year, and Johnson was a liar and a hypocrite. They twisted harder: It was now or never for the conservatives, they told him. Think of all those young people who have so cheered you on, they said. You can't back out now.

After a couple of days' reflection, Barry called Kitchel and said okay. But he told his wife that he really didn't want to run, he didn't want to be president, but that he did want to give conservatives a cause and a voice. "Lose the election," he said, "but win the Party."

On December 11, at the request of our candidate, the Draft Committee met to assess the full impact of Kennedy's death and Lyndon Johnson's ascension. Naive, lacking Barry's personal insight, we believed that Johnson would be easier to beat because he would not enjoy much support from women, Catholics, veterans, intellectuals, African Americans, the media, or the northern liberals who dominated the Democratic Party. We believed that the Democratic Party would fragment into special-interest groups and expose weaknesses—scandals, moral or financial—that we could exploit. Johnson would have to turn left to get his party's nomination, giving Goldwater a further advantage.

Someone suggested that we get Len Hall on the team. Bill Rusher called him "the classic image of the political pro" but nevertheless didn't want much to do with him. Stets reminded Bill that Len was sixty-five years old and didn't want to run a campaign, just to help out, and suggested we involve Len in helping round up delegates. "We've got all of the delegates we're going to get with emotional appeals," he said. "Now we have to bring in the pros." Besides, Stets added, "I'd rather have him with us than against us, in whatever capacity."

What we didn't know was that Len's potential involvement was a moot issue: He already had told Barry that he was "going to sit this one out," at least until after the convention. Rockefeller had offered him a blank check, but Len said "not interested."

The Draft Goldwater team had more or less decided to stay out of all primaries except California, which had been Barry's position before he'd actually decided to become a candidate. *Newsweek* political columnist Raymond Moley advised Goldwater—in person, not in print—to stay out of New Hampshire; he didn't need the exposure. If he won, it would be insignificant. If he lost, it could be devastating. But Barry's Arizona friends convinced him that primaries were important, and a bunch were put on the schedule.

So we parsed New Hampshire. Rockefeller and Nixon (who was being supported as a write-in candidate) would tend to cancel each other out. Senator Margaret Chase Smith from Maine was flirting with presidential destiny and many observers thought she might enter the primary; we heard a rumor that Rockefeller had asked her "to get out of New Hampshire," probing for "her price." And despite what John Tower had told us at the November 16 meeting—that Scranton "did not seek" the office—we thought the Pennsylvania governor might be the real threat. An attractive candidate with an attractive wife and no known enemies, he would provide an acceptable rallying point for the eastern wing. There was also a rumor that astronaut-hero John Glenn had considered offering himself as a candidate, though no one knew to which party: Like Eisenhower in the early stages, it appeared that he could go either Democrat or Republican. RNC chairman Bill Miller had taken Glenn to lunch but didn't learn anything useful.

When the one-month mourning period ended and the voluntary moratorium was lifted, we learned that a new player was being entered in the game: A group called "Friends of Henry Cabot Lodge" was opening campaign offices. However, Lodge—former senator, Nixon's vice-presidential running mate in 1960—sent a letter to a radio station saying, "I have no intention of running for any office." It was another "draft" movement.

We also learned that Rockefeller had been very busy during the moratorium. Frank Shakespeare let me know, sub rosa, that the governor was planning five fifteen-minute "New Hampshire" broadcasts on CBS or ABC beginning the last week in January and continuing through February. Each would focus on a specific topic: foreign affairs, domestic policies, his wife "Happy," why he got into politics, and why the country needed him. If memory serves, scheduling problems kept the programs off the air. It was just as well for Rockefeller: At a projected cost of $250,000, the scheme—targeted at just one small primary—would have triggered legitimate charges that he was trying to buy the White House.

However much he planned to spend or did spend, Rockefeller faced legal limits on the amount that could be spent within New Hampshire. His team avoided the limits by putting spots on Massachusetts and Vermont TV stations that were picked up in New Hampshire, and by sending mailings from New York. So did we.

Barry made the formal announcement from his home in Phoenix on January 3, 1964. Phoenix, pardon the expression, was from nowhere. The media were concentrated in Washington and New York. And January 3 was a Friday—a day of the week best suited to burying, not encouraging, media coverage. No matter. Barry wanted to show that he was his own man.

Still, the announcement itself was nicely worded:

> I will seek the Republican Presidential nomination. I have decided
> to do this because of the principles in which I believe and because
> I am convinced that millions of Americans share my belief in these

principles. . . . I have been spelling out my position now for ten years in the Senate and for years before that here in my own state. I will spell it out even further in the months to come.

I was once asked, what kind of Republican I was. I replied that I was *not* a "me-too" Republican. That still holds. I will not change my beliefs to win votes. I will offer a choice, not an echo. This will not be an engagement of personalities. It will be an engagement of principles.

No members of the Draft Committee were invited to the event. None. We had expected that, in announcing his candidacy, Barry would also announce a campaign organization that would in some respects be a combination of our committee and Kitchel's team. We had assumed, not unreasonably, that we would simply change the name of the Draft movement to something like "Goldwater for President" and soldier on. Not to be.

Goldwater was uncomfortable with people he didn't know well, and (perhaps in part because of the misinformation he had been given about Clif's motives) he was suspicious of some of the Draft Goldwater people. This was made quite clear in the selections for the top campaign staff, a close-knit palace guard—largely drawn from Phoenix—that came to be known as the "Arizona Mafia." The term was obviously pejorative—and, in my opinion, somewhat unfair. There is no question that the members of this inner circle ran protective interference for Goldwater and at times made decisions for him that they were not qualified to make. But I found them all to be men of honor and goodwill, if at times a bit naive.

Denison Kitchel was campaign manager, and Dean Burch was Kitchel's administrative assistant. Dick Kleindienst (a Harvard classmate of mine, although we didn't know each other at school) was director of field operations. Of the three, only Kleindienst, a former member of the Arizona House of Representatives and Republican state chairman, had any practical experience with political campaigns, although Burch was the most knowledgeable of the three; he had previously been Barry's chief administrative assistant, which gave him at least some understanding of what went on in Congress. When Burch returned to Tucson to practice law in 1958, he continued to assist part-time in Barry's local office. I don't believe he met Denny Kitchel until Barry asked them to be on his team.

The rest of the immediate staff was to include Bill Baroody, Ed Mc-Cabe, and speechwriter Karl Hess. But where the Draft Committee had built a solid infrastructure and established personal connections with Republican leaders throughout the nation, these men were largely unknown and had no significant influence in the world of politics—except with Barry.

A few days after Barry's announcement, during preparations for a meeting of Republican state officials, Kitchel asked Clif White for advice on working with the Republican National Committee. Clif gave Kitchel, Kleindienst, and Burch a thorough briefing on personalities, home-state connections, and attitudes toward Goldwater as determined through earlier Draft Committee contacts. After the presentation, Kitchel said, "As you know, Clif, Barry has asked Dick to be director of field operations for the Goldwater for President Committee. He will report to me. I guess the best thing for you would be to serve as sort of an assistant to Dick."

Clif—the only man in the room who had ever participated in a presidential campaign on any level and who had naturally expected to be given a significant role in the campaign—was stunned, and he declined the insult. Hundreds of people had been working for him, he said: "When they find you have made me somebody's assistant, I will lose their confidence, I won't be any help in this campaign."

Kitchel said, "Well it might be helpful if you would stay on with us until Friday."

Kleindienst intervened. "We need you. . . . We can work it out."

Burch suggested that Clif be designated coordinator of field operations, which seemed to be met with agreement by all in the room.

Yet just minutes later, in front of members of the national committee who already had been brought aboard the Goldwater train by the Draft Committee, Kitchel introduced Kleindienst as director of field operations and Clif as an assistant. The next day, Kitchel added to his rapidly growing reputation for poor judgment by telling Peter O'Donnell there was no place for him on the Goldwater for President Committee.

In truth, I can't say that Kitchel alone was responsible for such poor judgment and bad manners, then or later. When Ione Harrington, head of the Draft Goldwater Women's Division, tried to brief Goldwater on her group's plans, Barry said thank-you-very-much but Arizonian Ann Eve Johnson would be heading up the women's committee. Ione put aside her disappointment, continued in a lesser role, and eventually picked up a comparable assignment with another group, Citizens for Goldwater.

Many key members of the Draft Committee were shunted aside, given subordinate roles, or ignored. I don't think Barry had any close friends who understood the duties and responsibilities of a campaign treasurer—I don't think *Barry* understood—so I was kept on in that capacity. For good or ill, I thus became the only Draft veteran admitted to the inner circle. Barry asked Daniel C. Gainey, who had been RNC treasurer, to serve as finance director; Gainey added G.R. Herberger, a department store operator and real estate developer, as assistant director. They joined the team we already had in place: Stets Coleman, Roger Milliken, Jerry Milbank, and me. We brought in some $3.5 million between then and the convention, and Henry Salvatori raised about $1 million to support the primary effort in California.

Clif swallowed his pride and tried to work with Kleindienst, with mixed results. They were both very good people, dedicated to the common cause and each with valuable skills and experience, but they did not enjoy a warm relationship, working or otherwise. At one point Arizona Congressman John Rhodes, having received an anonymous letter highly critical of Kleindienst, shared the contents with Kleindienst, who then called Clif on the carpet and accused him of responsibility for the complaint. Clif denied the charge. They agreed to divide their responsibilities state-by-state—more so they wouldn't have to work together, I suspect, than for any administrative efficiencies. Clif came out ahead on points, as he was put in charge of all planning and operations at the convention. This was significantly more important than rounding up a few stray delegates in states where he already had closed some deals.

When told about what had happened, Kitchel was not pleased. He told Kleindienst that Clif should have been fired. Not quite two months into the marriage of Draft Goldwater and Goldwater for President, we were ready for a divorce.

In his 1988 autobiography, Barry acknowledged that he didn't know Peter O'Donnell, Clif White, or the others of the Draft movement very well, and since he didn't expect to win anyway, what difference did it make? It made a lot of difference to us, because we did not share his pessimism.

CHAPTER 8

The Runner Stumbles

THE NATION'S FIRST PRIMARY—by tradition always in New Hampshire—was to be on March 10, 1964. Though not part of the official team, in December 1963 Peter O'Donnell walked the ground and discovered that the Goldwater supporters were underfinanced and ill-equipped to handle a campaign. The campaign director and the committee chairman (who happened to be Senator Cotton) did not agree on how to run the campaign, or even, apparently, how to talk about it. Peter reported this to Kitchel, who told Peter to relax.

Barry made his first foray into New Hampshire on January 7. He would ultimately spend some twenty-three days there—eighteen-hour days clumping through the snow with a cast on a foot painfully sore from an operation, making as many as eighteen appearances, each time meeting with a handful of people hardy enough to brave the winter weather. He would shake hands, give a ten-minute talk, and answer the same questions over and over again. At some stops, there was a ratio of one newsman per voter in attendance. Once he addressed a group of eight-year-olds at a primary school. This was a campaign so disorganized that the very term "campaign" seems out of place. As Theodore White noted, "For mismanagement, blundering and sheer naiveté, Goldwater's New Hampshire campaign was unique."

He was woefully unprepared. At the beginning of this campaign, Clif put together a briefing book—itinerary, names of officials, names and vitae of people he would be meeting—but the "staff" had not passed it on to Barry. Five days before the primary, Mary McGrory of the *Washington Star* would write, "Senator Goldwater has yet to give a statistic about New Hampshire. He does not even trouble to mention the town in which he finds himself."

During two press conferences on his first day in the state (January 7), Barry pushed what would become the two most troublesome buttons of the campaign. More to the point, they were the two issues that, in hindsight, sank his candidacy before it even left the dock.

At the first meeting with the press, in Concord, he was asked whether he was in favor of continuing Social Security. His views on Social Security—then and now "the third rail of politics"—were no secret: He had long believed it to be an underfunded pseudo-insurance program; though it was originally developed as a safety net in the depths of the Depression for elder citizens who had no savings and little hope, he felt the program was barely adequate and that now, with the Depression long past, every worker was being taxed to fund something that many of them would not need. Therefore, he responded, he would offer "one change"—make participation in the program voluntary. "If a person can provide better for himself, let him do it. But if he prefers the government to do it, let him." There were many better ways to invest the same amount of the payroll tax, he suggested, and "get a better Social Security program."

Responding to a question that referenced the botched Bay of Pigs invasion of Cuba that had taken place three months after JFK took office in 1961, Barry opined that Cuban exiles ought to be given another chance—with better training and support from the United States.

Headline-writing is an art, not a science; the people who write headlines try to boil a story down to an attention-getting essence. They are often not the people who write the stories. Thus, above an account that largely was accurate, the *Concord Monitor* headline of the day said: "GOLDWATER SETS GOALS: END SOCIAL SECURITY, HIT CASTRO." Copies of the article were distributed by the Rockefeller team to every Social Security beneficiary in the state. The Rockefeller team knew that people who read headlines don't necessarily read the articles.

At another press conference later in the day, Barry was asked about nuclear weapons in Europe. He gave about the same answer he had given in Hartford some two months earlier: "I have said, the commander should have the ability to use nuclear weapons. . . . Former commanders have told me that NATO troops should be equipped with nuclear weapons, but the use should remain only with the commander."

As before, he meant, of course, *the* commander of NATO, not unit commanders in the field. And he meant tactical nuclear weapons of limited reach—with a yield equal to perhaps 40 metric tons of TNT over a radius of about a mile (minuscule compared with the 12,000-ton and 15,000-ton weapons that had devastated Hiroshima and Nagasaki, and submicroscopic against the 50 million–ton weapons available in 1963). But it did not matter what he really meant: His comment was interpreted to mean that any hotheaded major could start a nuclear holocaust. Nor did it matter that NATO had long been equipped with tactical nukes, and the commander already had authority to use them under certain conditions.

Rockefeller took advantage of the misunderstanding at his own Concord press conference, asking: "How can there be sanity [in the campaign] when he wants to give area commanders the authority to make decisions on the use of nuclear weapons?" Goldwater's campaign managers did not even try to put this in perspective until the end of September. This was much too late. It wasn't just that the water had already gone over the dam—the dam had burst.

These two issues, more than any others—and with more significant impact than any others—dogged Barry to the very end, when a touring Lyndon Johnson would exhort the crowds: "Vote Democratic on November 3. Vote to save your Social Security from going down the drain. Vote to keep a prudent hand which will not mash that nuclear button."

But again, I'm getting ahead of the story.

The National Draft Goldwater organization met for the last time on January 12, 1964, to arrange for the formal transition to a newly constituted Goldwater for President Committee. We had loose ends to tie up dealing with finances, staff assignments, and coordination with state organizations. Finances were the easy part; the Goldwater for President Committee would absorb the assets and liabilities of the Draft Committee. There were some legal formalities, and my attorney brother, Harry S. Middendorf, who had been providing advice and assistance, would draft a "Resolution to Dissolve" and a "Constitution and By-Laws" for the new organization. The Draft Committee would send a letter to each state organization thanking everyone for their support and alerting them to the forthcoming changes. The new director of field operations, Richard Kleindienst, would follow up with a "welcome aboard" letter.

Denny Kitchel and Dean Burch had been invited to our meeting, and Peter O'Donnell—in charge of one last session—had a few things to say. First, putting on his hat as Texas Republican state chairman, he reported on the mood at a recent RNC meeting. Officials from around the country had been following the Draft Committee's efforts with great interest and some support, but the new campaign team breezed through the winter meeting as if nothing had yet been accomplished, denigrating—if they were mentioned by anyone—the efforts of Draft Goldwater. Kitchel and friends did not mix with the crowd, did not make their manners to important officials (did not, in fact, seem to know who was, or who was not, important). Not a good beginning. "Keep in mind," Peter advised, "all state officials are prima donnas. They want to know that we want their help—and that we'll be there to help them, when needed."

Our guests remained quiet, and if body language means anything—that is, two guys sitting there with their arms folded across
their chests—I sensed an emotion somewhere between defensive and
defiant. Or a mix of both.

Peter then brought up two increasingly familiar topics: Goldwater's tendency to speak his mind rather than shape his comments to
the audience, and the inexperience of our two guests. Peter suggested that Barry had to start thinking nationally, even globally, and
not as a candidate for senator from Arizona. His team had to welcome, not exclude, advice. Peter said, "I have never thought of anything but success, but I'm beginning to see clouds." It was, he said,
"Goldwater or Bust" for the conservative movement. Conservative
politicians had begun gathering under the Goldwater banner, but
they easily could be spooked back into safe burrows.

John Ashbrook offered a few reasons for the success, to date, of
the Draft movement: candor, honesty, and the ability to give—and
take—criticism. "A rare quality," he said, "in a political organization."
He urged Kitchel to include tough and honest politicians on his
working staff and exclude yes men. John Tower suggested that Kleindienst, at least, would not hesitate to tell Kitchel "how the cow ate the
cabbage." A bit of colorful Texas talk, but the meaning was clear.
Tower may have surmised that Kitchel and Kleindienst were not Arizona clones. As it turned out, he was right: They would soon have a
falling out, and by the end of July, Kleindienst would leave the campaign to make an unsuccessful run for governor of Arizona.

Through it all, Kitchel sat, stone-faced, just listening—like a lawyer in
court. Then, when it came his turn, he stood up—like a lawyer in
court—and delivered a calm, measured response. "No one is more ap-
preciative of your efforts than Barry Goldwater," he said. He noted that
Goldwater had been a "reluctant dragon" until he had told him, "It's
now or never." Barry had responded, "Okay. Let her rip." Now that he'd
made the big decision, Kitchel said, Barry was all fired up. "Your mission

had been not just to draft him, but to elect him. You feel pushed aside; you are let down, wondering where to go. This soon will be dispelled." He pledged to continue the spirit of openness and candor, but asked that private communications "not be let outside of the room." Then he and Burch, who had said little between "Hello" and "Goodbye," left.

They left us more than frustrated, and the meeting turned a bit sentimental. Clif gave a little speech, taking us back to the beginnings of the movement. Peter offered thanks all around and said, "Now I'm off to be a good Texas chairman." John Ashbrook expressed his appreciation for the "wonderful associations" we'd all had and said, "The Republican Party will be the beneficiary." Ione Harrington was "happy to have been on the team." In short, they said the sort of things people say when they have just been fired.

John Tower brought us back to business. "We must nominate Barry Goldwater," he said. If the country was going to elect a liberal Republican, it might as well elect a Democrat. The diminutive Tower rose to his full height and said, "I will throw myself in front of any on-rushing competitors." He paused, then said with telling emphasis: "Barry has wrapped himself up in his security blanket and is sucking his thumb." The only people Goldwater would listen to were on the Arizona team, and it was obvious that he was not getting good advice. On the recent visits to New Hampshire, he had not even reached out to enlist the support of the state leaders. Tower said Barry needed a speaker's bureau to coordinate schedules and a "delegate advisory committee" to coordinate the precinct-by-precinct search. Len Hall, perhaps, could be the chairman.

Jerry Milbank said that Len appeared to be leaning toward Barry; in a conversation at the RNC meeting, he had suggested a Goldwater-Scranton ticket. Peter reiterated that Goldwater (the strong, silent cowboy) would not break down and ask Len for help. Tower said, metaphorically, that Barry must "make league with the devil to beat Hitler." We needed to have, he added, a united front: We should give Barry our estimate on the delegates, then tell him that the issue was in doubt, that the top campaign leadership must reflect a national, not regional, base, and that one step would be to include Len, perhaps as chairman of a delegate advisory committee.

Peter took it all in and put it down in a letter to our candidate, opening with one of Barry's favorite phrases:

> We'll probably "catch hell" for saying this, but we want to offer these observations. They were reached after considerable discussion and are the unanimous opinion of our Committee.
>
> The survival of the conservative element in our Party depends on your success in obtaining the nomination. In each state, conservative Republicans have committed themselves to your candidacy. Should your drive for the nomination fail, they will be buried, politically. It will be a long time before a new generation of conservative leadership asserts itself, particularly in the Northern and Eastern states.
>
> The grass roots of the Republican Party is overwhelmingly in your corner. However, the next six months must be a single-minded quest for delegates, which requires concentration on the leadership elements of our Party.

Peter included our recommendations: Give the campaign team a more national flavor; add an advisory committee with Len as chairman; hold regular weekly meetings of senior staff; and put one person in charge of the presently chaotic scheduling (this last step, he said, was "essential to proper coordination of the tremendous demands on your limited time"). He once again reminded the senator that "shooting from the hip" could prove fatal, adding, "We do not mean to suggest that the witty and spontaneous way in which you answer questions should be changed. We strongly suggest, however, that you control the issues by only discussing those things which you have considered in advance. Helpful to this aspect would be the development of a series of position papers." He closed with a pledge of our complete support and expressed gratitude that Barry had agreed to accept "this tremendous responsibility."

In the middle of his first New Hampshire swing, Barry took a short detour to New York to be the speaker and guest of honor at an Economic Club dinner. In advance of the event, Robert B. Anderson, secretary of the treasury under Eisenhower (and a Middendorf family friend), sent me a list of talking points he knew would be of interest to the audience, such as:

- We should get control over our balance of payments.
- We should stimulate the economy to encourage capital investment and spur expansion.
- We should export far and wide the American economic concepts of freedom of the individual, protection of property and investment, and the right to earn profits.
- We should remember that economic development comes from incentives—when people can enjoy the fruits of their own initiative. Otherwise, they become dependent on the government or someone else. We needed to find ways to help the underdeveloped nations of the world—and not just by extending lines of credit. "It is only when people are paying their own money," Anderson wrote, "that at some point they become interested in fiscal responsibility."

I passed the talking points to Kitchel, along with a few other suggestions. Barry seems not to have noticed—all things considered, I doubt that he ever saw them. According to one critical observer—my brother "Took" (W. Kennedy B. Middendorf), vice president of the Bank of New York and a certified member of the economic community—the speech was bland and lacking in memorable phrases, ideas, or emotion. Blinded though I was by my respect for Barry, I had to agree.

Oh, there were a few good points. Barry affirmed his belief that the nation had an obligation to provide help and opportunity for the poor, but said, "I do not believe that the mere fact of having little money entitles everybody, regardless of circumstances, to be permanently maintained by the taxpayers at an average or comfortable standard of living." He said that people now on public welfare should, if physically able, "be put to work to earn their benefits at a specific rate per hour" on community projects. There was no need for "gaudy" new federal programs.

But then he laid another "Goldwater" on the crowd. "We are told," he said, "that many people lack skills and cannot find jobs because they do not have an education. It's like saying that people have big feet because they wear big shoes. The fact is that most people who have no skills have no education for the same reason—low intelligence or ambition."

After the dinner, economics of a different sort were clearly on Barry's mind when, bothered by his foot and unhappy with his performance in New Hampshire, he sat down with a few of us—including Kitchel, Jerry Milbank, and me. "Get out if we can't raise $1 million," he said. "If there's no dough, Goldwater runs for the Senate. We'll spend $150,000 in New Hampshire; beyond this is not worth it." He looked at me and said, "To you it's money. To me it's my neck." Then he offered a rambling, but not incoherent, discourse: "I thought Peter O'Donnell was an idiot to start this, but this thing done by amateurs, great job. I haven't gotten here by my own efforts. You young fellows have done it. . . . This is a new party."

He gave credit to Peter because when the Draft organization was formally announced in April 1963, Peter had been in charge. And Peter's name was first on the "National Draft Goldwater Committee" letterhead. It was not until much later that he realized the depth of Clif's involvement, or that he should have credited the seminal contribution of Bill Rusher. And I'm not sure whether, at this point, Barry knew that Peter had essentially been kicked off the team. And I'm almost certain he had not yet seen Peter's letter, mailed only a couple of days earlier.

Someone suggested that we bring Len Hall aboard to get a steady hand at the tiller. Barry was clearly ambivalent. "He's already turned me down. . . . I'm not going to kiss Len's ass. . . . Len Hall may be 'the old pro' but he's not available, so what's wrong with having a young pro, Dick Kleindienst?"

I didn't say so, but a few days earlier Len had told me he was disturbed about the "provincialism" of Goldwater's team. He also left me with the distinct impression that he had pretty much been told that his services weren't going to be needed. I would later learn that Denny Kitchel and Len had had lunch together; Kitchel had expected Len to volunteer, and Len had expected to be invited. The mating dance ended without result, at least for now; Len would join us much later in the campaign.

Meanwhile, things were picking up in New Hampshire, where Barry was now drawing record-breaking crowds, holding the largest rallies in the history of some New Hampshire towns—some of them even taking place in the middle of a snowstorm. One week, he appeared before 17,500 people; he told me he "shook every hand; at least, I feel like it." There were record-breaking crowds in other places, too. A Lincoln Day rally in Chicago drew 3,600 people, and almost 8,000 attended an event in Portland, Oregon; both were the largest ever of their kind. Barry's speech at the Commercial Club of San Francisco drew the largest audience in the history of the club.

Record-breaking crowds, but a poor report card. His speeches were dull, and his delivery was flat. He got restive saying the same things over and over again, so he tried to vary the pitch, so to speak, which left him open to charges of inconsistency. At four stops on one day he gave four versions of his position on the United Nations. First, he said he would be inclined to withdraw from the UN if Communist

China were seated. Then, he affirmed that the United States must stay in the UN. By the third stop, he was saying that if the mainland Chinese supplanted the Nationalist Chinese at the UN, it would blow U.S. participation in the UN to pieces. That evening, he said, "I've never said, 'Let's get out of the UN.' I don't know how that rumor ever got started."

All of this triggered plenty of advice—some of it bang-on and powerful—from experienced Republican campaign officials. A few samples, from memos sent in to campaign headquarters:

"Goldwater gave a scattered type of talk. He must have an organized speech—and speak it, not read it."

"If the subject is dull—make it lively. People are impressed with examples, not statistics. . . . Is the government overstaffed? Don't just say so, tell a story: 'I walked into the office of a Cabinet member and two secretaries were doing their nails.'"

"Don't tell him what to say—but make sure that what he says works with the audience."

"On a national speech, stay away from arcane local issues such as reclamation in Arizona. In Arizona . . . talk about local issues."

"Barry told me people get elected because of what they are AGAINST not what they are FOR. He is wrong. . . . He needs to tell us where he stands, not what the Democrats are doing wrong."

These outside suggestions were seldom, if ever, given appropriate attention. One longtime Goldwater supporter, a Republican official in Illinois, had good suggestions for working with the press while on the road: Enlist the assistance of volunteers who know the local reporters; provide timely transcripts of press conferences (derived from a human stenotypist or a tape recorder); provide reporters with adequate desk space, typewriters, and telephones; and have someone standing by to answer simple questions, such as "What time is the briefing?" or "Where can I get a cup of coffee?" Follow up with brief

thank-you or commendatory notes to individual journalists, to let
them know you read their stuff. This official sent a detailed letter to
Kitchel and was answered with the standard brush-off: "Mr. Kitchel
has asked me to reply to your very helpful letter . . . "

Along the way, Barry continued to hand fat, juicy, unscripted
sound bites to the media. Some were vintage Goldwater and merely
controversial, as when he said that government couldn't stop economic depressions but could only start them, or that he had voted
against federal aid to education because he didn't think educators
could spend the amount of money they were seeking. Some of his
comments contained easily exposed errors: He said that 11 million
Americans were unemployed on the eve of World War II; the actual
number was almost exactly half that.

In meetings with college students he suggested that medical care
for the aged would undermine the American family and filial love.
He said that some people did not want to work. The Nuclear Test Ban
Treaty made it impossible to test the reliability of our guided missiles;
Secretary of Defense Robert S. McNamara had destroyed military
morale more than any of his predecessors; and trends toward "handouts and circuses" were threatening the United States with a fate comparable to that of ancient Rome. He told one group, "If some of these
colleges you fellows go to would start paying attention to the Constitution, I would feel safer about the future of the country."

In one forty-five-minute off-the-cuff meeting at the home of a
local family—joined by thirty neighbors and fifteen national reporters—he advocated the abolition of the Electoral College; complained that our nation had the lowest tariff in the world ("about 8
percent") and was a trillion dollars in debt; promised, if elected, to
cut federal spending by $7 billion to $8 billion a year; proclaimed
that the Great Depression had started in Austria because Austria did
precisely what America was doing today; advocated carrying the war
to North Vietnam; said no state in the Union discriminated against
blacks more than New York ("I am half-Jewish and I know something

The Publisher's Newspaper Syndicate, courtesy of Estate of Karen Fischetti

"OF COURSE YOU'RE PREJUDICED—
YOU PRINT EVERYTHING I SAY"

about discrimination"); and defended an earlier position about sending Marines into Cuba (when Fidel Castro cut off the water supply to the U.S. base at Guantanamo) by saying that "a dictator was able to push the United States around and get away with it; sooner or later we must stop this, our embassies being burned up, our flag being torn down and scoffed at."

He ended the meeting by saying how happy he was to have had this opportunity "to find out what's on your mind and you to find out whether I have one." He was off-camera but not off the record. Much of the press coverage virtually ignored a fine speech that same day, warmly applauded by the audience, that was filled with rational thoughts on civil rights, morality, and the need for law and order—and played up the unfocused, trigger-happy cowboy.

In early February, our eighteen-member campaign finance team held a one-day meeting in Phoenix. The outlook on the political side was good overall. A *Newsweek* poll agreed with our estimates of convention delegates in Barry's corner: 425 probable, 124 leaning in that direction. We were bringing some top-level leaders aboard, but our greatest strength lay in grassroots support, which was better than it had been among Republicans at any time since the first Eisenhower campaign. We also had good control of the fund-raising effort—someone joked that we would be able to get away with almost anything except a lack of cash. Rockefeller, we had heard, was planning to spend between $15 million and $20 million, $6,000 a day in California alone. It was an exaggeration, but it seemed plausible at the time (he actually spent about $5 million). We were reasonably on target toward Clif's original estimate of $3.2 million. However, the campaign had no comprehensive budget and was spending in scattershot fashion. Too many advertising dollars went to some places, and not enough to others. Too much money went to charter aircraft, and we were spending money on polls in areas like the District of Columbia where we didn't need the information.

This latter point sent my brother Harry off on a moderate tirade. "What on earth," he said, "is the reason for wasting money on polls?" Barry, he suggested—a creative politician with fresh new ideas—should create opinion, not try to conform to the popular notions of the day. "When moving into an uncharted sea, polls are useless," he said. Harry had a point, but he was fixated on the Edsel debacle—the failed Ford product that had been designed by polls. He didn't understand the tactical value of political polling.

When our candidate joined us for lunch in early afternoon, he told us he was bothered by the media's concentration on what seemed to be irrelevant comments, and its predilection for giving coverage to Rockefeller propaganda. "I have never in my life seen such nonsense," he said, but added, "I don't intend to butter up the press." He proposed that we go over the heads of the media with paid television and a brigade of speechmakers. Yet, he didn't want to launch any sort of "publicity" campaign. "I've made 125 speeches in Los Angeles, 125 in San Francisco, 250 in New York," he said. "If I'm not well known now, I never will be." From this I could only assume that Barry didn't understand the tactical value of working with the media—a rather scary thought, later proven to be true.

Barry believed that Scranton was angling for the VP slot but was doing so in a rather weird fashion, by "using every pressure known to keep people from working for me." As for the other side's VP selection: "If Johnson picks Bobby Kennedy, the South comes back to us. I don't know how he can avoid it, if Bobby wants it, with millions invested." Barry added, "I hope he picks someone like Hubert Humphrey."

A week or so later, with three weeks to go in New Hampshire, the campaign staff and all Goldwater national and state leaders gathered in Chicago for a full-scale "progress review." Clif White made the arrangements and prepared a briefing that he expected to deliver. As it turned out, he was asked to deliver it physically to Kitchel, who gave the briefing. It was another insult to Clif, but the briefing went so well that it may have preserved Kitchel's job, which was in jeopardy because of growing dissatisfaction with the direction of the campaign—a great irony.

Before that meeting began, however, some members of the original Draft group (most of whom had not been at the finance committee meeting in Phoenix) arranged for a private session with Barry. And it was very private. We posted a guard at the door to block any interlopers. The reports from New Hampshire were troubling; we wanted Barry to understand that his apparent lack of focus, his scattershot approach to campaigning, was becoming a serious liability. In the event, however, we backed down. The rigors of his last swing through snowbound New Hampshire had taken a toll; Barry came into the room looking tired and distraught. His hands were shaking. This was not the time to add to his misery. Charlie Barr called off the confrontation, and the meeting became a desultory conversation on unimportant matters.

I think that Barry knew he had escaped a bullet, because while speaking to the full assembly later in the day he once again acknowledged the Draft movement's efforts in bringing him to this point; in essence, he promised to do better in the future. "I thank the group that met here in Chicago at that *secret* meeting that the whole world heard about. There were times when I wished that Peter O'Donnell, White, Middendorf, Millbank, and their group would go home and run their cattle ranches, but now I'm grateful to them. Now, I want this job. And when I want something, I go after it."

Our fervor, he said, reminded him of a religious movement, and he admitted that he had not been doing a very good job. "I'm a clumsy idiot," he said, "with five feet and six hands." He pledged: "This is a campaign I intend to win. I have never lost a campaign and I'm too old to go back to work and too young to quit politics." Moreover, "my tail's too big to put between my legs."

And, he laughed, "Reporters throw up at the thought of me being nominated."

Three days before the voting in New Hampshire, Barry, seduced by the roar of the crowd—a common failing of politicians—and encouraged by an optimistic Kitchel, told a group of reporters, "I've got it made."

This was a big mistake. Yes, Barry was drawing large crowds—but the crowds too often saw an exhausted and irritable candidate. At one stop he told his audience, "I'm not one of these baby-kissing, hand-shaking, blintz-eating candidates. I don't like to insult the American intelligence by thinking that slapping people on the back is going to win you votes." Rockefeller shook hands, kissed babies, slapped a few backs, and charmed everyone. His campaign strategy was perfectly tuned to New Hampshire: Where Barry flitted about in a chauffeur-driven Cadillac, Rocky rode on a bus with the press; where Peggy Goldwater wore mink, Happy Rockefeller wore tweedy cloth. But, while Goldwater and Rockefeller tried to outdo each other with public meetings and paid media, they succeeded only in pushing the "undecided" vote up to 50 percent.

The members of the team pushing Henry Cabot Lodge spent their time and money rounding up supporters and sending out sample ballots that showed how to vote for a write-in candidate. They also demonstrated how to hoodwink voters. They brought out a five-minute TV endorsement of Lodge that had been made by Eisenhower four years earlier, when Lodge was Nixon's vice-presidential running-mate. In the 1964 version, references to Nixon had been edited out; a blast of trumpets cleverly drowned out the word "vice" in Ike's spoken introduction, thus creating the impression that the endorsement was current.

Lodge—who had not left his post in Saigon—had not set foot in the state, said nothing, and charmed no one. Nevertheless, he captured many of the "undecideds" and won the race with 35 percent of the vote. The final tally: Lodge, 33,007 votes; Goldwater, 20,692; Rockefeller, 19,504; Richard Nixon, also a write-in candidate, 15,587; Maine's Senator Margaret Chase Smith (who had visited New Hampshire only once during the campaign), 2,120; and perennial presidential candidate Harold Stassen (who entered the race nine times between 1948 and 1992), 1,373.

We watched the returns on TV in a room at the Madison Hotel in Washington, while reporters waited downstairs. Not more than eighteen minutes after the polls had closed, the networks announced the results. Barry took the news quietly, went down to face the cameras, and offered one of the more honest comments ever spoken by a politician: "I goofed."

Time, in the postelection issue, summed up the campaign to date:

Touted as the front runner at the start of the campaign, he hobbled into New Hampshire with one foot in a cast (a minor operation) and the other in his mouth (a major affliction). He showed no knack for person-to-person politicking, and his formal speeches

were stilted. His argument that social security should be made voluntary was confused, leading New Hampshire's sizable number of
retired persons to believe that Barry was against the whole pension
program. Sensing that he was slipping, Goldwater began to depre-
ciate the importance of the New Hampshire primary. Said he:
"The person who wins in California will win the nomination." He
may have been right, but he did not endear himself to Hamp-
shiremen, who think highly of their little primary.

Privately, Burch said, "We all underrated the New Hampshire primary, but the one error which cost us the election comes back to the
candidate himself. He was not psychologically attuned to a presidential primary." Kleindienst called New Hampshire a "catalytic agent"
that drew the Goldwater team together. Kitchel said, "In one way, New
Hampshire was a good thing for we learned so much."

Publicly, Kitchel—the lawyer dabbling in public affairs—issued a
press release: "It is most gratifying that a candidate from the Far West,
Senator Barry Goldwater, could do so well in the New England state
of New Hampshire." No one was fooled. Some of the Draft Goldwater
veterans asked for Kitchel's resignation. He declined.

CHAPTER 9

The Spoilers

PETER O'DONNELL SHARED his anger and disappointment in a letter to Dan Gainey, John Tower, John Grenier, Jerry Milbank, Stets Coleman, and me. Goldwater's response to the January memo, he said, virtually had been no response at all: Barry had ignored the Len Hall recommendation; the top campaign leadership remained almost exclusively from Arizona; and weekly meetings were not being held. Therefore, confusion reigned at the Washington headquarters. Since the fundamentals of the campaign were not periodically reviewed, there was neither a sense of direction nor strategic planning. Candidate scheduling was disorganized. No position papers had been developed, and Barry continued to shoot from the hip. "The general impression created was that Goldwater was too reckless or even dangerous to turn over the running of the country to him," Peter wrote. He continued:

> The foregoing deficiencies result from Goldwater's apparent attitude toward this campaign. . . . His laissez-faire attitude of "pooping along" will fail to commit a sufficient number of delegates to assure the nomination. Unless those commitments are obtained prior to the convention, the nomination will be left to chance rather than direction. It is a direct result of Goldwater's attitude toward the campaign that mistakes were made. In the final analysis

Senator Goldwater has failed to accept the *responsibility for leadership* of this campaign.

What is at stake? An unsuccessful drive for the nomination will provide the vehicle and excuse for the Republican liberals and moderates to *purge* the Republican Party of conservative officials and not a few conservative officeholders.

What can be done? In summary, 1. Candidate attitude must change. 2. Campaign leadership must be changed. I recommend Len Hall. If that is not possible, I recommend Bill Miller.

As before, nothing happened.

Clif almost quit—several times. No one listened to his suggestions, and he could do nothing without first getting permission. Things came to a head in the middle of March, when he sent Goldwater a letter critical of the organization (or lack thereof) in the delegate hunt. To his surprise, he was promoted, in a manner of speaking, to "co-director of field operations." He continued to be responsible for the caucus states, where the process had begun, and for making preparations for the Republican National Convention.

Goldwater was scheduled to make one major appearance in Illinois, April 14. After talking with some voters, Kleindienst was convinced that the charge that Barry had planned to "abolish Social Security" had to be confronted head-on. He brought this up during a strategy session with Baroody, McCabe, Kitchel, George Humphrey (Eisenhower's close friend and his first secretary of the treasury), Arthur Summerfield (Ike's postmaster general), and Barry. No dice, they said; the speech was already set. After the meeting, Baroody accused Kleindienst of disloyalty. "Don't you know what it is to have teamwork? We've decided what Goldwater is going to do in Illinois. You knew the decision, and yet you brought up this Social Security business in front of all the other people." Kleindienst affirmed his loyalty to Goldwater, then added, "If disagreeing with you is being disloyal,

then I don't understand the definition." He wasn't invited to any
more of Baroody's "strategy" meetings. Although he made some solid
contributions through the primaries, he dropped away from the
Goldwater for President Committee when he went on to his unsuccessful run for governor of Arizona.

From the last weekend of February through April, we enjoyed victories in Oklahoma, North Carolina, South Carolina, Wisconsin, North
Dakota, Kentucky, and Illinois—although press coverage of the Illinois primary was bizarre. Goldwater had a big win against six declared
or write-in candidates. Clif said, "It was the first contest I have ever
been involved in where the candidate got 62 percent of the vote—
and still came out a loser in the press." As *Washington Star* columnist
David Lawrence offered: "Maybe two and two don't make four, after
all, in national politics. Judging by some of the TV and radio broadcasts on Tuesday night and subsequent comments in the press, Senator Goldwater got the highest number of votes . . . but nonetheless
suffered a 'setback.'"

Victories in Arizona, Louisiana, New Jersey, Iowa, Texas, Ohio, and
Indiana came in short order, and Clif's unofficial reckoning soon put
the total number of committed delegates at more than 400. I should
note that, while Clif White justly gets a lot of credit for building grassroots support, many of the victories were due to the efforts of Peter
O'Donnell and John Grenier, a pair of political geniuses who really
knew how to work with state delegations.

On May 8, *Time* magazine wondered at Goldwater's momentum:
"It seemed hardly possible. Here was Arizona's Barry Goldwater, who
only a few weeks ago appeared to be flat on his back in his quest for
the GOP Presidential nomination. . . . Yet, as of last week, Goldwater
was clearly the man to beat [at the convention] in San Francisco."
Time ascribed his swift rise in popularity to "the national preoccupa-
tion with primaries, which usually make more headlines than delegates" and to an "obsession with the polls." "But," the writer mused,

"no pollster ever nominated a Presidential candidate." Slowly and steadily, *Time* noted, "Goldwater kept collecting delegates while the unavowed and disavowed collected press clippings."

In the West Virginia primary, Rockefeller was unopposed, and write-in votes were not permitted. Rocky took all the votes, but they were nonbinding on the delegates. Ten of fourteen went for Goldwater.

On May 12, 1964, we held another "monster" rally, this time in Madison Square Garden, to show the nation that even in Rocke-feller's home town, Barry had pull. The *Daily News*—the tabloid with the trademarked slogan "New York's Picture Newspaper"—carried the banner headline "18,000 CHEER BARRY IN GARDEN" and filled the rest of the front page with a marvelous shot of the band playing, the crowd applauding, balloons dropping, Barry and his wife at the podium—and, standing with them and looking quite happy, yours truly.

The *Daily News* called the rally "a totally unprecedented personal political triumph" and reported that the forty-five-minute speech "was interrupted 108 times, by meticulous count, by bursts of applause [and] small demonstrations." The paper also noted that the rally was "snubbed by local GOP leaders in deference to Governor Rockefeller."

Or perhaps they were put off by admission fees, which ranged from $2 to $1,000 (adding some $100,000 to the campaign). The pols need not have worried: We would have let them in free. Barry shrugged off the snub, commenting to the press: "Any Republican who would rather fight fellow Republicans than fight Democrats is doing nothing more or less than pinch-hitting for Lyndon Johnson. I want to find ways we can work together as a team."

There was another snub that took place that day, though behind the scenes. Kitchel-Baroody managed to keep Bill Buckley off the program even though the *National Review* had played an important role in organizing the event. Kitchel believed that *National Review* readers would be with us anyway, and he wanted to appeal to people who didn't like the *National Review*. Having Buckley up on the podium, he reasoned, would cause some of the less conservative voters to turn away.

The Oregon primary came three days later, May 15. It did not go well for Barry, who had barely visited the state and had not endeared himself to the natives. On a scheduled visit in April, he had been greeted at the airport by 500 people who had been waiting for some time—his commercial flight had been delayed. Goldwater got off the plane, marched though the crowd, gave autographs to two eight-year-olds, then climbed into a waiting car for the drive to his hotel. The next day he gave a speech at noon, and that evening he gave a televised address from the hotel ballroom, with 300 supporters as a live audience. Afterward, he spoke briefly to one person on the edge of the crowd before retreating to his suite. When challenged about this lapse of manners, he said he was tired and wanted to call his wife.

Steve Shadegg, recovered from his disconnect with Barry and serving as regional director for most of the western states, learned that the Lodge team planned to re-run the New Hampshire "Eisenhower endorsement" clip during the Oregon primary. He sent a telegram to Eisenhower, asking him either to authorize or condemn the spot. Ike responded that he had "high esteem" for all of the "individuals prominently mentioned as possible nominees for the presidency in 1964. I respect each and oppose none." He went on: "The film in question I have never seen, nor have I been contacted in any fashion in respect to its use prior to your communications. If it expresses my high respect for Cabot Lodge, it is accurate and I do not object to that esteem being reaffirmed in any place in America. If it suggests that I have given any public indication of a preference for any person over any other in the current contest, then it is a definite misrepresentation."

We wondered if it was possible that Eisenhower had been completely unaware of the fraud in New Hampshire. In any event, the telegram was made public, and the Lodge manager in Oregon pulled the broadcast schedule.

Another scheduled visit to Oregon was canceled, rescheduled, and canceled again. Steve Shadegg complained to Dean Burch, who said that it was hard to reach Oregon on a commercial airline, and Barry needed to focus on California. The campaign would later issue a press release citing the need for Barry to participate in debate on the pending civil rights bill. So much for honesty in campaigning.

When Rockefeller learned of Goldwater's dropped schedule, he more than doubled his planned appearances in the state, telling voters, "I am the only man who cares enough about your votes to come to Oregon." He had a point, and he won. Lodge, still in Vietnam, finished second. Goldwater was third.

Barry's reputation for not bothering himself much with good manners was growing. *Time* reported on a visit to Atlanta, just a week earlier:

> Barry Goldwater ordinarily is an amiable sort, a man with an earthy sense of humor who enjoys a drink with friends. With delegates entering his camp in ever-increasing numbers, he ought to be feeling good. He isn't. The hard campaign for the Republican nomination is getting on his nerves. On a recent trip to Atlanta, Goldwater stepped from his plane, strode wordlessly through a cheering crowd. A radio reporter popped up with a microphone, asked: How was the trip, Senator? Goldwater just scowled. An admiring girl tried to clap a big white hat on his head. Goldwater shoved it away, snapping: I don't want that. The radio reporter tried again. Goldwater spoke a few words, but the reporter wanted more. Goldwater pushed the mike away and growled: Get that damn thing out of here.

Next up was the big one, California—a state with eighty-six delegates—on June 2. We knew this primary could be the final key to

Barry's nomination. But Rockefeller went after the prize with a vengeance, blanketing the state with broadcast and print media. His crackerjack PR firm, Spencer-Roberts, had a $2 million budget in the state and—according to Stuart Spencer—one goal: "We had to destroy Barry Goldwater as a member of the human race." He and his team set out to portray Goldwater as a dangerous extremist, an enemy of the elderly, the thief who would take Social Security checks away from the needy, the man who would "turn back the clock of social progress."

One brochure featured portraits of Nixon, Lodge, Romney, and Scranton grouped together on one panel, above text implying support for Rockefeller, and Goldwater, alone, on the facing panel. The headline was, "Do You Want a Leader or a Loner?" But no one had asked those four men for permission to use their names, and each in turn repudiated the assertion that he was supporting Rockefeller. Goldwater's California supporters saw a golden opportunity and twisted the premise into "Do you want a leader or a lover?"

This was a brilliant stunt, but it wasn't enough to offset a very slow start. When Dick Kleindienst arrived to assess the efforts in California, he discovered that the campaign had plenty of door-to-door and phone-bank volunteers but no radio or TV spots. The scripts were either still being developed, or being developed by someone else, or delayed for some other reason. Time had been purchased for three half-hour shows, but no one had given any thought to their content. Kleindienst called in a crew from Washington, including Lee Edwards and speechwriter Chuck Lichtenstein, to join a West Coast team of Rus Walton, Dick Herman, Steve Shadegg, and a host of others. They set to work in a three-bedroom Los Angeles apartment that had been built to order, they were told, for Greta Garbo.

Meanwhile, during a television interview with Howard K. Smith on ABC, taped earlier and broadcast May 24, Barry opened the "nuclear wound" about as far as it could go. Smith asked about interdicting enemy supplies headed south along the Ho Chi Minh Trail in

The Charleston Gazette

"THE CONFUSED OLD MAN ON THE FLYING TRAPEZE"

Vietnam. Barry replied, "Well, it's not as easy as it sounds because these aren't trails that are out in the open. . . . There have been several suggestions made. I don't think we would use any of them. But defoliation of the forests by low-yield atomic weapons could well be done. When you remove the foliage, you remove the cover." The wire services, working from a prebroadcast transcript, ignored the "I don't think we would use any of them" and reported that Barry, who was only explaining possibilities, had advocated the use of nuclear weapons in Vietnam.

When notified of the error, the wire services issued corrections, but the damage had been done. They had already dumped gasoline onto the "Goldwater is trigger-happy" fire. The headline in the *San Francisco Examiner* read "Goldwater's Plan to Use Viet A-Bomb." The *New York Times* made note of the correction in its report, which also included Goldwater's exact words, but the story was headlined "Goldwater Poses New Asian Tactic; Says A-Arms Could Be Used to Expose Supply Lines of Reds in Vietnam." It was a repeat of the Concord Social Security flap: Headlines are noticed, but disclaimers buried in the text are not. Spencer-Roberts spent $120,000 to distribute a scurrilous pamphlet to California's 3 million registered Republicans: "Who Do You Want in the Room with the H-Bomb?" it said.

In prior years, Barry had not endeared himself to Ike. In fact, he had once called Eisenhower's "modern Republicanism" a "Dime Store New Deal." But changed circumstances often lead to changed behavior, and Barry made proper obeisance to the general during the campaign—who nonetheless held himself above the fray, insisting that he was not going to be a partisan until after the convention.

Walter Thayer, the president of the *New York Herald Tribune,* tried to change that. Thayer didn't think much of Rockefeller, but he thought a great deal less of Goldwater and was determined to block Barry's nomination. Someone prepared a letter to be signed by Eisenhower outlining the qualities he would like to see in the party's nominee. It could have been written by Eisenhower himself, but since he had spent most of his adult life supported by a staff, I doubt it. However it was generated, it ended up on the front page of the *Herald Tribune* as a statement by Eisenhower. Some of the qualities it mentioned

were fairly neutral; others seemed to describe Rockefeller more than
Goldwater. "I do fervently hope," the letter said, "that the person selected . . . will be a man who will uphold, earnestly, with dedication
and conviction, the principles and traditions of our party . . . responsible, forward-looking Republicanism." On civil rights, it stated, "The
nation has a profound moral obligation to each of its citizens, requir-
ing that we not only improve our behavior but also strengthen our
laws." And on international relations, it recommended "loyal support
for the United Nations in its peacekeeping efforts."

Eisenhower seems not to have been aware of the slap at Goldwater
until the letter was published on May 25. An accompanying sidebar
proclaimed, "If former President Eisenhower can have his way, the
Republican party will not choose Sen. Barry Goldwater as its 1964
presidential nominee." Not content with just reaching readers of his
own newspaper, Thayer had Ike's letter passed to a wide range of
news organizations—including the Associated Press, United Press International, the *Los Angeles Times,* and the *New York Times,* which also
gave it front-page treatment. All on the same day that the latest
"trigger-happy" flap created headlines.

Rockefeller was overjoyed, viewing the letter as an endorsement.
Barry took the insult with uncommon good humor. Addressing a college audience in California, he stuck an arrow under his arm and
turned sideways to the audience so that he appeared to have been
shot in the back. Eisenhower was stunned. He was not a fan of Barry
Goldwater but had vowed to remain neutral; now he had been ma-
nipulated into the appearance of disfavoring a leading candidate.
George Humphrey advised him to set the record straight.

In the meantime, an invitation for Rockefeller to speak at Loyola
University was withdrawn six hours before the scheduled May 27
event, because (according to the board of regents) his appearance so
close to the election might be viewed as an endorsement of his candidacy. The matter of his divorce and remarriage—anathema to the
Catholic Church—was not mentioned but more likely was the cause,

thanks to a bit of arm-twisting administered by the solidly Catholic (and solid Goldwater supporter) Dick Herman.

Barry was scheduled to do a "family" theme TV show on Thursday, May 28. This would be similar to programs he had made during his successful runs for the Senate—he would be grouped with his family in a living-room setting to discuss the issues, his vision, and what he might do as president. He would be introduced on camera by John Wayne. On the appointed day at the appointed hour Wayne was at the studio, ready to work. But the filming had been canceled the night before. No one had thought to tell Wayne. A fog of reasons was given for the cancellation: Barry was too tired, Barry didn't have the time, the show was too complicated. In truth, what it didn't have was Kitchel's approval.

Later that day, sixteen Protestant ministers condemned Rockefeller's divorce and instant remarriage as a "serious blow against the Christian concept of marriage." Nevertheless, on Friday, a Louis Harris poll had Rockefeller ahead in California 49 to 40 percent. On Saturday, Happy Rockefeller gave birth to Nelson A. Rockefeller, Jr. You may be sure the matter was addressed from many a pulpit on Sunday.

On Monday, June 1, Eisenhower followed George Humphrey's advice and told a group of reporters that any implied effort to "read anyone out of the party" was a "complete misinterpretation. . . . You people tried to read Goldwater out of the party, I didn't." Primary day was Tuesday.

By one estimate, two weeks before the election, Barry trailed by 200,000 votes. The efforts of Kleindienst and friends pulled him closer, and the efforts of Goldwater volunteers sent into battle to get supporters to the voting booth were critical. But in my judgment, Rockefeller himself put Barry over the top. "Only Rockefeller," as Bill Rusher had said, "could turn motherhood into a liability." Goldwater squeaked by with a margin of 68,350 votes out of 2.1 million cast—which was an astonishing 72 percent turnout.

It was not much, but it was enough—especially when the week's other victories in Nebraska, New York, and South Dakota added

twenty-nine more delegates. These successes were followed by more
the next week in Alabama, twenty delegates; Colorado, fourteen; four
of eight in Hawaii; and four in Virginia. By this point, 532 delegates
(of the needed 655) were publicly or legally committed to Goldwater.
Then, on June 16, Texas brought in fifty-six more. On June 18, Utah
came in with fourteen; and Arkansas contributed nine of twelve. And
there were more to come. Goldwater won all but two of the primaries
he entered and piled up 2,150,000 votes—more votes than all the
other candidates combined.

Somewhere along the way, we thought the other potential candidates
realized they had lost out and pulled back. Nixon never declared but
was open to suggestion. Romney might have been a factor but was
never really in the hunt. Scranton, who had been enjoying a run of
good press, formally entered only one primary, Oregon, where he received a minuscule 2 percent. Then, in the first half of June, with only
a handful of delegates yet to be selected and the convention only a
month away, all three were back.

First, Scranton sought an endorsement from Eisenhower, with whom
he had very cordial relations. On June 6 they had a meeting at Ike's Gettysburg farm, only a short hike from the governor's office in Harrisburg.
Afterward, Scranton released a statement saying that Ike had encouraged him to make himself "more available" for the nomination.

Romney's turn came the next day. At a governor's conference in
Cleveland, he challenged Goldwater to explain himself. "If," Romney
said in a press statement, "his views deviate . . . from the heritage of
our party, I will do everything within my power to keep him from becoming the party's Presidential candidate."

Scranton, meanwhile, had just arrived at the conference when
Eisenhower called to suggest that Scranton must be mistaken; he was
supporting no one until after the convention, and, further, he was
not going to be part of any cabal against Goldwater. Why did Eisenhower call? He'd had a conversation the night before with George

Humphrey, and George had suggested he continue in his avowed "neutral" stance.

Scranton, who had planned to use a scheduled appearance on the TV show *Face the Nation* for a formal announcement of his renewed candidacy, now shifted gears. He followed Romney's lead and challenged Goldwater to state his views—as if, after more than eleven years in the Senate, his newspaper column, hundreds of speeches, and a best-selling book, his views were not already widely known. The demand made Scranton look foolish. Even Rockefeller, speaking with reporters later in the day, said as much.

Then Nixon joined the fray. At breakfast on Monday, June 8, he tried to convince Romney to really make a run, perhaps hoping to put the convention into the deadlock that would be Nixon's only hope. He also spoke out on the "views" question: "Looking at the future of the party, it would be a tragedy if Senator Goldwater's views as previously stated were not challenged—and repudiated."

Like a dog worrying a bone, Scranton would not let go. On June 12, at the Maryland convention, he officially offered himself as a candidate for the nomination. Without mentioning any opponents by name, he took a broad swipe at Goldwater's supporters. He warned them not to "let an exclusion-minded minority dominate our platform and choose our candidates." He then went out on what was left of the campaign trail, where he drew respectable crowds and comment (although one newspaper editor mused, "I fail to understand why the hesitant gentleman from Harrisburg is suddenly the hero of the hour in most of the press, and Goldwater the leper").

Scranton now had the backing of Rockefeller, who, after having thrown away some $5 million of his own money, threw in the towel and quit the race on June 15. The entire Rockefeller campaign staff was turned over to the gentleman from Harrisburg.

A week later, Henry Cabot Lodge resigned his post in Vietnam and joined the Scranton effort. President Eisenhower's brother Milton agreed to place Scranton's name in nomination (Ike remained neutral). Scranton began rising in the polls as former Rockefeller, Lodge, and Nixon supporters saw him as the moderate's last hope. None of it helped very much. Scranton couldn't make a dent in our numbers; delegates who were committed to Goldwater remained committed. Scranton addressed the Illinois convention on June 30; of the fifty-eight delegates, forty-eight announced for Goldwater, and the rest declined to commit to any candidate. At the Utah caucus a few days later, Scranton learned, to his dismay, that the Young Republicans had captured the delegates almost a year before. He found a similar story in Washington state, where twenty-two of the twenty-four delegates had been committed for more than a year. In Delaware, the favorite-son candidate gave Scranton a hearing and then dropped out, announcing his support for Goldwater.

In desperation, Scranton pulled out the Rockefeller song sheet: Don't send an impulsive man to the White House, he said. Don't send a man to the White House who "has no part of the heritage of a true conservative like Bob Taft. Would Bob Taft destroy Social Security?"

Incredibly—to us—Goldwater was leaning toward Scranton as his running mate. Barry had been Scranton's commanding officer in the Air National Guard and was one of the first people to encourage him to run for the governor's office. He did admit that Scranton might have become "too willowy," whatever that means.

Scranton appealed for support from Illinois senator Everett Dirksen, certain that he would find a willing ally in the coauthor of the civil rights bill (against which Barry had just voted; see next chapter). Dirksen not only came out for Goldwater but announced that he would place the senator's name in nomination at the convention. Scranton's next big hope was the Ohio delegation—until Governor John Rhodes, the designated favorite son, released his fifty-eight delegates and announced his personal support for Goldwater. As Bob Novak was to write, "All that now was left for Scranton was . . . some kind of 'incident' that would miraculously change the mood in San Francisco."

CHAPTER 10

Civil Rights

IN FEBRUARY 1964, the House of Representatives had passed a major piece of civil rights legislation and sent it on to the Senate, where it became subject to eighty-three days of scrutiny and debate filling almost 3,000 pages in the *Congressional Record*. The Senate passed the Civil Rights Act of 1964 on June 19 by a vote of 73 to 27. Barry Goldwater was one of the 27 voting against it, and his vote laid down one more roadblock to his election.

It made no political sense for him to vote against a controversial but popular social issue on the very eve of a national campaign. Barry did a lot of things that made no political sense, though, because he believed they were right. He was not alone in his opposition to the bill: He was joined in dissent by, among others, Albert Gore, Sr., of Tennessee (the father of Clinton's vice president), Sam Irvin of North Carolina, and J. William Fulbright of Arkansas—but they, after all, were Democrats and southerners. Five other prominent Republicans also voted "nay": Norris Cotton of New Hampshire, Bourke Hickenlooper of Iowa, Edwin L. Mecham of New Mexico, Millard L. Simpson of Wyoming, and John Tower of Texas. Also opposed: George H.W. Bush, candidate for the Senate from Texas.

Goldwater voted against the 1964 civil rights bill because he questioned the constitutionality of two sections, those relating to fair employment and public accommodation. The latter—the so-called "Mrs.

Murphy" clause—held that you couldn't refuse to rent your home or
a room in your boardinghouse to anyone. The goal was to ensure that
blacks could not arbitrarily be excluded, but as written the law also
forbade discrimination against drunks, felons, wife abusers, and people who smoke in bed.

"I am unalterably opposed to discrimination of any sort," Goldwater said from the floor of the Senate. "I believe that, though the problem is fundamentally one of the heart, some law can help; but not law
that embodies features like these, provisions which fly in the face of
the Constitution." He argued that the Constitution gave the states all
powers not specifically reserved to the federal government, and that
employment and accommodation were local, not national, issues.

He was swimming against the current and knew it, but he stood on
principle. "If my vote is misconstrued," he said, "let it be, and let me
suffer its consequences." The opposition—Democratic and Republican alike—took turns polishing his image as a racist. It mattered not
that he had voted for the Civil Rights Acts of 1957 and 1960, that he
approved of the other nine sections of the act of 1964, or that he had
offered four amendments to the Youth Employment Act of 1963 to
forbid discrimination because of race, color, creed, or national origin—which had been rejected by the Democrat-controlled Senate
Committee on Labor and Public Welfare on the grounds that the ad-
ministrator of the program, the secretary of labor, "could be trusted
to bar discriminations without the guidance of specific legislation." A
forthcoming election makes a world of difference: Politicians can be
so remarkably inconsistent.

It mattered not that Barry had integrated the employees of his
family department store before World War II, or that as the organizer
of the Arizona Air National Guard after the war, he had ensured and
enforced integration two years before President Truman ordered de-
segregation of the armed forces. It mattered not that he had been active in desegregating the lunch counters of Phoenix or that he had
been a member of the NAACP and the Urban League. Barry's Senate

staff put together a memo outlining these and other efforts. It seems largely to have been ignored.

Based on no known evidence, the nation's best-known political pundit, Walter Lippmann, took an egregious leap of judgment and wrote, for the *Newsweek* issue of June 22: "In his extreme views on states' rights, [Goldwater] is in fact one who would dissolve the Federal union into a mere confederation of the states. . . . He would nullify if he could the central purpose of the Civil War amendments, and would take from the children of the emancipated slaves the protection of a national union."

Another media titan reacted, not to Goldwater's vote, but to the torrent of abuse being heaped upon him. Newspaper publisher John S. Knight offered an apology, of sorts, for his brethren:

> Barry Goldwater is not my candidate, and I have done nothing to promote his Presidential aspirations, but I do think the Arizona Senator is getting shabby treatment from most of the news media.
>
> Some of the television commentators discuss Goldwater with evident disdain and contempt. Editorial cartoonists portray him as belonging to the Neanderthal age, or as a relic of the 19th Century. It is the fashion of editorial writers to persuade themselves that Goldwater's followers are either "kooks" or Birchers. This simply is not so. The Goldwater movement represents a mass protest by conservatively minded people against foreign aid, excessive welfare, high taxes, foreign policy and the concentration of power in the federal government.

Barry told a number of people that if he were challenged on this vote, he would trot out Lyndon Johnson's voting record, "the phoniest individual who ever came along." Johnson, he noted, had been opposed to civil rights until 1964. In 1960, LBJ had campaigned for reelection to the Senate in Texas on an anti-civil-rights platform, while at the same time he was running for vice president on a pro-civil-rights platform. As a senator he had voted six times against proposals to abolish the poll tax; twice against legislation to make lynching a federal crime; twice in support of segregation in the armed forces; and once in support of the perpetuation of segregation in the District of Columbia. "Let them make an issue of it," Barry said. "I'll recite the thousands of words he has spoken."

Barry never put Johnson in his place on the issue, however, because just after Barry accepted the Republican nomination in San Francisco, riots broke out all along the East Coast. They had nothing to do with Goldwater but were in protest of the killing of a black youth by a New York City policeman. On July 24, Barry met with President Johnson at the White House to propose a racial truce, if you will, to which he added an offer to avoid discussion of the divisive war in Vietnam, since American fighting men at the front needed whole-hearted support at home. The two men issued a joint statement agreeing that from then on, "race" would be off-limits in the campaign. They more or less held to that, although every time Barry spoke of "crime in the streets," it was interpreted by some as a thinly veiled appeal to racists. This was despite the fact that Barry, recognizing that the riots largely had been "Negro against Negro," had said, "The people who have suffered as a result of these riots are the Negroes." To further clarify his position, he said, "I'm not solely concerned about crime in the ghettos or slums. I'm talking about the general increase in crime."

Barry's vote on the Civil Rights Act of 1964 was of more interest to the media (then, and now) than to the voters, many (perhaps most) of whom were opposed to the same aspects of the act that Barry was—and the results on November 3 offered proof of this, at least in California. In the Senate race, the well-entrenched Democrat Pierre Salinger (the former Kennedy press secretary, appointed to the Senate in August to fill the unexpired term of Claire Engel, who had died) was opposed by movie song-and-dance man George Murphy, who had never before run for public office. The California ballot also included Proposition 14, which would overturn a state fair-housing law that was more or less equivalent to the "Mrs. Murphy" title of the Civil Rights Act. The Democrats campaigned long and hard for Salinger and against Proposition 14, and lost on both counts. Twice as many Californians voted to overturn the law as voted to elect Barry Goldwater, with whom they more or less agreed on the civil rights issue. Some 98.5 percent of the national African-American vote went to Democrats, proponents and opponents of the Civil Rights Act alike, including sixteen Democratic congressmen in Texas who had voted against the Civil Rights Act. Barry's problem with the voters had nothing to do with civil rights. Yet his vote against the act became inextricably linked to a "southern strategy" that was not, in fact, predicated on civil rights.

A comment Goldwater had made in 1961, which became a catchphrase of American political discourse, did not help. Arguing that the Republicans might as well write off the "Negro vote" for 1964 and 1968, he said, "Let's go hunting where the ducks are"—that is, where we could bag some voters. The Democrats had long since captured the overwhelming majority of blacks, and Barry could not see much point spending a disproportionate amount of campaign time and money on that portion of the electorate—nor on trying to convert eastern liberals. But the comment was widely interpreted as a bid for the votes of southern segregationists.

The South had been moving toward the Republican Party for some time, and there were a lot more potentially conservative ducks in South Carolina than in New York, Connecticut, or Massachusetts. World War II had brought a mixed economy to the agricultural South, and modern communications had brought greater homogenization. Bill Rusher had described the changes in his article "Crossroads for the G.O.P."

"In scores of Southern cities today," he wrote, "white-collar and professional workers drive home to split-level suburban ranch houses every evening, looking and acting for all the world like their northern and western counterparts. *And they are voting Republican.*" In the 1962 U.S. Senate race in Alabama, Rusher noted, Republican James Martin, who never before had run for public office, had lost to incumbent Lister Hill by just 0.7 percent—and carried every major city in the state. In the House races in the eleven states that had constituted the Confederacy, twice as many people voted Republican in 1962 as in 1958.

From such musings was evolved a strategy that recognized the broad economic shifts in that once solidly Democratic stronghold—a strategy that had been laid down during the earliest conversations among Ashbrook, Rusher, and White.

It was not Barry's intention, but indeed was a fact, that racists thought he was their friend. While we tacitly accepted their support, to charge Barry with consciously appealing to racists was specious. As the *New York Times* correctly noted in an editorial just a few days before the election: "Their embrace does not, in and of itself, signify that he returned their affections or shares their beliefs—any more than do the unsolicited endorsements the Communists have been so prone to shower on some Democrats." In the next sentence, however, the editors warned of the danger that "a Goldwater victory would create a political climate of increased respectability for these spewers of rancor." Ergo, better not vote for Goldwater.

At a press conference back in July 1963, a newsman had asked President Kennedy "whether you plan to either repudiate or reject the support and the votes of segregationists in the South." As *Time* magazine noted, "Since the power of the Democratic Party over the past hundred years has to a large extent rested upon the votes of segregationists in the South, Kennedy could hardly be expected to answer yes." In fact, he made "a neat little speech" about his administration's position on equal opportunity. But he didn't answer the question.

CHAPTER 11

The German Connection

W E THOUGHT THE STRIFE was over, the battle won. We were wrong. Upon his arrival in San Francisco for the Republican National Convention July 6, Scranton announced that he would continue his fight to keep the GOP from becoming "another name for some ultra-rightist society." Rockefeller told the Platform Committee that the party could not win if it was focused on "the narrow interests of a minority within a minority." Lodge said, "We must never countenance such a thing as a trigger-happy foreign policy which would negate everything we stand for and destroy everything we hope for—including life itself." Romney urged that the party "unequivocally repudiate extremism of the right and the left and reject their efforts to infiltrate or attach themselves to our party or its candidates."

The convention was Clif White's baby, and in San Francisco, at least, the Goldwater campaign was organized as never before—or after. State coordinators were assigned to monitor each delegate's arrival, assisted by a volunteer staff in a Goldwater "Welcome to San Francisco" suite at the airport. We had a command center at our main hotel, the Mark Hopkins, with at least one direct telephone line to a room in every one of the thirty-six hotels where Goldwater delegates were staying. We had locator boards to track the movement of each delegate and campaign staffer—with phone numbers at each known stop, restaurant, meeting room, and hotel—should immediate communication be needed. It was like the combat information center on a warship, complete with edge-lighted plastic panels upon which we scribbled data with grease pencils.

Another command center was built into a fifty-five foot trailer parked just outside the convention hall (an overgrown Quonset hut known as the "Cow Palace," site of rodeos and other western-style events). Direct telephone lines connected the site to Goldwater's suite at the Mark Hopkins, the other hotels, and leaders of key delegations on the convention floor. Three-channel walkie-talkie portable radios were assigned to every driver. Walkie-talkie operators were stationed at strategic points on the convention floor as back-up should the telephone connections "fail," and a specially designed jam-proof antenna was installed just under the roof to ensure uninterrupted radio communications, since jamming had been a problem at conventions past. Supporters were stationed around the city and convention site to report on the movements of any person of interest (such as Governor Scranton). Charlie Barr was in charge of a security detail armed with portable tape recorders and Polaroid cameras. No incident would go undocumented.

Clif had been working Republican National Conventions for sixteen years and knew all the tricks a desperate opposition might employ to disrupt, derail, or steal a nomination. Some tactics were mechanical, directed at disrupting the process, while others were psychological, directed at co-opting delegates. The best example was the Eisenhower-Taft convention of 1952. The conservative Ohio senator Robert Taft was the favorite going in and probably had the votes, but members of the eastern elite saw Eisenhower as more compatible with their agenda. They were better organized and played "divide and conquer" with the uncoordinated Taft delegations. They would persuade groups of delegates to vote a certain way on a motion, only to have it come out later that this was against their candidate's wishes. Or they would challenge the seating of Taft delegates, knowing that the unprepared Taft campaign would respond too late. Clif made sure that we were covered on any possible legal challenges. We had a

lawyer on the scene, with a full set of law books covering delegate selection in every state.

Everyone was on the alert for a wide range of dirty tricks from the
opposition. Some were basic espionage: Plant microphones, intercept
radio communications, or tap telephones. Or plant spies: waitresses,
delivery men, messengers, or chambermaids to report on anything
that seemed of interest. Some possible tactics were just plain disrup-
tive: Make the candidate and key staffers late for meetings by leaving
phony phone messages saying a meeting had been moved or canceled. Get to the drivers and pay them to get lost, hire other drivers
to tie up traffic with fake breakdowns.

As for manipulating the delegates, a determined opposition could
build a dossier on each one's outstanding debts, assets, business aspirations, civic identity, school and church ties, personal weaknesses of
the delegate and close relatives, and police records, if any. The information could be used either as a carrot or a stick. As a carrot, imply
that if the delegate voted the "right" way, he or she could get an ex-
tension of a loan. The stick: Threaten to call the loan. Offer or withdraw business franchises, promise a patronage job or suggest that
none would ever be forthcoming. Offer to hide—or threaten to re-
veal—a little-known family problem. None of this was theoretical; Clif
had seen it all done at the 1952 convention. Not all forms of bribery
involve envelopes stuffed with cash.

Our delegates were warned to be suspicious of any unexpectedly easy
companionship. Clif may have gone a bit overboard when he set up a
"buddy system" pairing the delegates: They roomed in the same hotel,
dined together, and went sightseeing together. But because of his pre-
cautions, none would be an easy target for a Scranton Mata Hari.

Drafting the platform, the document upon which the campaign
would stand, is always a battleground for the heart of the party, and
we were prepared to forestall any attempts to turn this statement into
something Barry simply couldn't work with. We had a pretty solid grip

The Sacramento Bee, 1964

"YOU MUST BE KIDDING!"

on the 100-member committee (one man and one woman from each state), but we knew efforts might be made to manipulate the proceedings. Challenges could arise against the seating of members, for example. Fortunately, Melvin Laird, a congressman from Wisconsin serving as committee chairman, kept a firm grip on the process. Our "Horatio at the bridge" was John Tower. "I am the last speaker," he said. "We can play it by ear."

As it turned out, he was the last of some 170 speakers who appeared before the committee in the week before the convention to offer one or another point of view. Past and present candidates dropped by to offer suggestions or make demands; and the liberal clique, which seemed to understand the controversies but not the facts, tried to insert a plank affirming that the president was solely responsible for any decision on the use of nuclear arms.

The most troublesome plank concerned civil rights. In his appearance before the committee, Barry was challenged by a representative from the District of Columbia, an African American, to affirm that he would "consistently, conscientiously and in good faith use the powers and prestige" of the presidency to enforce the law. Barry was a bit taken aback, but he replied, "When you use that argument, you are questioning my honesty. I should resent it, but I won't." After another delegate asked a similar question, many on the committee groaned in protest. But Barry said, "Now, wait. Let's be fair about this. That was a sensible question and I'm glad it was asked."

One of the more interesting participants in the debate was Martin Luther King, Jr., who had almost taken Barry's side in opposing the Civil Rights Act of 1964, but for different reasons. He felt it didn't go far enough and was a "cruel jest . . . [like] giving a pair of shoes to a man who has not learned to walk."

I believe the Platform Committee did a reasonably good job. In the section addressing civil rights, the plank that emerged called for:

— full implementation and faithful execution of the Civil Rights Act of 1964, and all other civil rights statutes, to assure equal rights and opportunities guaranteed by the Constitution to every citizen;

— improvements of civil rights statutes adequate to the changing needs of our times;

— such additional administrative or legislative actions as may be required to end the denial, for whatever unlawful reason, of the right to vote; . . .

— continued opposition to discrimination based on race, creed, national origin, or sex. We recognize that the elimination of any such discrimination is a matter of heart, conscience, and education, as well as of equal rights under the law.

This wasn't enough to satisfy the anti-Goldwaterites, who asked General Eisenhower to intervene. He did not. They offered a number of amendments, but none were approved. Scranton proposed an amendment attesting to the constitutionality and desirability of the

Civil Rights Act. The amendment was declined and the plank affirmed as offered—and publicly supported by Goldwater.

I arrived for the convention on July 7, doing double duty as campaign
treasurer and as a member of the Connecticut delegation. I had been
nominated for this honor by Henry Cabot Lodge's brother, Governor
John Davis Lodge. I say I was "nominated," but in truth Governor
Lodge jammed me down the throats of the Rockefeller-leaning selec-
tion committee. "Middendorf goes in!" he shouted, and that was that.
As it turned out, I was one of only four Goldwater delegates in all of
New England; the others were also from Connecticut.

Once in San Francisco, I learned that a media firestorm was in
progress. The German magazine *Der Spiegel* had just published an instantly controversial interview with Goldwater. Scranton called a press
conference and challenged Goldwater to hand over a transcript of the
interview; Barry suggested that Scranton go out and buy a copy of the
magazine. The *New York Times* grabbed the story, printed excerpts from
the article as published, and a day later published a transcript of unused portions of the conversation. Both contained reiterations of already known Goldwater positions on a variety of topics: his views on the
Civil Rights Act (there were some constitutional issues, but if elected he
would enforce it), for example, and on control of tactical weapons in
NATO (the supreme commander should be given great leeway).

But since Barry never hesitated to tell the truth as he saw it, there
were also a couple of fresh thoughts. To the question, "Do you think
you would have a chance to win over Johnson in November?" he
replied, "No, I don't think any Republican can, as of now." Scranton
countered, "How could the delegates nominate someone who says he
can't win?"

Asked what he would do, as president, about the problem of South
Vietnam, Barry said, "I would turn to my Joint Chiefs of Staff and say,
'Fellows, we made the decision to win, now it's your problem." Scran-
ton sneered, "That is another example of his failure to comprehend

that being President of the United States is not the same as being a benevolent chairman of the board, letting others decide when nuclear destruction shall be released."

Barry may have been pandering to the German readership—but he may also have been correct—when he said, "With all due respect to American military leaders," Germany would have won both world wars if it had not been badly led. And he offered a fresh take on the Civil Rights Act: "If they could have locked the doors to the Senate and turned the lights off, you wouldn't have gotten 25 votes." Good old Barry. For good or ill, he certainly was not a typical politician.

CBS took its cue from the *Times* and decided to give the Goldwater campaign a "German connection." Daniel Schorr, reporting from Munich, stated with authority that right after the nomination, Barry would "be starting his campaign here in Bavaria, center of Germany's right wing" as a guest of Lieutenant General William Quinn, commander of the U.S. Seventh Army in Europe. The Goldwater "interview with *Der Spiegel*," Schorr said, "with its hard line appealing to right-wing elements in Germany, was only the start of a move to link up with his opposite numbers in Germany." Less than twenty years after the end of World War II, it didn't take an expert to know what "right-wing elements in Germany" meant, or the implication of calling them Barry's "opposite numbers."

Someone made certain that a transcript of the broadcast was slipped under the hotel room door of every delegate. In fact, this was how the CBS network reporter assigned to cover the convention learned of the allegations. Not only had his editors not bothered to check with him on the story—which he knew to be false—they even neglected to warn him that it was coming.

After Goldwater denounced the CBS report ("the damndest lie I ever heard"), the *New York Times* noted that "Senator Goldwater has decided not to take a post-convention vacation in Germany," citing as a reason, "a Columbia Broadcast System news report yesterday that asserted Mr. Goldwater's trip signaled a link between the 'right wing' of the United States and that of Bavaria." He did not feel he could go to Germany, the *Times* explained, "without embarrassing the friend who asked him to be a vacation guest," General Quinn.

The only truth in the story was that the Goldwaters were thinking about taking a vacation in Europe after the convention. They had made no overtures to any "elements in Germany," right-wing or otherwise. Or, according to Barry, to his friend General Quinn, with whom he had not been in contact for over a year. Neither Schorr nor anyone at the CBS network or the *New York Times* made any effort to verify the story with Goldwater. Some years later, when Barry questioned Schorr about the broadcast, he admitted he had been "guilty of sloppy writing."

One bit of fallout was that LBJ may have taken revenge on Quinn for no reason other than that he was revealed to be a friend of Barry's—at least, that was what Barry was told by senior officers close to the throne. Despite a brilliant record in the Army, Quinn was eased into retirement without being considered for promotion to full general.

On Wednesday, July 15, the day of voting, the *Times* added insult to injury with a report on a Goldwater interview with the "extreme rightist weekly" *Zeitung und Soldaten Zeitung.* Goldwater had been "in frequent and friendly correspondence for some time," the *Times* noted, with right-wing elements in Germany. This was not correct: Barry had never given an interview with *Zeitung und Soldaten Zeitung.* That newspaper had taken excerpts from a Goldwater campaign brochure, changed a few words to suit its own interests, and published the result under a Goldwater byline. To their credit, the *Times* editors acknowledged the mistake a couple of weeks later, long after the convention was over. But an apology or retraction after the fact is of little merit.

An error in the file is a fact forever.

CHAPTER 12

The Incident

THE SCRANTON FOR PRESIDENT Committee published a daily *Convention News* that out-hectored the worst of the national media. "News" reports in the issue of July 12 included "VICIOUS DRIVE FOR GOLDWATER OPENED BY RADICAL BACKERS" and "GOLDWATER'S POST CONVENTION PLANS RAISE QUESTIONS OF NUCLEAR SANITY," illustrated by a photo of an atomic explosion.

That evening, the Scranton team created the "incident" that they hoped would change the governor's fortunes: They tried to force a debate with Barry, with an inflammatory letter delivered to all delegates that began, "As we move rapidly towards the climax of this convention the Republican Party faces a continuing struggle on two counts. The first involves, of course, selection of a candidate. Will the convention choose a candidate overwhelmingly favored by the Republican voters, or will it choose you?" The letter continued:

Your organization does not even argue the merits of the question. . . . They feel they have bought, beaten and compromised enough delegate support to make the result a foregone conclusion.

With open contempt for the dignity, integrity and common sense of the convention, your managers say in effect that the delegates are little more than a flock of chickens whose necks will be wrung at will. . . .

I have double-checked the arithmetic of my staff, and I am convinced that a true count at this minute puts your first ballot strength at only some 620 votes.

Our count differed from that of your managers because we have calculated an important element which you are incapable of comprehending. That is the element of respect for the men and women who make up the delegations to the convention.

We are not taking them for granted. We are not insulting their intelligence or their integrity.

We're not counting noses, we're counting hearts.

We're not issuing orders, we're providing a rallying point for responsibility in the Republican Party.

Having set Scranton up as the honest broker between the people and the villainous Goldwater, the letter proclaimed, "You will be stopped on the first ballot because a sufficient number of your nominal supporters have already indicated to us that they will not vote for you." And it explained why:

You have too often casually prescribed nuclear war as a solution to a troubled world.

You have too often allowed the radical extremists to use you.

You have too often stood for irresponsibility in the serious question of racial holocaust.

The "radical extremists," the letter said, were attempting to steal the soul of the Republican Party by promoting "Goldwaterism" rather than "Republicanism." The ideology of Goldwaterism stood for "nuclear irresponsibility," for "being afraid to forthrightly condemn the right-wing extremists," and for "refusing to stand for law and order in maintaining racial peace." In short, the letter charged, "Goldwaterism has come to stand for a whole crazy-quilt collection of absurd and dangerous positions that would be soundly repudiated by the American people in November."

The letter was full of stirring phrases, but was sent to the wrong crowd. Those delegates were *our* delegates, Goldwater delegates, because that's where they wanted to be.

In closing, the letter challenged the senator to open debate before the assembled convention (and the several millions in the television audience). "Certainly you should not fear a convention you claim to control, and I would hope that we have not reached the point where you fear to face the nation."

Not surprisingly, the senator was not interested.

As soon came to light, Scranton didn't write the letter and apparently had not even read it before it was distributed. He went on television, trying to distance himself from the content while taking "full responsibility."

This bit of handiwork by an overzealous staffer was variously interpreted by the pundits as "a plan to ensure that Scranton would not be drafted as Goldwater's running mate" (*New York Times*); an attempt to make Goldwater "so mad that he would agree to a debate" (David Reinhard); a way of destroying Goldwater's chances in the election (M. Stanton Evans); or an attempt to make a last stand, "to go down bloody, in defeat" (Theodore White). In fact, it was nothing but a dumb mistake. Up to that point—even afterward, to a point—Scranton had remained on Barry's list for VP; now Kitchel and friends objected so vehemently that Barry backed off.

The Convention Gala was held that Sunday night, July 12—all were welcome, for a $500 contribution to the Congressional Campaign Committee. It was more gala for some than for others. The Scranton letter took the edge off the festivities, and Barry chose not to attend. I certainly found it exciting to be mingling with the party's certifiable stars. I even managed a few moments with President Eisenhower, gaining his instant respect by mentioning that my father—a gentleman farmer as well as investment adviser—had been providing prized Black Angus for Ike's Gettysburg farm.

At mid-morning on Monday, July 13, the convention formally opened with a program of ceremonial and procedural folderol. To get into the Cow Palace we had to pass through a throng of semiprofessional demonstrators of the sort who even today turn Bay Area events into theater. They chanted "Barry Goldwater must go" and carried placards reading "Defoliate Goldwater," "Vote for Goldwater—Courage, Integrity, Bigotry," and "Keep NATO Fingers Off the Nuclear Button."

Although Barry did not yet have the nomination, we had little doubt that he would get it, and the finance committee began working on transition details. We would be going from a preconvention focus to a full-up campaign; there were fiscal and legal considerations and, as before, my brother Harry was right there with us. We mulled over our recommendations for the next chairman of the Republican National Committee (to the victor goes the choice): Peter O'Donnell, Clif White, Wayne Hood, Len Hall, or Dean Burch.

The next day was taken up chasing down details. Denny, Jerry, Cliff Roberts, and I met with an Eisenhower staffer to work on some campaign issues. Cliff also spoke with a Scranton staffer, urging Scranton to withdraw before the balloting as a gesture of unity. George H.W. Bush, preparing his Senate run, visited with Barry in his penthouse suite. I doubled as a spokesman-pitchman in an ABC-TV interview, during which I briefly outlined the history of the Draft movement and praised the exceptional support we had been getting from small contributors—a dollar here and a dollar there. One woman in Omaha, I noted gratefully, had been sending us twenty-five cents a week.

On Tuesday night it was Eisenhower's turn to address the delegates. He sounded a lot more like Barry Goldwater than he sounded like either Rockefeller or Scranton. "Let us not be guilty," the general said, "of maudlin sympathy for the criminal who, roaming the streets with switchblade knife and illegal firearms seeking a helpless prey, suddenly becomes, upon apprehension, a poor, underprivileged person who counts upon the compassion of our society and the laxness or weakness of too many courts to forgive his offense." Ike ended with a few well-chosen words of his own, not from the speechwriter: "Let us particularly scorn the divisive efforts of those outside our family, including sensation-seeking columnists and commentators, because, my friends, I assure you that these are people who couldn't care less about the good of our party. . . . [Let us] renew our strength from the fountain of unity, not drown ourselves in a whirlpool of factional strife and divisive ambitions." A consummation devoutly to be wished. And not achieved.

The best-remembered point of Rockefeller's failed two-year effort to get the nomination was his podium plea for an amendment to the platform, proposed by Pennsylvania Senator Hugh Scott, denouncing "extremist" groups. Eisenhower may have appealed for unity, but Rockefeller was not in a conciliatory mood. He claimed that his headquarters had received more than 100 bomb threats. "We repudiate the efforts," he said, "of irresponsible extremist groups—such as the Communists, Ku Klux Klan, the John Birch Society, and others, to discredit our party by their efforts to infiltrate positions of responsibility in the party or attach themselves to its candidates."

His remarks were interrupted by waves of angry booing, twenty-two times in five minutes. He smiled, looking brave in the face of such humiliation. "This is still a free country, ladies and gentlemen," he said, and television carried the spectacle, live and in countless replays, across the nation. He repeated his earlier critique of the Goldwater campaign, condemning "infiltration and take-over of established political parties by Communist and Nazi methods."

The booing intensified. "Some of you don't like to hear it, ladies and gentlemen, but it's the truth," Rockefeller said. The television cameras, focused on Rockefeller at the podium and on some frenzied dissidents, did not show all of what was happening in the hall—it was not delegates demonstrating, but spectators in the gallery. Clif White and his team, operating from the communications trailer outside the convention hall, were in touch with all of their floor leaders. "Knock it off," they ordered, but all floor leaders reported back that it was not our people.

Was this a put-up job, rigged by Rockefeller himself? Barry seemed to think so, but he had no hard evidence. Clif White thought so, too; otherwise, he wondered, how did these spectators get so many highly coveted gallery tickets? But Theodore White reported that the crowd was truly angry. "As he taunted them," he wrote, "they raged." But at what? They didn't seem to know, he wrote, whether they were raging at "the East; or New York; or Communists; or liberals." That they were supporters, followers, worshippers of Barry Goldwater he had no doubt. But he also knew that unlike the majority of men and women associated with the campaign, the members of this angry group really were out on the fringe.

The amendment was not passed. The "sensation-seeking columnists and commentators" were quick to pile on, although the Rockefeller story soon was replaced by the story of Goldwater's victory.

Wednesday found the Goldwater team milling around the fifteenth floor of the Mark Hopkins. At 1:00, I was in the radio-TV studio set up at one end of the hall, doing another pitch on behalf of "Box 1964." Send in your money, folks, it's for a good cause. At 2:00, we had a friendly, relaxed meeting with Barry. Ike had called him the previous night, he said. We had been winning every attempt to change the party platform, and Ike asked, "Can't you let these fellows have something?" But he already knew the answer. Perhaps we should have let the other side win something, since many of the suggestions were perfectly benign, but our collective anger against Rockefeller and Scranton was too great to admit of any compromise.

Barry asked me how we stood on finances and smiled broadly at my report: We would have about $120,000 in the bank after the convention. "There is nothing I enjoy more," he said, "than being in politics and being solvent at the same time." Then he presented each of us with a gold Rolex wristwatch, his thank-you gift; mine was engraved "To JWM from Peggy and Barry, July 15, 1964."

And I headed out to the Cow Palace to cast my vote.

Eight names were placed in nomination (even though Rockefeller had withdrawn from competition, he held on to his pledged delegates, hoping to forestall a first-round Goldwater victory). Once the counting began—after seven hours of de rigueur speeches—it took twenty-four minutes for Barry to reach the magic number—655; six minutes later, the roll call was over. The result: Goldwater, 883; Scranton, 214; Rockefeller, 114; Romney, 41; Margaret Chase Smith, 27; Walter Judd, 22; Hawaii Senator Hiram Fong, 5; Lodge, 2. Scranton made the *amende honorable* and called for the nomination to be made unanimous. I suppose that it was, but some delegates were already walking out of the hall.

Back at the Mark Hopkins, we celebrated with champagne all around, and Barry shaking hands with everybody. Rocky and Scranton both came up with their families—and their best manners. Barry held a news conference and said: "I wouldn't be in this thing if I thought I was going to lose because, as I've said, I'm too old to go back to work and too young to get out of politics." He had said this before, but now he seemed to mean it.

CHAPTER 13

Extremism . . . No Vice?

I STOPPED SMOKING AT 3 A.M., Thursday, July 16, 1964. This moment is easy to remember because I was locked in a bathroom at the Mark Hopkins, helping to screen potential candidates for vice president. In fact, a small crowd of us was in there for several hours. We couldn't leave because reporters were everywhere—trying to get an angle, trying to get interviews—and they were all desperate for information. The bathroom was the only place we could be alone. Although "alone" is a relative term. I was one of two or three members of Barry's team assigned this task, and each potential VP had a team of sponsors. There were two or three people standing in the bathtub, someone sitting on the edge, and everyone was talking so loud that in order to be heard, someone else would have to talk louder. And everyone was smoking. In those days, we all smoked (I got started in the Navy, where cigarettes were free, and worked up to two packs a day)—we thought it was glamorous, made us feel mature. And we didn't just smoke. We held our cigarettes in a certain way, trying to look sophisticated, like some character in the movies.

The smoke grew so thick I could hardly see across the tiny room. By midnight, I was coughing so much that I resolved that if I got out alive, I would never smoke again. And I never did.

Barry had sent us into the bathroom with a list of possibles and the instruction to "narrow it down." I don't remember how many were on the list at the beginning, but in the end there was only one: Bill Miller, chairman of the Republican National Committee. The runner-up was Walter Judd, endorsed to us by seven Minnesota congressmen led into the bathroom by Clark MacGregor (it got really crowded). They put in a strong pitch for Judd, a true icon of the party. But Judd had hung on right through the voting as Minnesota's "favorite son" candidate, keeping twenty-two votes out of the Goldwater column. Not a good way to win favor with the nominee.

We picked Miller the way a Wall Street analyst picks a stock: run the numbers. It's a good tactic for picking stocks, but probably not so useful in politics. In Miller's case, the "numbers" included personality, religion, and home state. Miller was a genuinely nice guy, Catholic (to balance Barry's Protestant faith with semi-Jewish roots), and a New Yorker. Barry, the westerner thought by some to be a "right-wing extremist," was out of the mainstream, and Miller, as chairman of the RNC, was smack in the middle of it. We figured that with Miller on the ticket, the New York vote would be locked up.

In hindsight, our attempt at balance stood for nothing. We should have gone with Judd—he stood for something more. As a medical missionary in China in the 1930s, Walter Judd had seen at first hand how the invading Japanese army operated; following his return home in 1938, he gave more than a thousand speeches, well before Pearl Harbor, trying to warn the American people and the Congress to stop trading with the Japanese, to stop giving them the sinews of war with which they may later fight us. He was right, but few people listened. He was elected to Congress in 1942 and served ten terms. In a losing race for vice president, Judd would not have gone quietly down to defeat but would have remained a strong conservative voice on the national scene. Bill Miller more or less disappeared. He later became one of the first participants in the "Do you know me?" American Express credit-card promotion celebrating forgotten public figures.

At 9:30 A.M. Peter O'Donnell, Ione Harrington, and I—a bit hung over from too much celebration and a bit groggy from lack of sleep—

served as the totally unnecessary "notification committee" to advise our candidate that he had won, and to offer our recommendation for vice president. Barry accepted the news with genial good grace, agreed with the recommendation, and called Bill Miller to give him his own good news. This was followed by a meeting with some twenty-five members of the finance team, where Barry thanked all of us for our efforts to that point, adding a charge that, in the event, was to prove more symbolic than real: "Don't bother telling me when I'm doing well," he said. "Call, anytime, and raise hell when I'm not."

Later that morning, at a meeting with Republican state chairmen, Barry described Miller as a man who had once called JFK the "foundering father of the New Frontier" and had advised that, if Lyndon Johnson was offering a "Better Deal," someone else should first cut the cards. "Miller," Barry said, "drives Lyndon Johnson nuts."

He announced that he wanted his "Middendorf-Milbank" team to run the financial show—I would be treasurer of the Republican National Committee, Jerry would be treasurer of the Goldwater for President Finance Committee—a marvelous vote of confidence for both of us. But then Barry added a shocker: Dean Burch would be chairman of the Republican National Committee, and Denny Kitchel would be campaign manager. Even though Clif White had played such a critical role, he once again was assigned to be Dean's assistant—this time, as director of field operations. After having pretty much invented the Draft movement and after more than three years of pulling the wagon for Barry—even after being in such an ambiguous position during the primaries—he hoped to be put in the driver's seat as chairman of the Republican National Committee, or at least as campaign chairman. Clif first heard that he had been passed over from someone in an elevator, who said, "Is this thing on Dean Burch a secret or can we let it out?"

I later found out that Barry had, in fact, suggested that Clif be appointed RNC chairman, but he had been dissuaded by Kleindienst,

Baroody, and others. Kleindienst, reflecting on his earlier disagreement with Clif, thought he was too independent, not a team player. Baroody saw Clif as some sort of stand-in for the dreaded *National Review* crowd. Maybe he was; putting Clif out to pasture certainly pushed Buckley and Bozell even further away from the campaign.

It was a busy day. At noon, I attended a meeting of the campaign inner circle with Barry, Miller, Kitchel, Burch, Baroody, and McCabe. Barry made it clear that the campaign would be run out of the RNC rather than, in the usual fashion, by a totally separate organization. About half an hour into the meeting, someone passed the word that Ike, who had not yet heard of the selection of Miller, had just suggested using the VP slot as a bridge across which the liberals might cross over to our side. He recommended Romney. Later, when told this would not be possible, Ike said, "Walter Judd would be terrific." He was right.

By that afternoon, Clif was ready to quit again. We didn't blame him, but we tried to find a bone that Barry could toss his way. We came up with "executive director" of something, as yet undetermined. It was a meaningless but face-saving title. Next, I once again practiced my skills as a TV pitchman, telling anyone who might be paying attention that we could use some money. I read some letters and asked for pledges, no matter how small. By 4:00 P.M., we were heading back out to the Cow Palace for Goldwater's acceptance speech. Dick Nixon made the introduction—unity was okay with him. It was time, he declared, not for the New Deal or the Fair Deal or the "Fast Deal of Lyndon Johnson, but for the Honest Deal of Barry Goldwater."

Barry took "freedom" as the theme of his acceptance speech. "This party," he declared, "with its every action, every word, every breath and every heartbeat has but a single resolve, and that is *freedom*—freedom made orderly for this nation by our constitutional government; *freedom* under a government limited by the laws of nature and of nature's God; freedom—*balanced* so that . . . liberty, lacking order, will not become the license of the mob and the jungle."

He indicted the Democrats: "Failure cements the wall of shame in Berlin; failures clot the sand of shame at the Bay of Pigs; failures mark the slow death of freedom in Laos; failures infest the jungles of Vietnam. . . . Tonight, there is violence in our streets, corruption in our highest officers, aimlessness among our youth, anxiety among our elderly, and there's a virtual despair among the many who look beyond material successes toward the inner meaning of their lives."

He gave fair warning: "Yesterday it was Korea; tonight it is Vietnam. Make no bones of this. Don't try to sweep this under the rug. We are at war in Vietnam. And yet the president, who is commander-in-chief of our forces, refuses to say, refuses to say, mind you, whether or not the objective over there is victory. And his secretary of defense continues to mislead and misinform the American people."

He invited support: "Anyone who joins us in all sincerity we welcome. Those who do not care for our cause, we don't expect to enter our ranks in any case." He called for clear thinking: "Let our Republicanism, so focused and so dedicated, not be made fuzzy by unthinking and stupid labels." And then, as he came to the end of his speech, Barry took on the major theme of the opposition's preconvention debate: that he and his supporters were "extremists" and the Rockefellers and Scrantons of the party were the voices of "moderation." In the original text, his answer is underlined: *I would remind you that extremism in the defense of liberty is no vice. And let me remind you also that moderation in the pursuit of justice is no virtue.*

Most of the delegates and spectators erupted in applause. Some listeners reacted with surprise or immediate disapproval. Clif White was "stunned"; Nixon felt "almost physically sick." It may have been at this point that a newsman in the press section exclaimed, "My God, he's going to run as Barry Goldwater!" NBC-TV reported that "Senator Keating of New York seems to be leading the entire New York delegation in departing from the convention hall," walking out on the speech, that is, in response to Goldwater's line about—NBC's misquote—"excess being no vice." Keating's staff later explained: As the speech was over (and the convention as well), he was merely trying to beat most of the crowd to the parking lot. Well, he may have been sending a signal—but he also beat the crowd.

The offending words, one of the best-known lines to emerge from any political convention and deserving of some comment, had been written for Barry by political science professor Henry Jaffa. But they instantly became Barry's own. In the firestorm that erupted among Democrats and liberal Republicans, he maintained that the sentiment was accurate, although widely misunderstood.

Whence this call to arms? Jaffa pointed to Thomas Paine's 1791 *The Rights of Man:* "A thing moderately good is not so good as it ought to be. Moderation in temper is always a virtue; but moderation in principle is always a vice." But I've seen so many attributions, ranging from Cicero, circa 100 B.C., to Wendell Wilkie in 1940, that I suspect it may have sprung full-blown from the professor's brow.

Writing for the *New York Times,* James Reston called the line a "jumble of high-sounding contradictions" and offered this parsing: "If 'extremism in the defense of liberty is no vice,' then surely the Negro extremists are justified in their civil disobedience. And if 'moderation in the pursuit of justice is no virtue,' then obviously Negro moderate leaders are to be condemned."

In counterpoint, editors of the *National Review* asked their readers to identify the source of two other quotations: "Justice too long delayed is justice denied," and "There comes a time when the cup of endurance runs over." The first is a paraphrase of the English jurist William Gladstone, but it was uttered—as was the other—by Martin Luther King, Jr. The editors offered a different sort of context: Battlecries, they noted, do not accommodate subtle distinctions. "Patrick Henry did not say 'Give me liberty—always understanding that liberty consists in a complex accommodation between the individual on the one hand, and the collectivity, plus objective reality on the other—or death.'" Goldwater, they said, had the right to indulge in "theatrical political expression." But considering recent experience along the campaign trail, where so many of his remarks had been misconstrued or taken out of context, the *National Review* suggested, he would have been better advised to "do the cautious thing" and not offer such a fat target for his opponents. "Extremism" had been, indeed, the opposition's rallying cry, and it remained an unhealed scab that he didn't have to scratch.

Barry and Denny parsed the phrase for Eisenhower and his brother Milton. At first, the general was angry with Barry for having given the "right-wing kooks" a leg up and everyone else a punch in the nose. The conversation was touch-and-go, with our side losing, when Barry had an inspiration. "There's no more extreme action than war," he said. "General, in June 1944 when you led the Allied Forces across the English Channel, you were an 'extremist,' and you did it in defense of liberty." The general thought about that for a moment, then exclaimed to his brother, "By golly, Milton, I'm an extremist—and damn proud of it!"

At a Republican "unity" meeting in August, Barry offered a paraphrase of "the two sentences in question . . . that wholehearted devotion to liberty is unassailable and that halfhearted devotion to justice is indefensible." That clarification pleased neither the moderates nor the conservatives. Later, toward the end of the campaign, a group of fighter pilots from both world wars were induced to sign their names to a full-page ad in the *New York Times:* "We were EXTREMISTS," the ad said. "We were civilians who served our country in wartime." Few people in the electorate seem to have gotten the message. Dean Burch put it in perspective: "Barry Goldwater could have recited the Lord's Prayer or the Twenty-third Psalm as his acceptance speech. He still would have been attacked."

After the acceptance speech, members of the original Draft group gathered at the Fairmont Hotel for a sentimental celebration. Emotions were mixed: Some were jubilant, some perplexed by Barry's appeal to coarse passions. Bill Rusher, who had been acting as our unofficial historian, made an eloquent little speech, reminding us of where we had started and how far we had come. Clif joined us, but I don't think his heart was in it. He said a few nice things and credited me with having held the movement together. (When I later read his own history of the Draft movement, *Suite 3505*, I was most flattered that he called me "the man who stood at the dike and prevented it from crumbling around our ears.") After a while he left—and left town, on his way to a vacation in Hawaii. I doubt that he had much fun.

Friday, July 17, was another full day, infused with the minutiae of setting up our new organization and making assignments. What should we call the two major campaign committees? One of them would be called Goldwater for President; proposals for the other included Americans for Goldwater and Citizens for Goldwater-Miller. Barry was not too keen on "Citizens" but liked "Americans" even less. He finally agreed to "Citizens." He said that he had a new job for Clif: executive director of that committee.

Unfortunately, Clif was not around to hear the news. Barry sent him a letter acknowledging "the deep debt that I feel in my heart for your wonderful efforts during the entire campaign." He said, "We want to get started on a number of things immediately that will require your continued attention. . . . As soon as you are back in Washington, I want to visit with you so please let me know when you are available. With best personal wishes, Barry."

"Deep debt" was simply good political manners—but offering an opportunity to devote "continued attention" to something unnamed, to a man as insecure as Clif, might have referred to a job running the mail room. The ambiguity just deepened Clif's depression.

Jerry and I collected recommendations and drew up a list of proposed appointments to various finance-related positions: Cliff Folger would be RNC finance chairman, and Henry Salvatori (a West Coast oilman and philanthropist) would be Goldwater television finance chairman, among others. We suggested that Barry give each a timely call inviting them to accept, and he agreed. We also suggested—strongly—that he call Ike immediately to seek his support. One of Ike's staffers had just called Jerry, saying, "Ike is extremely upset because he feels his recommendations have been snubbed." I was not privy to whatever conversation may have ensued. But I think Ike was regretting his earlier detachment from the campaign, which had essentially nullified any influence he might otherwise have been able to exercise.

Most journalistic reaction to the nomination was negative, and, I suppose, predictable. Walter Lippmann claimed that electing Goldwater would lead to "a global, nuclear, anti-Communist crusade." Drew Pearson wrote, "The smell of fascism has been in the air at this convention." The *New York Times* said Goldwater's nomination was "a disaster for the Republican Party, and a blow to the prestige and to the domestic and international interests of the United States." The *Chicago Daily News* judged that Goldwater had "the invaluable ability to give a latent, fear-born prejudice a patina of respectability and plausibility"; and, according to the *New York Post:* "The Birchers and racists have never before enjoyed so big a night under such respectable auspices." The *Louisville Courier-Journal* predicted: "This will be a campaign to sicken decent and thoughtful people." (It certainly was, though not in the way the *Courier-Journal* had in mind.)

Time—which reprinted the above comments in its postconvention issue of July 24, 1964—interjected some balance: "Who are the Goldwaterites? They wear tennis shoes only on tennis courts. They don't read Robert Welch or hate Negroes. They aren't nuclear-bomb throwers, and they don't write obscene letters to editors who disagree with them. They are reasonably well-educated and informed. They are, in fact, nuts about Barry Goldwater without being nutty in the process."

And *Newsweek,* in its postconvention issue, offered another portrait of the Draft Goldwater movement: "Jack Kennedy wanted the nomination, recruited his cadres, planned his own strategy, his eye always on victory. Goldwater had a nationwide organization handed to him while he remained aloof, longing to remain in the Senate. Kennedy captured his supporters; Goldwater's supporters captured him." The magazine defined those supporters as "mostly obscure, humorlessly efficient, faintly Puritanical . . . propelled by motives as mixed as any revolutionary's. Some thirsted for authority, others delighted in the IBM technology of the new politics, still others yearned for a Free Enterprise Eden."

As for me—obscure, yes, but "humorless" and "Puritanical"? (Although I do confess to a yearning for a "Free Enterprise Eden.") I much preferred *Newsweek*'s description of me as "an eager young giant of a man (6 feet 4, 215 pounds)." The magazine was fascinated with our fund-raising success ("300,000 individual contributions, most of them $1, $2, and $3") but overlooked Jerry Milbank, Frank Kovac, and others, giving me unwarranted credit as head of the fund-raising effort.

Newsweek let two young members of Congress speak to our effort. John Ashbrook said, "Most older politicians are afraid to make decisions. 'Well, son,' they always say, 'I've been that route before.' We haven't had that inbreeding." And Bob Dole told them, "We're not trying to turn back the clock, we're just trying to sound the alarm."

PART II

And so the battle was joined between a candidate for whom winning the presidency was not everything and a candidate for whom winning the presidency was the only thing.

LEE EDWARDS,
Goldwater: The Man Who Made a Revolution

CHAPTER 14

Musical Chairs

HEADING INTO THE PRESIDENTIAL campaign, the sitting president had momentum; Barry took a vacation. Rather than capitalizing on whatever public interest had been generated in his candidacy, our public campaign went into hiatus for almost six weeks. I suppose this was traditional—wait until Labor Day or thereabouts—and it did not seem inappropriate at the time, as we were focused on building and housing a working staff.

The "new" Republican National Committee met on July 27–28. Clif White was hanging around, looking rather dejected, waiting for a call from Barry. He had received the letter ("As soon as you are back in Washington, I want to visit with you"), but he didn't know what it meant. In the meantime, a few of us were still discussing job titles for Clif. We had already suggested "executive director," and Barry had agreed, but the days were passing without resolution. Maybe Clif should be chairman of a Goldwater-Miller Victory Committee. Maybe he should be Barry's liaison with the media. In the end, he was designated national director of Citizens for Goldwater-Miller, nominally assisted by Lieutenant General James H. Doolittle, USAF (Retired), and Clare Booth Luce, who would be cochairs. It was a significant assignment, in which Clif continued to make a significant contribution.

The RNC had a lot of work to do, some physical—rearranging offices, installing new equipment, increasing the staff from about 100 people to almost 700—and some philosophical, as in, "Where do we go from here?" Rearranging and installing came first. The RNC offices had been on one floor of the Cafritz Building, 1625 Eye Street NW, Washington, D.C. We took over space on nine floors. The political staff was on the second floor, the brain trust (Baroody and friends) was on the third. I was on the ninth, but in truth I spent a lot of time on the second floor. Communications at the RNC had stumbled along with as many as six telephones sharing one line; following Clif's convention example, we installed dozens of new lines, many connecting directly through a twenty-four-hour manned switchboard to the hotels and apartments where the executive staff was staying. We established a communications center linking nine area communications centers and all state headquarters to pass along news releases, itineraries, advance copies of speeches, and the like and to take aboard feedback from the field. Even with the limited technology of the day, campaign aircraft had contact with headquarters, aloft and aground.

Increasing the staff was not as easy. I used to think that as one went higher in life, dealing with ever more senior and experienced people, one would eventually reach a point where everyone was mature and fully qualified for the positions they held. Sadly, I have never gotten to this point. At the RNC headquarters, staffers came in a whirlwind, scrambling for office space like children playing musical chairs. One man introduced himself to another, saying, "I'm the finance director of Committee X. What's your job?" The other man was greatly upset, because he thought *he* was slated for that position. In the event, neither man became finance director.

When an incompetent national committee holdover was fired for what was deemed to be good and sufficient reason, he triggered a telephone daisy-chain through George Humphrey to Kitchel to Dean Burch to me, all within thirty minutes. George—at home in Cleveland—was the 800-pound gorilla, and I immediately called him, only to be treated to vituperation for another thirty minutes; we were "stupid, youthful, unlegal." And those were the nice things he said. When he finally calmed down, I explained what was at issue; he listened and came on board.

Charlie Mohr must have been listening at someone's keyhole and had a relevant note in the *New York Times* of August 11: "The former officers of the Committee have had to move out or downward to make room for the new Goldwater team. Some observers have characterized this as a 'purge,' but Mr. Goldwater has appeared more interested in surrounding himself with his personal staff than in driving out the former jobholders. The omelet-making process has, nonetheless, resulted in many broken eggs."

As regards the "philosophical" aspects, we knew where we wanted to go—to victory—but we never agreed on how to get there.

Our new finance chairman, Ralph Cordiner, was the recently retired chairman and CEO of General Electric—a businessman, not a politician. In a departure from the usual method of campaign financing, he insisted that we run on a pure cash basis, not committing any money we did not already have in the bank. That made it difficult to plan for an uncertain future. Since radio and TV companies required funds in hand at least forty-eight hours before broadcast, our ad agencies had to have the monies perhaps seventy-two hours in advance. Therefore, we had to have the money in hand at least four days before each planned broadcast. Then there was the issue of booking a slot; other than for one-minute or thirty-second "commercials," broadcast schedules were set at least a month ahead of time. Unless we knew that we definitely would have the money three weeks after the booking, we couldn't plan the broadcast.

Welcome to "Ralph's Rules."

Ray Collet joined us as comptroller. He quickly set up controls to run the campaign, with clear organization charts and budgets for each department—to great applause from Peter O'Donnell, who continued working on Barry's behalf despite being cut out of the formal organization and who insisted that we should do no campaigning until we had established an agreed-upon budget. A firm budget makes candidates think before committing funds (Goldwater had just returned from the convention in a chartered plane, at a cost of $4,500) and establishes a target for fund-raising.

Ray also set rules for hiring and firing, job descriptions and pay rates, and expenditure authorizations. Credit-card use was more or less limited to telephone charges and auto rentals. Requisitions of $2,000 or above could be approved by one of only four people: Chairman Burch, Deputy Chairman Grenier, Comptroller Collet, or the treasurer, me.

We gave Ray plenty to chew on, right from the start. On August 17, he sent me a memo: "How are we going to get Dean Burch and Kitchel to stop signing contracts for commitments or money without bringing us into these matters beforehand?" The off-budget expenditures for which "authorization" had not been obtained included $75,000 for private security for Barry and $25,000 for the lease of air-to-ground radio equipment.

There was also the question of Nixon's travel expenditures. He had agreed to travel far and wide to speak in support of Barry. The budget did have a line item for charter aircraft for Nixon, $64,000, and personal travel expenses (hotel, meals) of $150 a day for forty days, which would add up to $6,000, for a total outlay of $70,000. But Nixon wanted to bring along a staff of six, including a speechwriter at $1,500 a month. It was up to me to break the news. "Sorry, Dick. Not in the budget." Nixon traveled alone, and I helped write his speeches.

Someone told a reporter that the Republican National Finance Committee had a $13 million budget for the campaign, and my brother Harry—the legal glue that held everything together—was mightily concerned. There were campaign finance laws—notably "An Act to Prevent Pernicious Political Activities, 1939, As Amended" (a.k.a. the Hatch Act), easily overlooked by the uninitiated—which we would have to follow. "It may be good public relations," Harry told us, "but as a legal matter any statement that over $3 million is to be raised and spent by any one organization could constitute an admission that an effort was being made to circumvent the law." Harry also reminded us that the law limited business done with any one supplier to $3 million. In other words, to spend an advertising budget of more than $4 million we would need at least two ad agencies. I don't think anyone had noticed this mandate before. Harry, may he rest in peace, was one of the most rigid men I have ever known, and he insisted that everyone meet his legal standard. There was no cutting corners when Harry was around.

While some members of the RNC staff certainly needed a reminder about the Hatch Act, most of us did not. For example—to the point that no one organization could raise and spend more than $3 million—we created perhaps twenty separate committees, each legally independent, although clearly operating in common cause. As RNC treasurer, I was involved in coordinating the finances of the Republican National Committee, the Republican National Finance Operations Committee, the Republican Campaign Committee, Citizens for Goldwater-Miller, Citizens Campaign Committee for Goldwater-Miller, T.V. for Goldwater-Miller, the National T.V. for Goldwater-Miller Committee, Women Voters for Goldwater-Miller, and perhaps a dozen others. Clif White's group had many more committees, including Pilots for Goldwater-Miller, Physicians for Goldwater-Miller, and Dentists for Goldwater-Miller; also Petitioners for Goldwater-Miller (those who had signed petitions and contributed $1.00 to the Draft movement) and Mothers for a Moral America. The multiplicity helped us target specific communities and incidentally give visibility to supporters by getting more names on the fund-raising letterheads (twenty-two dentists on the Dentists for Goldwater-Miller solicitation, for example).

Besides the spending limit of $3 million by any one group, there was a statutory limit of $5,000 on individual contributions to any one

group. The greater the number of committees, the more money we
could have going in or out.

The rules were sometimes ambiguous, however, and Congress
seemed to like it that way. The $5,000 limit did not apply to contribu-
tions made to or by any state or local committee or organization.
Twelve states had no limit and no reporting requirements—and contributions were not limited to residents of those states; an outsider
could make a huge contribution to any state or local committee, for
either state or national candidates, and the contribution need not be
reported.

Most of our committees were headquartered in Washington, although the TV committee headed by Henry Salvatori was based in
Los Angeles. All but the two RNC committees were devoted almost
exclusively to the presidential campaign. A multitude of state and
local committees, supporting both the presidential and local races,
were not under our supervision.

For the record, I think the Democrats had thirty-two national-level
committees: These included specialized ones for artists and entertainers, district attorneys, women, senior citizens, independent citizens, builders, and so forth, all "for Johnson-Humphrey." And all
created to get around the $5,000 and $3 million caps.

During the campaign, we received checks made out to 114 different payees. I didn't know there were so many ways for contributors to
specify "Pay to the order of." Some were obvious—"Republican National Committee" or "Republicans for Goldwater" or "Goldwater-
Miller." Others were imaginative ("Gold for Goldwater"), cumbersome
("National Sustaining Program for Republican Party Headquarters"—how do you get all of that on the payee line?), or simple
("G.O.P."). And it was surprising how many variations the mind could
conjure between "The Honorable Senator Barry M. Goldwater" and
"Mr. Goldwater."

The problem was not in cashing the checks but in deciding which
committee account to deposit the money into—divining the intent of

the contributor, if you will. It was important to get it right, both to protect the contributors from being put over the limit through no fault of their own, and to avoid going over the limits ourselves, since transfers between committees were subject to the same $5,000 limit.

But the fund-raising effort was exceptional, and the techniques we pioneered during the primaries and the campaign set the standard for all who came after. Big money is usually easy to come by, but it gets very few people involved with the candidate. In our fund-raising so-licitations, we emphasized our eagerness to accept small donations through the mail. I called it "a buck for Barry," and I was happy with twenty-five cents. "But," someone complained, "it costs nearly that much for the mailing." This was true, but each mailing that brought in a contribution added a member to the campaign, likely not only to vote for Goldwater but to work to convince their friends and neigh-bors to do so as well.

Frank Kovac assembled mailing lists of known conservatives and probable supporters; Barry's 500,000 volunteers gave us a head start. Overall, we generated 1.5 million contributions for the primaries and the campaign, as against the 50,000 supporters who contributed to the 1960 Nixon campaign. Was this emphasis on small-dollar donors a breakthrough? I can't say—history is long and details are often ob-scure—but it certainly launched a tradition within the modern con-servative movement. After the election, Richard Viguerie, who already had cut his fund-raising teeth on telephone appeals, turned lists of Goldwater contributors into a national direct-mail network of conservative donors. And political fund-raising was never the same again.

In 1963, the J. Walter Thompson advertising agency had provided ad-vice and assistance to the Draft Committee pro bono. When the Ari-zona team took over, J. Walter Thompson was ignored, and the Leo Burnett agency was brought aboard, as a consultant without fee, in anticipation of big commissions during a presidential campaign. But once Barry had the nomination, Burch wanted to make L. Richard Guylay director of public relations and advertising—a job he had held during the 1960 campaign. Guylay now worked for Thomas Deegan's firm, and Tom Deegan was a close personal friend of Lyndon Johnson. Guylay could get a leave of absence, but only if the lucrative advertising contract would go to some sister agency under the umbrella of the Marion Harper Interpublic Group. Sometime in the middle of August, Burch broke the contract with Burnett and hired Interpublic subsidiary Erwin Wasey, Ruthrauff & Ryan. As compensation, they would rebate $200,000 in commissions to Leo Burnett. I don't know if Harry ever heard about this move.

This, by the way, was not the first "unusual" advertising contract that Kitchel and friends had awarded. Back in February, they had engaged the services of another agency to handle the Goldwater for President account. That agency had never handled a political candidate or campaign, yet they were handed a sweetheart contract that paid $45,000 a month above all costs of production and in addition to whatever commissions they earned. Peter O'Donnell objected so strenuously and so persuasively that the contract was canceled, but not until the agency had collected three months' worth of free money. Perhaps this was when Burnett was brought in—I don't know, but I do know this was not the way to run a railroad—or any legitimate business.

The PR staff offered guidelines to the local campaign organizations—including, for the naive volunteers among them, a dose of Advertising 101: "Watch billboard copy for too many words. Over seven gets beyond the comprehension of the fast moving public." "Brochures and pamphlets should have plenty of 'white space'" and the copy should be "set in large, well-chosen type." "Consider cost-per-thousand as a rough rule of thumb for evaluating different media."

Leo Burnett came up with the slogan "In your heart you know he's right."(A proposed alternate, not adopted, was "Freedom is his flight

Barry Goldwater "official"
campaign photograph
(HIRO OF PHOENIX)

Richard Kleindeinst
and Bill Middendorf

Prime mover F. Clifton White

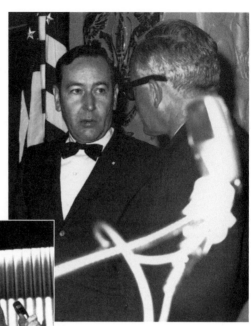

Campaign manager
Dennison Kitchel

Campaign Fnance Committee: from left, Jeremiah Milbank, Robert Herberger, J. Stetson "Stets" Coleman, Barry, Peter O'Donnell, William Middendorf, Jack Pew, Daniel Gainey

Former vice-president Richard Nixon, introducing Goldwater at the San Francisco convention

Texas Senator John Tower with Barry

Intellectual guru
William Baroody

Goldwater with
Pennsylvania Governor
William Scranton, a rival
but a friend

A study in body language? President Dwight D. Eisenhower and Barry, just after the filming of the unsatisfactory "Conversation at Gettysburg" TV program

George H.W. ("Poppy" to his friends) Bush, (unsuccessful) candidate for the Senate from Texas

Ray Bliss,
RNC chairman 1965–1969

The set of the unconvincing "Brunch with Barry" TV program

The Cow Palace, just south of San Francisco, site of the 1964 Republican National Convention

Moira O'Connor, a
Democrat "dirty tricks"
operator, after being
discovered and ejected
from the campaign train

President Lyndon B. Johnson and Mrs. Johnson (press secretary George Reedy in the
background) caught off-guard by campaign photographer Don Dornan. Johnson, who once
had been "advised" by a Hollywood photo stylist never to be photographed from his right
side, was not amused

Ronald Reagan, Peggy, and Barry Goldwater at a Dodger Stadium rally in Los Angeles during the first week of the campaign

Lee Edward's billboard, a form of "welcome" for delegates to the Democratic National Convention in Atlantic City

Air Force Reserve Major General Barry Goldwater

There were many commercially offered promotional gimmicks, not the least of which was "Gold Water," an orange-flavored beverage for people who "think." Barry said it tasted "like warm piss."

Atlanta, Georgia—
"no left turn"

Goldwater at a campaign
rally in Albany, with New
York Governor Nelson
Rockefeller looking on—
and looking bored

San Antonio,
Texas

Corpus Christi,
Texas

Indianapolis, Indiana

Marion, Ohio

Teaneck, New Jersey

An "unfriendly"
slipped into the
adoring throng in
Lewiston, Pennsylvania

The crew of the chartered campaign airplane gave it a symbolic touch in Boise, Idaho

Not to be outdone, Assistant PR Director Vic Gold set up this "eyeglasses" shot in Montgomery, Alabama, which appeared in several hundred newspapers

Barry said—more than once—that he wasn't a baby-kissing, back-slapping kind of candidate, and he refused to be "packaged" by some Madison Avenue agency. However, a few PR shots found their way into the kit. In Phoenix, with running mate Bill Miller, he donned a gift Mexican sombrero

Except for the "official" portrait, all photos were taken by campaign-photographer Don Dornan

Middendorf escorts President Eisenhower at a Military Preparedness Meeting, after which an ill-prepared Ike told a reporter that he didn't think control of nuclear weapons would be an issue in the campaign!

New Orleans, Louisianna

Last campaign stop: Fredonia, Arizona, election eve

Speechwriter Karl Hess, Barry, and Middendorf at the last stop on the last day of the campaign. A few moments later, Barry asked, "How are we doing?" and Middendorf predicted, "It's in the bag." It was. For Lyndon Johnson

Barry's final campaign press conference, the day after his defeat. The tears were real

plan." Subthemes, not used all that much, were "Put Conscience Back in Government" and "A Leader—not a Dealer.") I offered this thought: If the Communists could give us the term "capitalism," why couldn't we turn the word "freedom" into an "-ism" of our own? Fight back on semantics, and let Barry coin the word "freedomism." Yes, I knew it was corny—I even predicted that it would thus be labeled, violently, by the media. But I believed the more publicity the media gave it, the more the name would stick. "The word should sweep the world," I wrote in a memo sent to everyone on the immediate campaign staff, "and replace the word 'capitalism.'"

I was passionate on the subject, but I stood alone. In truth, I still think the *idea* was valid—to find a positive term the equal of "communism" (the people, come together in common cause) to replace the money-centered connotations of "capitalism." But, as some wise fellow noted, the pronunciation of "freedomism" was awkward, at best. And so my great idea fell by the wayside.

Nevertheless, we did think we had scored one early advertising coup: For the Democratic National Convention in Atlantic City at the end of August, Lee Edwards leased a 106-foot-long billboard on the roof of a building a few blocks from the convention center. It carried a portrait of Barry and the slogan "In your heart you know he's right." It turned out to be only a semi-coup. On the *Today Show* broadcast August 24, Hugh Downs announced: "It's a rumor around here that somebody's going to sneak up at night with a bucket of white paint, and pencil in the word 'far' between 'he's' and 'right' so it'll read 'In your heart you know he's far right.' If that happens you heard it here first." Two days later, a sign was found appended to, but not painted on, the billboard, reading, "Yes—extreme right."

A case of life imitating art? Teenage vandals? Not really. The miscreants, identified in the *New York Times,* included Newton Minnow, former head of the Federal Communications Commission, and Robert Tish, president of Loew's (later appointed postmaster general by Ronald Reagan, who perhaps was unaware of Tish's reprehensible behavior).

The campaign assembled the usual paraphernalia, although there was one unusual departure: We had two "official" portraits of the candidate. One, a bland photo of Barry wearing glasses, was issued by the RNC. The other, a dynamic photo taken by the Karsh brothers of Ottawa, Canada (Barry without glasses), had originally been commissioned by the RNC, but our ad agency apparently didn't like it. Perhaps they thought the glasses were iconic; without them, Barry just wouldn't look like Barry. Rus Walton pulled the Karsh photo out of the files and it was quickly adopted by Clif White's "Citizens" group, to be used far and wide.

There were trinkets galore. In this, the RNC was forbidden by law from selling buttons, bumper stickers, and the like, but it could (and did) operate as a clearinghouse. We screened the offerings for suitability, narrowed down the list of companies offering them to about fifteen suppliers, and sent samples and a catalog to officials in the field. In addition, while Citizens for Goldwater-Miller also was not allowed to "sell" materials, they could exchange them for "contributions." It was a distinction without a difference.

The usual trinkets included gold-colored elephant cuff links, earrings, and pins; campaign buttons with a gold-colored elephant wearing Barry's famous glasses; inflatable elephants (in three sizes); and clocks, boxes, and playing cards adorned with pictures of the candidates. There was Goldwater Taffy, touted as a "Golden Opportunity to sweeten your campaign fund . . . a delicious confection, made with fine ingredients [that] will never require an apology for its quality." The manufacturer had useful suggestions: Use it as a giveaway at rallies; as a door-opener for voter canvassing; or as a fund-raiser—we could buy it for 63 cents and sell it for $1.25 a bag. And there was "Gold Water," an "orange flavored soft drink for conservative tastes," 25 cents a can. Barry was induced to take a sip at a rally in Georgia; he spat it out and exclaimed, "That tastes like piss; I wouldn't drink it with gin!"

Among the not-quite-so usual trinkets were elephant-print boxer shorts. And there were campaign portraits that glowed in the dark, available in two sizes, 8 x 10 and 16 x 20 inches. I suspect they were most useful as a surprise gag gift, surreptitiously hung in someone's bedroom.

And while Barry had cautioned against "puff pieces," a few slipped into the official photo file: Barry the ham radio operator "since age 13," working his set; Barry the outdoorsman with a just-hooked sword-fish; Barry the major general climbing into the cockpit of an Air Force jet. Mrs. Barry was not overlooked: Under a photograph of her in the kitchen, a caption said she "loves to cook for her family of four. She enjoys preparing salads most of all."

I should note, in fairness, that the Democrats had their share of campaign dreck. Let one stanza of their convention anthem, "Hello, Lyndon," suffice (words and music by Jerry Herman, set to the tune of his Broadway hit "Hello, Dolly"):

We hear the band playin'
And the folks sayin'
"Let's all rally 'round the one who knows the score" . . . *so*
Be our guide, Lyndon,
Ladybird at your side, Lyndon,
Promise you'll stay with us in '64.

There were trinkets of a different sort as well, a string of virulent books written, published, and generally sold by people not connected with either campaign. Millions of copies were printed—one estimate for those on the Goldwater side was 16 million in total. Some were purchased in bulk by local organizations for free distribution; the Goldwater campaign endorsed none and kept them at arm's length. Most popular were *A Texan Looks at Lyndon* by J. Evetts Haley, which portrayed LBJ as a compulsive wheeler-dealer and political fixer; *None Dare Call It Treason* by John A. Stormer, which found a Communist under every bed and a one-world government just around the corner; and *A Choice Not an Echo* by Phyllis Schlafly—a reasoned argument against the Country Club Republicans.

The other side had *Barry Goldwater: A Political Indictment. A Moderate Republican's Critical Appraisal of the Man and the Issues,* by Edward Paul Mattar III; *An Answer to Goldwater,* by Millard L. Howell ("The purpose of this book is to help the American people understand and realize the inherent dangers of 'rugged individualistic' Conservatism and thereby make certain that it remains obsolete"); and *Barry Goldwater: Extremist of the Right,* by Fred J. Cook (which portrayed "Goldwater—the man, the myth, the menace," insensitive to the lot of common people, preoccupied "almost exclusively with the selfish interests of his own well-placed class, . . . surrounded by henchmen like the wily Clif White."

The only one of these with any claim to lasting relevance was Schlafly's book, which helped to launch her career as a conservative activist.

The basic campaign strategy remained "Go hunting where the ducks are." Except for a few token visits, Barry wouldn't spend much time on New England, New York, or Pennsylvania; instead, he would concentrate on the South (127 electoral votes), the Midwest (especially Ohio and Illinois, 52 votes), a smattering of traditional Republican states (Oklahoma, Kentucky, Arizona, 22 votes; Nebraska, Kansas, Indiana, Wyoming, Colorado, the Dakotas, and the smaller mountain states, perhaps 50 or 60 votes), and, of course, the big prize: California, 92 votes. It was basically the same plan we'd had ever since Clif White's initial presentation at the December 1962 meeting.

Among the issues to be addressed were America's loss of international prestige, the Berlin Wall, the repudiation of the Monroe Doctrine, the situation with Cuba, the war in Vietnam (which by that point had taken the lives of only a few hundred Americans but threatened to grow—Barry was opposed to the war but believed that if we were going to do it, we should do it right), the scandals that swirled around the Johnson administration (especially the tale of Bobby Baker, LBJ's protégé when he was Senate majority leader, who had become very rich through what is generally termed "influence peddling"), the continuing shift of power from the people to the federal government, the "dismal failure" to enforce law and order, and "the discouragement of individual initiative and responsibility among our people."

Barry wanted to engage LBJ in a televised debate—as he had earlier planned to do with Kennedy—but we had to overcome some impediments. The first was Section 315 of the Federal Communications Act, which allowed all announced candidates, of whatever political party, or of none at all, to claim the privilege of "equal time" to respond to an opponent's broadcast political address, unless the air time had been purchased. Because the application could be so cumbersome—nine or ten candidates all demanding to be heard, free of charge—debates between major candidates rarely happened. To allow the historic 1960 Presidential Debate between Nixon and JFK, with no other candidates involved, Congress had voted on a one-time suspension of the rule.

Barry's supporters introduced appropriate bills into the House and Senate to do likewise, and there arose the second impediment. On August 18, the Senate shelved the measure by a vote of 44 to 41, a Democratic party-line majority. Senator Cotton said the Democrats were acting on "orders from high up to junk this bill." There would be no debate in this campaign.

There were complaints that Barry was being two-faced, as earlier he had refused a challenge to meet Rockefeller in debate in New Hampshire. "I see no sense," Barry had said at the time, "in Republicans berating other Republicans." Rockefeller himself had refused a debate with an opponent in 1958: "I cannot believe," he wrote at the time, "that a series of debates between Republican candidates is the best way to strengthen the Republican Party."

We hired the Opinion Research Corporation (ORC) to do biweekly surveys of voters to determine public attitudes and alert us to what we were doing right and wrong. The report delivered August 26 told us, right at the start, that Goldwater needed more exposure—46 percent of respondents knew very little or nothing about the candidate. In addition, Goldwater needed humanizing—only 17 percent rated him as warm and friendly, compared with 49 percent for Johnson. LBJ was also rated high for "good judgment" but was seen as a politician who made deals and would promise anything to get votes. Goldwater's strengths, according to the survey, were that he spoke his own mind and had strong convictions. As for his weaknesses, he was seen as acting without thinking, as a politician who would promise anything to get votes, and as too conservative. Miller was practically unknown.

In identifying key issues on the public mind, ORC named the rise in government spending, the rising cost of living, handouts to the poor, and foreign affairs (45 percent believed the United States should get tougher with Cuba). One-third of respondents believed Johnson pushed civil rights for political gain; 62 percent believed that changes were needed in the law and that the Democrats were pushing for too much, too fast. Goldwater positions, all.

While we were getting organized, LBJ was grabbing headlines. Worried that people would think that he was just a vice president filling in until a real president could be elected, Johnson had set about in a most aggressive fashion to put his mark on the office. From the start of 1964, his legislative batting average was extraordinary; while Barry was battling other Republicans, Johnson was engineering congressional approval of forty-five out of fifty-two major proposals—in addition to the Civil Rights Act, voter-friendly legislation such as a civil service pay raise, support for mass transit and hospital construction, and antipoverty legislation.

On August 4, the president announced that North Vietnamese patrol boats had twice attacked, without provocation, U.S. Navy destroyers in the Gulf of Tonkin, and he was ordering retaliatory air strikes. (In fact, as Johnson knew, the destroyers had violated territorial waters to collect intelligence for South Vietnam.) There has long been doubt that the attacks happened at all; reports from the scene were ambiguous and may—or may not—have been honestly misinterpreted by our leaders in Washington. However, this controversy falls outside the scope of this memoir.

Goldwater offered immediate support. "We cannot allow the American flag to be shot at anywhere on earth if we are to retain our respect and prestige," he said. On August 7, Congress passed a nearly unanimous joint resolution—only two senators abstaining—authorizing the president "to take all necessary measures . . . to prevent further aggression." Within a month, the president would be planning a series of air raids against North Vietnam—to begin after the election. The president, of course, did not share information about these plans with the public or acknowledge his tacit agreement with Barry on the subject.

Meanwhile, the press was working a number on Barry. Columnist Walter Lippmann called him a "war hawk." Joseph Alsop—writing in the August 8 *Saturday Evening Post*—suggested that opposition to Goldwater rose out of "fear of an itchy finger on the nuclear trigger." Another article in the same issue warned that Goldwater was "impulsive, intuitive, indifferent to advice, and capable of both great charm and great rudeness." The *Washington Daily News* implied that Ralph Cordiner, now finance chairman of Goldwater for President, was responsible for a General Electric price-fixing scandal and predicted that "Cordiner's lack of popularity in large sections of the business community will hardly inspire voluntary gifts for the Goldwater campaign coffers." The *Washington Evening Star* quoted Steel Workers Union leader David J. McDonald as saying that Goldwater "actually despises poor people

THOMAS JEFFERSON'S HAIR

GEO. WASHINGTON'S CHIN

NATHAN HALE'S ROPE

BETSY ROSS'S FLAG

NO LEFT

RADICAL RIGHT

JOE McCARTHY'S LIST

GOLDWATER'S DEP'T STORE

NEANDERTHAL SIMPLICITY

WELCH'S BIRCH STICK

KNEE-JERK CONSERVATISM

ISSUES BLACK AND WHITE

"THE COMPLEAT BARRY GOLDWATER"

and wants to destroy unions. . . . If you want to be unemployed and live in filth and degradation, go out and support Goldwater."

White House staffer Jack Valenti advised Johnson to treat Goldwater "not as an equal who has credentials to be President, but as a radical, a preposterous candidate who would ruin this country and our future" and to act as if Bill Miller were "some April Fool's gag." Johnson offered a hint of his campaign strategy in his acceptance speech at the Democratic National Convention August 27. He condemned the tactics of "fear and smear" and warned that "one rash act, one thoughtless decision, one unchecked action" could leave the world in ashes.

As headlines advanced Johnson's cause, we stood mute. As the national staff dawdled, getting organized, state and local Republican organizations—full of energy, well-funded, ready to work—were given no guidance and were cut adrift. They called, they wrote, they affirmed their readiness to launch the charge. But calls were not returned and letters went unanswered because the national staff was not yet in place; the designated leaders of the campaign were not ready to lead. Clif White's legions, carefully assembled precinct-by-precinct, were in limbo, and no one at the top seemed to notice or care. And things went on this way not just until Labor Day, but for much of the campaign.

CHAPTER 15

On the Road

I T HAD BEEN BARRY'S practice to begin his Senate campaigns on the steps of the courthouse in Prescott, Arizona—where his Uncle Morris had served twenty-six years as mayor—and end in the northern Arizona hamlet of Fredonia, population 300, a town so isolated that the only reasonable access was from a small airport in Utah, two miles to the north. He wanted to follow this tradition for his national campaign; it was a talisman, of sorts.

The Prescott event was scheduled for September 4, but if there were portents, they were not encouraging—there were enough foulups to get us off to a confused start (or, perhaps, to signal a continuation of "business as usual"). A fully equipped pressroom had been set up in leased space at the Westward Ho motel in Phoenix, although the reporters were staying at the Valley Ho in nearby Scottsdale. No one was sure whether the Prescott airport could accommodate the campaign airplane, a Boeing 727 (which Barry had named *Yai Bi Ken,* Navajo for "House in the Sky"), until it had safely landed. The date was moved up by one day, September 4 to 3, on short notice. The advertised time was moved up two hours, from 4 P.M. to 2 P.M., a decision announced too late to make the local afternoon papers the day before the event. The change may have been for security (there were rumors of a planned protest by black militants), but more likely it was to accommodate eastern newspaper deadlines. No one had thought about that when the speech was originally scheduled.

158

Nor had anyone thought to arrange national broadcast coverage. That was probably a good thing, since the crowds that would have been there for the four o'clock event hadn't yet left home and the actual spectators were pretty thin on the ground, perhaps 4,000 instead of a predicted 20,000 to 50,000. Of course, given the local population of 13,000, one might wonder how the prediction was arrived at.

Portions of the speech, written by Karl Hess, one of the best in the business, were a pretty good exposition of Barry's views. Barry called for an end to the draft and advocated shifting to reliance on a professional, all-volunteer force. He said the federal government should undertake a prudent, slow, but steady withdrawal "from its many unwarranted interventions in our private economic lives." The process would have to be gradual so that the private economy could smoothly adjust to the changes without "the extra burden of sharp and erratic shifts" in policy. There were, however, some things that could be done immediately, he said: "We can start at once to slow down the expansion in federal spending. We can start at once to foster an economy that will provide jobs for our growing population. We can and will see to it that the job-making sector of the economy—the private sector—flourishes and absorbs the unemployed, particularly among our youth." Toward that latter end, following a suggestion made by University of Chicago economist Milton Friedman, Barry said he would call on the Congress to enact across-the-board tax cuts to stimulate growth in the economy, which would then lead to growth in tax revenues to offset any short-term losses.

And he spelled out his core beliefs, shared by the Republican conservatives who had maneuvered him to this point in history:

That each man is responsible for his own actions.

That each man is the best judge of his own well-being.

That each man has an individual conscience to serve and a moral code to uphold.

That each man is a brother to every other man.

"America's greatness," he said in closing, "is the greatness of her people. Let this generation, then, make a new mark for that greatness. Let this generation light a lamp of liberty that will illuminate the world. Let this generation of Americans set a standard of responsibility that will inspire the world. We can do it. And God willing, together, we will do it."

LBJ delivered his campaign opener in Detroit on Labor Day, September 7, 1964—although, in what was either typical LBJ dissimulation or a clumsy attempt at humor, he told a group of reporters that this appearance was not "political," it was just a traditional Labor Day address to 100,000 "working men." Nevertheless, travel expenses were covered by the Democratic Party.

In his address, LBJ spoke of many things in largely glittering generalities; on September 8, the *New York Times* called them "abstractions." He had a "dream" centered on the "simple wants of the people," which, he said, "is what America is all about." But the headline focused on the "key theme": "President Vows to Keep Control over Atom Arms." How did the editors know it was "the key"? Because the president said so, having devoted "fully half of his formal speech to the theme of peace" and affirming "the inviolability of Presidential control over nuclear arms." He declared:

> For nineteen peril-filled years, no nation has loosed the atom against another. To do so now is a political decision of the highest order. It would lead us down an uncertain path of blows and counter-blows whose outcome none may know. . . . Modern weapons are not like any other. In the first nuclear exchange 100 million Americans and more than 100 million Russians would all be dead. And when it was over our great cities would be in ashes, our fields barren, our industry destroyed, our dreams vanished."

Perhaps because of the high cost of operating Air Force One, LBJ's traveling party had been relegated to a pair of twelve-passenger Air

Force Jetstars. In addition to LBJ and his immediate staff, his plane
was occupied by five members of Congress from Michigan, two labor
union officials, and a speechwriter. There was no room for the officer
who carried the top-secret codes (in a briefcase dubbed the "football") that the president would need in event of a national security
emergency. That guy flew on the other plane. The other plane had a
minor mechanical problem. The White House announced that no
hazard had been involved. Except, of course, to the concept of the inviolability of presidential control of nuclear weapons.

The first Democratic TV commercial—produced under the direct
supervision of the White House—was shown a few hours after the
speech. It picked up the theme: Barry was a bomb thrower who would
ignite World War III. The commercial was brilliant, devastating, and
thoroughly dishonest. This was the infamous "Daisy" TV ad, broadcast, as a paid spot, only one time, in the middle of NBC's *Monday
Night at the Movies,* and it was seen by an estimated 50 million viewers.

The scene opens with a little girl picking the petals off of a daisy as
she counts, "One, two, three . . . " As she reaches "nine," a somber
male voice cuts in and counts down, "Ten, nine, eight, . . . " and the
camera zooms into the girl's eye. Then, the image explodes in the
mushroom cloud of an atomic blast. The viewer hears the voice of
LBJ: "These are the stakes, to make a world in which all of God's children can live, or to go into the dark. We must either love each other,
or we must die." The voice-over announcer closes the spot: "Vote for
President Johnson on November third. The stakes are too high for
you to stay at home."

To a nation that had not yet fully recovered from the nightmare
days of the Cuban Missile Crisis of October 1962, it was a powerful
message. The members of the White House team liked the nuclear
issue so much that they trotted out more commercials; the next appeared five days later. A little girl is licking an ice-cream cone. A kind-
sounding woman's voice-over warns about the dangers to children of
radioactive fallout and says that Barry Goldwater voted against the

Nuclear Test Ban Treaty. Then there is a sound effect: rapidly increasing clicks from a Geiger counter. A male voice-over says: "Vote for President Johnson on November third. The stakes are too high for you to stay at home." The problems with the Nuclear Test Ban Treaty—that the Soviets may have been ahead in weapons development, that there was room for cheating, that we would be forestalled from testing our own intercontinental ballistic missiles and thus wouldn't know if they would really work, and that rogue nations were not covered, all of which put our country at a disadvantage—were not, of course, explored.

LBJ's assistant, Bill Moyers, bragged that they had "hung the nuclear noose around Goldwater and finished him off." He was right, but what right did he have to be so proud?

Dean Burch and his Democratic counterpart, John Bailey, met on September 11—between the broadcast of "Daisy" and "Ice Cream"—to sign the "Code of Fair Campaign Practices" issued by the ten-year-old Fair Campaign Practices Committee. The idea, of course, was that everyone should agree to abide by rules of fair conduct.

But the season was off to a rough start. Bailey, after signing the code, announced to the press corps assembled for the event "that purveyors of bigotry and hate and fear and suspicion are already at work," whereupon Dean invited the attention of the committee "to the opening shot on the Democratic television campaign . . . these ads which depict a small girl pulling daisy petals, an atomic bomb, and then a voice persuading voters to vote for Lyndon Johnson. This, to me, is not exactly in the highest traditions of campaigns and fair practices." Bailey countered, "We think they are within the purview of fair campaigning. . . . In a 60 second spot . . . you have to get your message over pretty quick."

Dean suggested "that if the Democrat Party is genuinely interested in a rational approach to the issues in this campaign," the most tried and true way to address them would be for the major candidates to have a debate. "Take 30 minutes, or an hour, or however much you feel is necessary to really get into these issues, and debate them on television." He reminded Bailey that NBC had offered time and the RNC had offered to pay half the cost. Bailey's lame rejoinder was, "I would be willing to pay half the cost for the debate that Rockefeller and Goldwater didn't have."

Dean reminded Bailey that the idea for a presidential campaign debate had originated with the Democrats "back in 1960 with significant results for your party." Perhaps it should be our turn? Bailey countered that the decision not to debate "was made by the president. . . . He knows the problems that might arise in that kind of debate and I am sure he decided it in his good judgment." (We had offered to have the debate filmed in advance of broadcast to forestall any inadvertent security leaks that might be sprung in the heat of the moment; nevertheless, LBJ's "good judgment"—not to debate—prevailed.)

Someone said, "May I ask you sir, does that mean there will be no debates?" Bailey waffled, blaming "the bill" authorizing a suspension of the "equal time" rule that "did not come out of Congress." Someone else asked Dean if he planned to file a complaint over "Daisy Girl," and he answered, "I will be delighted to do so." Bailey jumped in: "It seems that the complaint is that they think we are trying to scare people with the image of Mr. Goldwater, and I think that any image of Mr. Goldwater has been created by Mr. Goldwater himself."

Burch noted that the Republicans had not much to do with the making of Democratic commercials and that "according to the *Wall Street Journal* . . . President Johnson is personally directing the television programs in this campaign and if this is a sample of the type of thing we can look forward to . . . this campaign ought to set a new high."

Indeed. Thus ended the press conference held to celebrate the signing of the Code of Fair Campaign Practices for 1964.

Dean Burch did indeed file a protest over "Daisy," and the Federal Campaign Practices Committee asked the Democratic National Committee to pull the ad. So what? The one-day commercial run was over, but free exposure on news and documentary programs was terrific. A large number of adult Americans even today certainly are aware of "Daisy" and have seen all or portions of the ad, which is often presented as a prime example of the thesis that "negative campaigning" works. A week after the first appearance of the commercial, a Harris poll reported that 53 percent of women and 45 percent of men believed that Goldwater would take the country to war.

A week after the results of the Harris poll appeared, our own pollster, Tom Benham, presented the results of his most recent interviews. They reflected the impact of the first active campaigning, but before Goldwater's main TV efforts got underway. Tom reported an improvement in voter "familiarity" with the candidate, and Barry was gaining among the better-educated, some 44 percent of whom said they favored him. However, there was no measurable upward trend overall from a June Gallup poll showing that 80 percent of voters preferred LBJ, compared to 20 percent for Barry. But Tom cautioned, polls are like icebergs, you can't see what's below the water line. In fact, when asked if they "knew anyone" who would not admit that they probably would vote for Goldwater, 37 percent of respondents said yes.

Barry's calls for eliminating the draft and cutting taxes were having little impact; ending the draft was "very important" to only 31 percent of respondents and almost twice as many believed that LBJ would do a better job developing a tax-cut program than Goldwater. The major issue of the day, the handling of nuclear weapons, was "very important" for 92 percent, and the Democrats' early and constant concentration on this issue—not to mention the damage done by Rockefeller and Scranton—was working. Benham's results reflected the Harris poll findings. When asked, "Do you think the chances of a nuclear war would be greater under Johnson or Goldwater?" 44 percent named Goldwater, whereas only 8 percent named LBJ; 48 percent offered no opinion.

"AND HOW WOULD YOU DESCRIBE
YOUR DOMESTIC POLICY, SENATOR GOLDWATER?"

At last, in an effort to blunt the "nuclear" attack and expose John-son's perfidy, we assembled a six-member advisory group on de-fense issues: former Secretary of Defense Neil McElroy, former senior Department of Defense official Wilfred McNeill, legislators Gerald Ford and Prescott Bush, and former chairmen of the Joint Chiefs of Staff Admiral Arthur Radford and General Nathan F. Twining.

All had been involved in the making of the NATO nuclear understanding, and they brought unquestioned authority to a report presented to Barry on September 29 and released to the public on October 6, 1964. Back in 1953, they wrote, because of a shortfall in NATO manpower, the United States had developed tactical nuclear weapons suitable for use on a limited battlefield. The advisory group estimated that the deployed "Davy Crockett" nuclear artillery shell had the punch of about ten salvos of regular heavy artillery. In other words, it was not exactly a doomsday device.

From the beginning, the group affirmed, it was fully understood that the NATO commander would be "given sufficient latitude by the President to permit timely response to an attack on NATO with battlefield nuclear weapons." "Sufficient latitude" might be translated as a situation involving incapacity of the president or disruption of communications. That policy continued through Eisenhower and Kennedy and into the Johnson administration, but by August, the need to hang the nuclear noose around Goldwater's neck had overtaken good sense—and truth. Secretary of Defense Robert M. McNamara told the Democratic National Convention Platform Committee, "We in Defense spare no energy to make certain that the president of the United States—and he alone—has complete control over the dispatch of our nuclear weapons." A few weeks after his campaign opener in Detroit (where the officer with the "football" had been shunted off to a separate but malfunctioning airplane), LBJ affirmed to a Seattle audience that "the release of nuclear weapons would come by presidential decision alone." This made our NATO allies, who read the newspapers, very nervous.

LBJ's national security advisor, McGeorge Bundy, tried to get the president to come clean, to admit that there were circumstances where authority should pass to commanders in the field. NATO was restive, and Bundy asked LBJ to issue "a statement in which you make clear that there are indeed very specialized contingencies for which certain presidential instructions already exist." Johnson declined and instead drove his point home with another TV spot. The viewer's vote, it said, was:

> a decision which can affect not only you and your children but the future of every country on Earth, and the fate of mankind itself. . . . Atomic weapons are not simply bigger and more powerful than other weapons. From the American Revolution until now, 526,000 Americans have died in battle. A single tactical bomb can kill more than that in a few minutes. A full-scale atomic war would destroy more than 300 million people around the world. Our great cities would be in ashes, our industries destroyed, our dreams vanished. . . . Our great nuclear power must not be placed in the hands of those who might use it impulsively or carelessly.

A "single tactical bomb," with a radius of destruction of less than a mile, could kill "more than" 526,000? That would have to be a pretty crowded battlefield. Facts and logic were on our side, and even a writer for the *New York Times* ventured to assume that our advisory group's report "should help to strip the campaign issue of the artificial Democratic sound and fury." But the nuclear horse was long out of the barn, never to be coaxed back in.

Other Democratic commercials picked up where Nelson Rockefeller had left off. On radio, one ad said, "Barry Goldwater's plan means the end of Social Security, the end of widows' pensions, the end of the dignity that comes with being able to take care of yourself without depending on your children. On November 3, vote for keeping Social Security." And a TV spot featured the "President of all the people" saying:

Over thirty years we have shaped a simple philosophy, those who have given a lifetime of labor to their country, who have fought its wars and built its strength, are entitled to live out their years in happiness and dignity. Our basic instrument has been the Social Security system. . . . Our opponent has called for an end to Social Security as we know it. He has advocated a voluntary program. He has said, and I quote him, "People can buy better protection privately than the Social Security law provides for them."

Now this is not just a single careless statement made by someone in the heat of a campaign. It is a conviction repeated many times. It is backed by a steady record of votes in opposition to almost every measure to help older Americans.

He did not point out that Goldwater had voted with the majority in every piece of Social Security legislation that had come before the Senate during his time as senator. And—how easy it is to make an accurate statement that is not honest—*any* change to the program would be "an end to Social Security as we know it."

But the best "Social Security" spot put out by the Johnson staff used few words. While a voice on the soundtrack declared that Goldwater would "destroy" Social Security, the video showed a pair of large, masculine hands searching for, and then tearing apart, a Social Security card. The spot was so effective that voters would swear that they had seen Goldwater himself tearing up a card on TV.

The answers to one running poll question—"Is Goldwater opposed to Social Security?"—told the story. At the beginning of September, 27 percent of respondents said yes. Two weeks later, that slice had increased to 36 percent. After another two weeks, 40 percent of all respondents agreed with the premise.

One five-minute TV spot combined grief for the martyred JFK and stern resolve from the current commander-in-chief. It opened with a shot of LBJ returning to the nation's capital just after the assassination, where he said, "We have suffered a loss that cannot be weighed.

I will do my best. That is all I can do. I ask for your help and God's."
A voice-over continued the message: "He came with grief in his heart.
But he also came determined that the young president he had served
did not live or die in vain." The spot went on to extol LBJ's legislative
victories: tax cuts, civil rights, antipoverty, five bills on education, protection of the wilderness, improvements in urban housing and trans-
portation. "When American destroyers were attacked in the Gulf of
Tonkin," the announcer noted, "he replied firmly and decisively and
Communist aggression was turned back."

And it may be pure coincidence, but we saw a flood of documentary television shows on Truman, Roosevelt, and Kennedy. "The
Young Man from Boston," an hour-long tribute to Kennedy, was run
on some TV stations as many as four times during the campaign, all
in prime time. (Viewers of a station in Austin owned by the LBJ family, however, were not able to see two nationally televised Goldwater
speeches as they were being broadcast. The general manager of
KTBC-TV didn't want to "disrupt" the station's regular programming.) And, of course, a president (any president) has instant access
to the airwaves. Johnson appeared on "live" television more than fifty-
eight times during his first two years in office, nine more times than
Eisenhower had during his eight years and twenty-five more than
Kennedy in nearly three years. LBJ had the bully pulpit and used it
for all it was worth.

With the campaign barely underway, editorial judgments of newspapers far and wide were already cast in stone—or, rather, set in type. By
September 8, the *Chicago Sun-Times* had said, "We cannot accept the
Goldwater philosophy. Neither do we believe the Arizona Senator has
the capacity to serve as Chief Executive of the nation." The *Chicago
Daily News* had said that it found "no traces" of the Republican principles of Abraham Lincoln or General Eisenhower, both of whom
they admired. In Vermont, three of eight traditionally Republican papers announced for LBJ; the *Brattleboro Reformer*, which had never

before backed a Democratic presidential candidate in its fifty-three-year history, noted that it could not "subscribe to the extreme conservatism" of the Goldwater-Miller ticket. The *Kansas City Star* came out for Johnson—the first Democrat it had backed since Grover Cleveland in 1892: "We are convinced that the cause of world peace would be better served by Mr. Johnson and his foreign policy. . . . It would be safer to keep his finger on the nuclear trigger than to place the awesome responsibility on Senator Goldwater."

C.L. Sulzberger of the *New York Times* fell for the gag and wrote: "The possibility exists that, should [Goldwater] enter the White House, there might not be a day after tomorrow." Barry said that as far as he could recall, he had never met, spoken to, or been interviewed by Sulzberger.

The newspapers were positively benign compared with the *Saturday Evening Post:* The Republican candidate, it said, was a man who

> is manifestly unqualified to be President and whose unsuitability
> for this awesome responsibility becomes clearer with every passing
> day and with every feckless word he utters. . . . Goldwater is a
> grotesque burlesque of the conservative he pretends to be. He is a
> wild man, a stray, an unprincipled and ruthless political jujitsu
> artist. . . . For the good of the Republican Party, which his candi-
> dacy disgraces, we hope that Goldwater is crushingly defeated . . .
> [to] drive the fanatic saboteurs of the Republican Party back into
> the woodwork whence they came."

Along the same lines—opinion pulled out of thin air—the September-October issue of a new magazine called *Fact,* published by a man who had earlier been convicted of peddling pornography, reported on its "survey" of more than 12,000 psychiatrists. The respondents had been asked: "Do you think that Barry Goldwater is psychologically fit to serve as President of the United States?" Most ignored the survey; a few hundred said "not enough information"; and more than 600 said that Goldwater was indeed fit to serve. But on the cover of the maga-zine, in big black type, was the answer from the rest: "One thousand one hundred eighty-nine psychiatrists say Goldwater is psychologically unfit to be President." The cover and its screaming message appeared in full-page ads that the publisher purchased in major metropolitan newspapers. Numerous newspapers all over the country published the results of the *Fact* survey, along with "diagnoses" offered by some of the respondents, who called Barry "paranoid," "megalomaniacal," and "unstable." Barry filed for libel against the publisher and won a finan-cial judgment, upheld through a series of appeals. But that was later, well after the damage had been done to his campaign.

At least one brave voice stood against the tide—the *Cincinnati Enquirer*:

> Barry Goldwater has become the most slandered man in American
> political history. . . . He is portrayed as a poisoner of children, as a
> creature of the night-riders, as a pawn of the militarists and the
> warmongers. To see the viciousness of the vilification heaped upon
> him is to begin to understand the desperation with which his ene-
> mies are trying to cling to the perverted political order they have
> been foisting upon America. Their purpose is to do considerably
> more than defeat him at the polls: they seek literally to crush him
> lest any other muster the courage to ask them to account for their
> sordid works.

From that point forward, whatever Barry did was a wasted effort. He might as well have conceded at that moment; the campaign, lost before it began, had been the victim of only two issues: the security of nukes and the insecurity of senior citizens. The Democrats didn't need a big team of researchers digging into Barry's past positions; all they had to do was read yesterday's press clippings. Every charge lodged by Rockefeller and Scranton was picked up and seamlessly in-tegrated into the Democrats' campaign.

That's hindsight, but we were still trying to look ahead, seeking a path to victory. To bypass the filters of publishers and editors and take our messages directly to the people, we created full-page newspaper ads, a bunch of one-minute and five-minute TV and radio spots, and in what may have been another political "first," a series of thirty-minute "TV talkers." The cost for the air time was $130,000 for thirty minutes on NBC, $140,000 on CBS (with more stations covered). This innovation was sound—witness Ross Perot's success with the format in the 1992 election—but our execution was spotty.

The first thirty-minute piece was a filmed address, but it was rambling and defensive: It opened with Barry repeating the charges his opponents were making, that he was impulsive, imprudent, and trigger-happy. The bright spot, so to speak, was a highly successful fund-raising appeal by the actor Raymond Massey tacked on to the end, which brought in $175,000 and more than paid for the show. This was another innovation, and it was done over the objections of both Kitchel and Baroody, who thought such public pleading for money was too undignified.

The second program, broadcast September 23, was a thirty-minute conversation with Ike. The plan was to show Goldwater and Eisenhower in easy conversation at the Gettysburg farm. They would discuss the issues, the future of the country, and whatever else they wanted to talk about. While the crew was setting up, General Eisenhower offered a thought that the show would be better if at some point they walked over a portion of the Civil War battlefield. This required us to rearrange the shoot and add an unplanned $20,000 to the production cost. Once the film was rolling, Barry and Ike didn't talk about much of anything—they might as well have been discussing the weather, while squandering thousands of dollars every minute. The program started with an inane question, "Well, Barry, you've been campaigning now for two or three weeks, how do you like it? And how does it seem to be going for you?"

From that point on, it was going downhill. Don Dornan—the photographer I had provided to the campaign—reported that the whole shoot was messed up. The Goldwater managers declined to manage and just let things bumble along even though it was obvious that Eisenhower kept missing the point. Barry tried to get someone to pay attention and offer some direction, but he was told, "It's okay, don't worry about it."

At noon, Ike went off to have lunch and a nap, leaving Barry standing without an invitation. He cadged a meal from the packed lunches brought along for the production crew; none had been provided for Barry. Things were no better after production resumed. The flash-finish went like this:

GOLDWATER: Now, General, this has been a very interesting day here with you at the farm. I've enjoyed it immensely, as I've always enjoyed visiting with you. There's just one question I might ask in leaving. I don't think anybody in this country wants war. I've been through one of them, and that's enough, and I don't want my children, or my grandchildren, or your grandchildren, or anybody's children going through war. But, in this campaign that Congressman Bill Miller and I are engaged in, for the presidency and the vice-presidency, because we constantly stress the need for a strong America, our opponents are referring to us as warmongers. And I'd like to know what your opinion of that would be. You've known me for a long time, and you've known Congressman Miller a long time.

GENERAL EISENHOWER: Well, Barry, in my mind this is actual "tommyrot." Now, you've known about war, you've been through one. I'm older than you. I've been in more. But, I tell you, no man that knows anything about war is going to be reckless about it. Now, certainly, the country recognizes in you a man of integrity, goodwill, honesty and dedication to his country. You're not going to be doing those things—what do they call it—"push the button"? That is just crazy. I can't imagine anything you would be giving more thought to than the president's responsibility as the commander-in-chief of all our armed forces, and as the man conducting our foreign relations. I am sure that with this kind of approach you will be successful in keeping us on the road to peace.

We had intended to close off with another Raymond Massey appeal, but Kitchell wouldn't allow it. The dignity of the former president was more important than the money, he said. I thought at the time that a fund appeal might have brought in half a million dollars, although that was before we saw the audience numbers. In a slot where *Petticoat Junction* pulled 27.4 percent of the viewers and 25 percent watched *Peyton Place*, "Conversation at Gettysburg" was seen by 8.6 percent.

I hate to say it, but in the end, Ike was not much help in the campaign—although much of it was our own fault. Kitchel not only refused the fund-raising appeal, he apparently didn't believe in prepping the ex-president. Fiasco number two occurred when we held a meeting to discuss military preparedness at New York City's Waldorf-Astoria with Ike, Senator Prescott Bush, Eisenhower's secretary of defense Neil McElroy, and others. When Ike came out of the meeting and a reporter asked about control of nuclear weapons, the general said that he didn't think it was an issue in this campaign.

Ike was our ultimate authority, the man we hoped would affirm that Johnson had been deceptive about the practice of giving limited authority to the NATO commander. Ike certainly noticed our stunned reaction, and after the reporters had left, he turned to me and said, "What was I supposed to say? Nobody told me."

Another thirty-minute talker was an unconvincing question-and-answer session called "Brunch with Barry." The stage directions began, "The set is a simulation of Goldwater's apartment. . . . We come in on a brunch in progress, Barry and seven women—Senator

Margaret Chase Smith, mothers from New York and San Francisco, a Vietnam widow, a senior citizen, an 'Outstanding Woman Leader,' and an 'Italian Nationalities Representative.' . . . No make-up or special hair dressing." Goldwater has a conversation with the women, and it covers all the bases: busing, Social Security, Vietnam, communism (ninety miles off our shore), crime, and drugs. The widow reads a letter from her husband and makes the statement, "I am for Senator Goldwater because he understands the current situation and the problem." And Goldwater makes a "peace through strength" statement.

But the program came across about as lively as the directions. One southern state chairman joked with us over the choice of "Brunch with Barry" as the title for a daytime TV show. "We have *dinner* at noon," he said. In the South, brunch was a foreign concept.

Opinion Research reported that the audience for these thirty-minute programs was minuscule—and most of those who did watch were either conservative junkies looking for a fix or Johnson campaign workers looking for fodder. Many who tuned in out of curiosity quickly went looking for something interesting to watch. However, of those voters who stayed the course and watched until the end, 67 percent of Republicans and 39 percent of Democrats came away with a more favorable impression of our candidate than they'd had before seeing the show.

I still had a job in New York, of course, but I also had an understanding business partner and was able to devote an increasing amount of time to the cause. The duties of RNC treasurer occupied only some of my time, and I was more than happy to be involved in a variety of activities, from helping with advertising to going out on the road with Barry.

On the finance side, Jerry Milbank and I worked as a team, but our duties are best described as "ad hoc." One day might be spent on finances; another on candidate scheduling. Then back to finances, with a quick detour to book time on a TV station in Detroit or

Charleston in response to an urgent request from some local volunteer—although in this, Ralph's Rules often got in the way. We couldn't schedule a program until we could show the money, and often, this came too late to permit adequate advance publicity to ensure a reasonable audience.

We discovered that we also had to accept interference from Kitchel and Baroody, who destroyed the format for a national broadcast of Barry at a Milwaukee fund-raiser on October 13. Jerry and I planned to feature shots of the live crowd and Barry for the full thirty minutes. Kitchel and Baroody insisted on cutting back on the crowd shots, showed Barry live for perhaps a minute, and filled in the rest of the time with a rehash of a previously broadcast "Visit with Barry." In the meantime, Barry went on speaking to a marvelously enthusiastic crowd of 8,500 people who had each paid $50 for the privilege, expecting that their event was going to be on national TV.

The audience didn't learn the truth until after the program had ended. According to one volunteer who wrote to complain:

> The calls, telegrams, letters and stopped payments on checks have been fantastic. Kitchel gave a reason that stems from sheer idiocy— "crowd reaction would hold up the meeting and TV viewers would not have heard the end of the talk." That is a complete admission of incompetency. Two nights later Hubert Humphrey spoke in the same arena with an enthusiastic crowd. He was televised from 8:30 to 9:00 and he concluded his remarks at nine o'clock. It was a crime that Hubert Humphrey's campaign managers are so much more intelligent than Goldwater's. . . . Many people I have talked to here are very concerned that if Goldwater is elected, he will continue to surround himself with unqualified people. . . . The entire thing was an insult to everybody.

When Jerry and I challenged Kitchel on this, he sang a different song. He didn't know it was a fund-raiser, he said, and the change in format had been Barry's decision. There had been a few incidents in New Jersey and Pennsylvania involving booing and a few tossed eggs and tomatoes. Barry was gun shy about being televised with crowds. He didn't want to take any chances on inviting "negative" images at this late stage of the campaign.

If that was true—and I have my doubts—it was ridiculous for Barry to be surprised or upset about an occasional burst of such behavior. It was a big stretch to think that a paying crowd would resort to (or tolerate) any booing, and foolish to pull back into a protective shell. What did he have to lose? Jerry argued that now was exactly the time to be taking chances. We were so far behind that we probably could never catch up unless we did.

For the record, it was true that there had been egg incidents, and they continued. But I doubt that they had any negative impact on the campaign—perhaps just the opposite. Three days after the Milwaukee event, during a motorcade in Sioux City, Barry was hit in the face by an egg. It had been thrown by "two youths on a roof," who were arrested. He later told a crowd of 6,000—"smiling," according to the *New York Times*—that "One of LBJ's boys hit me with an egg. All I can say to LBJ is just keep them fresh."

Since I wrote the checks that covered their expenses, I was in regular communication with some of our surrogates in the field, especially Ronald Reagan and Dick Nixon, and soon was helping to arrange their schedules. Aside from the team working with Barry, there was no effective speech bureau. Requests would come in from the field—could we send in a celebrity for a rally or a banquet?—and many ended up on my desk. And, because Barry's speechwriters were too wrapped up with his needs—and, as noted earlier, since the campaign had declined to provide Nixon with a designated speechwriter—I also found myself in the part-time speech-crafting business, heavy on party-line talking points for both Nixon and Reagan.

I called Reagan almost every day and found him willing, with great good spirit, to take on any assignment at a moment's notice. Reagan, serving as cochair of the Goldwater campaign in California, didn't like to fly and usually stayed in that state, always delivering a great message. He may have given some 100 speeches.

And, while most of the "establishment" were taking a walk, Nixon gave his all for Goldwater, more than 237 speeches in thirty-six states, half again as many speeches as either of our candidates. Once, without mercy, I asked him to go to Hawaii, then to San Francisco, then to Los Angeles, then to Kansas, and then to somewhere I have forgotten, all in a two-day period. Once, when I complimented him on his ability to talk without any apparent notes, he said, "I do all those speeches without any notes, no Teleprompter. . . . It's a discipline. I make very heavy notes in advance and then think 'em through and then because of my long experience I just speak 'em off the top of my head."

He never complained, which didn't hurt his own standing with the party. Or, more to the point of this memoir, with Jerry Milbank, Peter O'Donnell, John Grenier, and me; he was to harvest that political capital a few years later.

CHAPTER 16

End Game

FROM SEPTEMBER 3 TO November 2, 1964, Barry covered 64,900 miles by air, 2,900 by rail, a dozen miles in a tugboat, a few hundred yards on a horse, and an unlogged number of road miles in and between stops. He visited forty-five states and more than a hundred cities. He was consistently met by gratifyingly large crowds: 53,000 in Los Angeles, 18,000 in Seattle, 16,000 in Minneapolis—where he outpulled the former two-term mayor and now Democratic candidate for vice president, Hubert Humphrey.

The crowds were there, but if, as Speaker of the House Tip O'Neill would later say, "all politics is local," the locals were getting the wrong messages. Kitchel, Baroody, and friends had decided that Goldwater should run a strictly "national-theme" campaign and never deal with local issues. That was a big mistake; people wanted to hear the candidate acknowledge their own problems and address their concerns, even if he couldn't offer to solve them on the spot.

In advance of a Goldwater swing through the South, Regional Director Sam Claiborne came to Washington, D.C., to meet with the speechwriters. He urged them to include those things that were most likely on the minds of the audiences—let cotton, peanut, and tobacco farmers know that Goldwater was sympathetic to their problems, and have Goldwater address the controversies surrounding the government-owned Tennessee Valley Authority (TVA), which provided electricity to some of the more poverty-stricken states in the nation. In particular, Barry needed to explain his suggestion that some portions of TVA be sold to more efficient private interests, a proposal that seems to never have been clearly articulated. (One woman vowed that she would not vote for Goldwater because he was going to take away her "TV.") The senior citizens in Sam's region were also concerned about the Social Security debate and needed to hear more about the voluntary program Goldwater was proposing.

Instead, Goldwater talked about rising crime rates, cutting taxes, administration policy on Vietnam, and ending the draft. They were important topics, and this was part of the overall strategy, but in many ways, it was New Hampshire all over again, where Clif's elaborate briefing books were not shared with the candidate. As Mary McGrory had said then, "He does not even trouble to mention the town in which he finds himself." McGrory may have known more about the fine points of campaigning than Kitchel and Baroody did. The political folks on the second floor prepared extensive briefing materials to assist the "think tank" people on the third floor in framing messages, and the speaker in reaching his audience. These included names of local supporters, analysis of local issues, and precinct-by-precinct demographics. The people on the third floor seem largely to have ignored the information, and there was no evidence that the speaker—Barry—ever saw them.

In the West, for example, the lumber industry was suffering from the high cost of shipping their product in American-owned and -operated ships—a requirement mandated by legislation passed by the largely Democratic Congress at the request of the maritime labor unions. It was cheaper for American customers anywhere to import lumber from Canada, carried in foreign-flag ships, than it was for them to purchase lumber from the American West. But Goldwater did not mention the timber industry when he visited western cities. Another controversy raged over a long-proposed dam on the Snake River in Idaho and whether it should be publicly or privately financed and constructed. But Goldwater did not address the issue.

Even issues important to voters in California—the state with the largest number of electoral votes—were neglected. Democrats in the state were opposed to the *bracero* program, whereby Mexican laborers were brought in under special permit to work the farms of California. Organized labor wanted an end to the program, too, arguing that it was taking jobs away from Americans. The Johnson administration announced that the program would end at the end of the year. Republican Senate candidate George Murphy, running against Senator Pierre Salinger, pushed for continuation of the bracero program at almost every stop. Goldwater never mentioned it. Murphy won.

Barry's approach to the sensitive issue of farm subsidies was not well understood either. It had been confused by various bits and pieces published over the years—many of which did not reflect his actual position. This was especially true of *The Conscience of a Conservative,* published in 1960, in which his ghost writer had Barry call for "prompt, and final, termination of the farm subsidy program" and said, "The only way to persuade farmers to enter other fields of endeavor is to stop paying inefficient farmers for produce that cannot be sold at market prices."

Goldwater's actual position was far less black and white. He proposed gradual change, not an abrupt end to the program. He believed that the federal government was responsible for the farmers' present problems and should accept responsibility for moving the farmer back into the free market, even if this would require substantial outlays of federal cash to train the farmers for new occupations. But that uncorrected snippet gave the Democrats a big hammer: If elected, they warned, Goldwater would immediately cancel the program under which farmers had been operating for the past thirty years.

Republican Senators Milton Young and Carl Mundt, from the farming states of North and South Dakota, leaned hard on Barry to attend the National Plowing Contest, September 19, and put his true position in perspective. The senators then offered advice and assistance to speechwriter Chuck Lichtenstein, who listened but didn't pay much attention. When Senator Mundt later saw a draft of the speech, he deemed it unacceptable and asked Lichtenstein for some changes. Dean Burch agreed and wanted the speech rewritten. For some reason, it was not revised, however, and four hours after Dean's request, the original, unaltered version of the speech was released as an advance to the press. An angry Senator Young, who had been asked to introduce Barry to the crowd, refused to even sit on the platform and later declined to campaign for him.

At the event, Goldwater reminded his audience that 17 percent of the farmers' income, amounting to $2.1 billion, came from federal subsidies, and asked, "Do you want that to continue?" It was probably not the best way to introduce the subject, although he added, "I have no intention of stopping supports overnight. . . . Nothing drastic will be done." He said, "We know in our hearts that you are plagued with special problems. And we know they are serious problems. We will work with you toward solutions, not schemes."

But he had lost that crowd before he began, because vice-presidential candidate Hubert Humphrey, addressing the same event earlier in the day, had already poisoned the well. The election of Goldwater would mean a "death sentence to agriculture," he said, and to make his point, he read a few lines from *The Conscience of a Conservative:* "There can be no equivocation here—prompt and final termination of the farm subsidy program." Humphrey spelled it out: If Goldwater carried out that promise, "it would impoverish farm people, wipe out billions in land values, ruin business on rural America's main streets, and solve absolutely nothing."

The headline in the *New York Times* was: "Humphrey Charges Goldwater's Policy Will Ruin Farmers." Game, set, match.

A month later, with time slipping away, a group of senators from farm states tried again—without Senator Young—and arranged a meeting with Barry and party leaders from eleven states. It was the opening of the mid-October National Corn-Picking Contest at Sioux Falls, South Dakota. They wanted this to be a meeting with Barry, not speechwriters, and they got what they wanted. Barry told some 20,000 farm folk assembled to watch people husk corn that price supports must go, but that changes could not be made overnight. Commitments already made must be honored, he said, and existing programs would not be scrapped until he was sure he had something better. In sum, he said, "I pledge to you . . . that I will never propose a change in the price support program until something better has been developed that can gradually be substituted for it." He promised, "I will never jerk the rug out from under the American farmer." But it was too little, too late, even if the farmers were paying attention. It was a message, like so many others, that should have been delivered, and a topic that should have been resolved, well before he had the nomination.

On September 18, the day before the plowing contest, Barry had taken on the Johnson $1 billion "antipoverty" program in the capital city of the impoverished state of West Virginia. Johnson's program, he said, was a "hodgepodge of handouts" really meant to maintain LBJ in power, a "great society" in which there would be no penalty for failure and no reward for success, an all-American version of the Marxist formula, "From each according to his abilities, to each according to his needs." He added, "Human misery is not to be trifled with just to get votes in an election." The program was a fraud; the government was not the answer. Only the "vast resources of private business" could truly tackle the problems of penury.

Audience reaction was muted. Barry was interrupted with applause about twenty times, but it was usually perfunctory and mild. Adding insult to injury, Barry ignored eighteen men who were waiting in a private dining room at the Charleston airport; each had donated $1,000 for the privilege of having coffee with the candidate. Goldwater shook hands with passersby in the lobby and boarded his plane without so much as a hello to the waiting contributors. It looked like a case of either bad manners or poor coordination. Though it was probably the latter, it didn't make much difference.

Goldwater speechwriting was neither an individual nor a team effort; it was more like serial exposition. One or two men would write a
draft, another would make changes, and yet another would bring his
own ideas into the mix before the text was turned over to the blue-
pencil brothers, Kitchel and Baroody. Throughout the entire campaign, the key speechwriter—Henry Jaffa, the man who had written
much of the controversial convention acceptance speech—was never
given the opportunity to discuss, with the candidate, the issues to be
covered in the speeches on which he was working.

This is not to imply that Barry was some sort of automaton, or a
prisoner of a mafia. He had control over what he said. He took what
he was given by his handlers and modified it to include specific issues
that he wanted to raise. He wanted to challenge people and make
them think, not spread political manure. He believed that people
would see him as an honest man, worthy of their votes even if they dis-
agreed with some of his positions.

In a thirty-minute TV address on October 9—probably the best
of the bunch, although Len Hall complained that Barry seemed to
be trying to cram too many things into the allotted time—Barry
acknowledged:

> You have probably been reading and hearing about some of the un-
> orthodox things I have been doing. I have gone to the heart of Ap-
> palachia and there I have deliberately attacked this administration's
> phony war on poverty. I have gone into the heart of Florida's retire-
> ment country and there I have deliberately warned against the out-
> right hoax of this administration's Medicare scheme. I have gone
> into the heart of our farm areas and there I have deliberately called
> for the gradual transition from a controlled to a free agriculture.

He also was going around the country blasting LBJ as a "liar," as
being "soft on communism," and as someone who was willing to sacri-
fice the national interest to "buy votes." In my judgment, and that of

The Courier Journal

"A CHOICE, NOT AN ECHO! AN ECHO! AN ECHO!
AN ECHO! AN ECHO!"

many of our people in the field, he was delivering too many defensive
messages—answering charges but not promoting changes. His greatest liability was the charge that he was "trigger happy" and might start

a nuclear war; this was so much on his mind that he couldn't stop talking about it. At a campaign stop in Hammond, Indiana, he mentioned nuclear weapons, war, "destruction," and "holocaust" twenty-six times in about as many minutes. Kitchel—to his credit—suggested it was time for Barry to find another topic. Barry said, in effect, "Okay. Get someone else to carry that message and I'll shut up." Dick Nixon stepped up to the plate; in a national TV broadcast a few days later, he offered a summary of the advisory panel's report on NATO and "presidential control."

With less than a month to go until the election, some of us wanted Barry to take the next step—to drop away from ad hominem attacks and a cornucopia of unrelated issues and return to basics: liberalism versus economic conservatism, a choice not an echo. We believed it was time for him to reemphasize those views on personal liberty that had made him such a public figure in the first place, and to affirm his interest in local issues. We wanted a reshuffle in the speechwriting department with a professional politician, like Steve Shadegg, in charge. The campaign was adrift, touching on no shore. This was no big secret—the *New York Times* reported on the internal debate in its October 6 issue. "One source said that it was possible that Mr. Goldwater would 'return to the basics' in the last month of the campaign. . . . But . . . there was no consensus today as to what the senator should do—except that he should do something, and fairly quickly."

Talking to the *New York Times* was one thing—engaging our candidate's attention was another. That should not have been much of a problem—after all, he was our candidate, and we were part of his campaign staff—but whenever I, Ralph Cordiner, or Wayne Hood, among others, made the effort, Kitchel or Baroody or someone close to them blocked the door or stifled the discussion. Ralph hopped a ride on the campaign plane when it was headed to Phoenix, hoping to catch a few minutes with Barry en route, or, better, have a private conversation with him after they arrived. But somehow, a meeting couldn't be arranged. Ralph reported, "It was obvious to me that

Goldwater did not want to see me. I suspect he knew the purpose of my visit, and I didn't think anything could be gained by forcing my ideas on him."

Back in San Francisco, Barry had said, "Don't bother telling me when I'm doing well. Call, anytime, and raise hell when I'm not." It had become virtually impossible to follow these instructions. Someone said it was similar to what had happened with Nixon in 1960; Bob Novak had written, "It was easier to gain an audience with the Pope than to see Nixon privately." As it turned out, Barry indeed knew what was going on but somehow didn't care. When Northern California field director Bob Mardian finally got a chance to grab a seat near Barry on a swing from Portland to Salt Lake City, he was told, "You go back and tell your crowd that I'm going to lose this election. I'm probably going to lose it real big. But I'm going to lose it my way."

Kitchel and Baroody had just been doing their job, the job Barry wanted them to do, which included shielding him from distractions. They came in for a lot of criticism, both at the time and in all of the postcampaign literature generated since—and some of it was justified. Kitchel was a cautious lawyer; the answer that first came to his mind in response to any question or suggestion was "no." Baroody was a deep thinker. Neither of them had the requisite political skills to handle such a large campaign, and they were not nimble enough to respond quickly to changing circumstances. But they were there because Goldwater wanted them there. Their actions—or lack thereof—lost a few votes and irritated a few people who "knew better," but they didn't cost Goldwater the election.

O'Donnell kept it all in perspective. He told us, "Well, we knew what we were getting into when we nominated him. We knew he'd speak his mind. I thought that's why we backed him. Now let's try to help him instead of bitching all day long."

We held weekly planning sessions in Washington, usually over a weekend, where we looked back to the events of the past week and ahead toward the election. Those in attendance usually included some combination of the following: Dean Burch, Denny Kitchel, John Grenier, Ralph Cordiner, Jerry Milbank, Len Hall, Bob Wilson, Bill Baroody, Bill Knowland, Wayne Hood, Bill Warner, Clif White, Stets Coleman, and me. To the best of my recollection, neither Goldwater nor Miller ever came to the weekly meetings. And a staff cannot plan strategy very well without the commanding general and his chief of staff.

We discussed advertising, personalities, and tactics—especially tactical errors, as in, neglecting to invite important local officials (governors, state senators) or top-dollar donors to join events or ride along with the candidate. On scheduling, we received sage advice from old pro Len Hall: "Go only where you have a chance to win" (another way of saying, "Go hunting where the ducks are"). Forget the Northeast, he advised, and keep out of Arkansas, but go into Virginia. Overall, he said, "We need four big states." "We must win California, Texas, Illinois, and Ohio."

Our electronic network kept us in constant communication with state and regional headquarters, but we also had a team assigned to survey key people in the field. They were to determine what was going well and what was not and suggest how things might be improved. We read and parsed the comments, but I'm not sure that Kitchel and Baroody did much of anything about them.

One report, for example, noted the complaint that too many people were handling advertising and that there were too many committees, with everyone and no one in charge. That echoed a Ray Collet comment of "too many fingers in this pie . . . too many fingers in the whole Barry Goldwater campaign—everyone telling him what to say and what to do. All the 'experts' are going to cause us to lose this campaign." Many local officials stopped using advertising materials from the national committee and were creating their own—not a good sign. Two weeks before the election, we learned of an unused inventory of 5,000 twenty-four-sheet billboard posters. The ad agency suggested an aggressive correction: Make arrangements and get 5,000 billboards mounted immediately. But by this time there were only two weeks to go before the election.

Meanwhile, Johnson played father of his country, invoking the memory of the dead president while campaigning with unabashed zest. He took on eighteen-hour days, giving twenty speeches a week. The man who had secretly ordered a great increase in troop strength in Vietnam offered public reassurance: "We are not going to send American boys nine or ten thousand miles from home to do what Asian boys ought to be doing for themselves." He was not averse to the nuclear issue. "By a thumb on a button," he told a crowd in New Orleans, "you can wipe out 300 million lives in a matter of moments." This was no time, he said, "to be rattling your rockets around or clicking your heels like a storm trooper. . . . Whose thumb do you want edging up that way?"

We heard that LBJ had a drinking problem, but we didn't know what to do about it. Neither did reporters traveling with the president. Some saw him reeling drunk on more than one occasion—the man whose finger really *was* on the nuclear button—but none reported on the behavior. After watching an obviously smashed LBJ give a rambling, incoherent speech at an unscheduled stop, at which there was virtually no audience, one reporter called the home office to ask for guidance; the response, "Oh, Christ, let's think about it and we'll call you back." The reporter was still waiting for that call when he wrote his memoirs twenty-five years later.

When Goldwater called for an end to the draft, he was accused of pandering for votes from parents. The Pentagon played one-up by reminding everyone that a committee appointed by LBJ had been studying ways to end the draft for four months. The Pentagon didn't mention that Goldwater had long been advocating increasing military salaries to attract more volunteers.

LBJ (perhaps the most political man of the century) announced he wasn't going to "play politics" with the draft. He wasn't going to do much else about it, either. His "study" wasn't made public until July 1966; it showed that 40 percent of volunteers enlisted because of fear of the draft, and it concluded that it was therefore necessary to keep the draft. After some public carping, LBJ called for another study—to be delivered in 1967.

On September 9, we announced the formation of a seven-man Task Force on Peace and Freedom, headed by Nixon and including former Undersecretary of State Herbert Hoover, Jr., along with General Lucius D. Clay, one senator, one congressman, one foundation executive, and one college professor. Three hours before our announcement, the White House reported that LBJ had created a sixteen-man panel of distinguished citizens to consult with him on international problems.

I suppose this synchronicity could have been the spontaneous, near-simultaneous eruption of a good idea, but it was almost certainly a simple case of cheating. We had issued advance copies of Barry's speech about the task force to the Washington newspapers—embargoed from publication until the speech had been given. The advance announced the appointment of "a task force on peace and freedom" but did not include the names of the members.

Writing for the *New York Times*, Arthur Krock offered comment on "yesterday's race between the Presidential candidates to announce the formation of a panel of non-Governmental consultants on international affairs, which Mr. Johnson won handily." Krock hinted that the embargoed text might have played a role: "The President, soon after the release had been generally circulated here, suddenly summoned the reporters to announce not only that he, too, had appointed a panel of foreign affairs consultants but gave their names."

On October 4, Barry decided that, if elected, he would ask President Eisenhower to go to South Vietnam as the head of a team of fact-finding experts. This was a clever echo of Ike's preelection promise in 1952 that—if elected—he would go to Korea. Barry was going to make a public announcement the next day, but again, Johnson beat him to it. LBJ had already called a rather puzzled Ike to tell him, "You don't have to wait for Senator Goldwater to get elected in order to go to Vietnam. . . . I'll send a helicopter after you any time you care to go."

Those are just a few of the more benign examples of White House "gamesmanship" during the campaign. There were many others. Johnson always seemed to have ready "responses" to points Barry would make in a campaign speech—but before Barry made the speech. In fact, a couple of such responses made it into newspapers printed before Barry was even in town. Once, during a private meeting in Grenier's RNC office, someone suggested that there was an opening in Barry's schedule for a stop in East St. Louis, Illinois. Thirty minutes later, headquarters had a phone call from a reporter in East St. Louis, who had heard that Goldwater was coming to town and wanted to know the details.

Although we were not aware of it at the time, we would learn long after the fact that Johnson had enlisted the assistance of both the FBI and the CIA to spy on the campaign. Barry had his suspicions, but never any solid evidence. In 1971, FBI chief J. Edgar Hoover admitted to Bob Mardian, then serving as an assistant attorney general, that the Goldwater campaign plane was bugged. "You do what the president of the United States orders you to do," he said. The chief of covert action for CIA domestic operations—Howard Hunt, later of Watergate fame—operated out of a phony news bureau in the National Press Building under the rubric "Continental Press," collecting whatever he could about our operations and receiving daily deliveries of materials purloined from our headquarters. When he complained to a superior that he was uneasy with the assignment, he was told that it was at the direction of the president. And some years later, former White House Press Secretary George Reedy confirmed that at least one hired spy had been planted at our headquarters.

It may have been mere coincidence, but might the president also have enlisted the aid of the Post Office Department? This agency, which Barry had suggested should be privatized, issued a most timely postcard in September with the stamp: "By the People—For the People—Social Security."

We had been guarding against potential dirty tricks by Scranton and others, but how do you guard against espionage by the premier law-enforcement and spy agencies in the world? Barry's initial reluctance to go up against an "unscrupulous" LBJ was not unjustified.

On a less ominous note, the June wedding of Barry's daughter Anne had been bugged, but probably by a newsman. On a somewhat more light-hearted note, a young woman named Moira O'Connor, passing herself off as a freelance reporter, bought passage for a September swing of the Goldwater campaign train—and was caught distributing copies of a scurrilous newsletter. Among other items—at a time in the history of our nation when paranoid elements on the fringe of the political spectrum were convinced that fluoridation of drinking water (to help prevent tooth decay) was a Communist plot to deaden American brain cells—the bogus newsletter proclaimed: "We are happy to report that the railroad has assured us that fluoride has not been added to the drinking water on this train." Assistant campaign PR man Vic Gold, who discovered the deception, thanked her for the $225 contribution that her ticket purchase had made to the Goldwater campaign, and then put her off the train.

The Democrats took a stab at laying a charge of espionage on the RNC. A man named Louis Flax (apparently a teletype operator at the DNC) publicly charged that, on or about September 28, he received an "anonymous phone call" in which the caller "said he understood that I was in financial trouble and that he knew how I could get some money." The caller apparently told him to provide the RNC with copies of messages, campaign schedules, and the name of an informer whom they believed was providing information to DNC headquarters.

DNC Chairman John M. Bailey issued a statement. The incident, he said, was "deeply shocking and disturbing." "Worst of all, to me," he added, "is that greed for political advantage could lead anyone to be so callous toward another human being."

Steve Shadegg thought that it was Flax who had made the contact, offering, for $1,000, to pass along the name of a spy planted at RNC headquarters, and if so, Burch and Grenier thought, well, why not? If there was a spy, and we had suspected as much, it would be useful to know who it was. However or by whomever the initial contact may have been made, the DNC notified the media and set up a sting, with reporters and photographers assigned to stake-out positions and security guards posted to block the escape route of whoever might show up as the RNC payoff artist.

Nothing happened. No payoff artist showed up. The *New York Times* had great sport, reporting "A 'Spy' Double-Crosses Party Lines." I presume that Chairman Bailey (who was a good friend of mine despite the fact that we had been political adversaries during the campaigns I managed in Connecticut) may have been unaware of the ongoing "greed for political advantage" and clandestine efforts of President Johnson.

CHAPTER 17

Finish Line

Good news! With three weeks to go, our pollster, Tom Benham, reported the beginnings of an upturn. Barry's position in the East was unchanged, but he was gaining in the South and even more in the West. In a trial heat—"If the election were held today . . . " —62 percent favored LBJ, 29 percent Goldwater, 9 percent "other" or undecided. To a pick-one-or-the-other question, however, it came out 60 percent to 40 percent. What polled "likely voters" liked most about LBJ was the good job he'd been doing since taking office. What they liked least was his lack of ethics. And what appealed to them the most about Goldwater was that they believed he would hold down government spending and clear up government corruption.

A concurrent Harris poll had it 58 percent to 34 percent, with 8 percent undecided; when the undecided were "allocated" by some abstruse formula, Harris's numbers almost matched ours, 61 to 39 percent. By our reckoning, defected Republicans were coming back at a rate of 6 to 8 percent a week. (Harris put the rate of return at 5 percent every two weeks.)

Tom pointed out that if the positive trend continued at this rate, we would win the election. If the election were held on April 1. We needed a breakthrough to leap ahead. Charles Mohr, writing for the *New York Times,* opined that a "dramatic event" might bring a flood of votes to Goldwater.

It came on October 12—or so it seemed. We received an anonymous tip: Walter Jenkins, LBJ's personal assistant for some twenty-five
years, had been arrested October 7 for committing a homosexual act
in the men's room of the YMCA, two blocks from the White House.
This was the man LBJ had called, right after the assassination, his
"vice president in charge of everything." The man who took notes at
highly classified meetings. It was the break we had been waiting for: a
serious security risk—easily subject to blackmail in the homophobic
climate of the times—working next to the Oval Office! We got a no-
tarized confirmation; we toyed with slogans, "Either way with LBJ."

We were gleeful.

Barry said, "Hands off."

Walter Jenkins had been a member of his Air Force Reserve unit,
and Barry would do nothing to add to the pain of his wife and six children. Here was a true paradox: The shoot-from-the-hip cowboy who
would "take Social Security away from the nation's old folks" and who
stood ready to "blow up the world" was refusing to take political advantage from a story concerning only one man.

As it turned out, this was not the first time that Jenkins had been
arrested for homosexual behavior—he had been picked up back in
1959, in the same men's room. In 1961, according to a report in the
Chicago Tribune, citing an unnamed government source, Jenkins had
"fought like the devil," without success, even invoking his connection
with then–Vice President Johnson, for reinstatement of an Air Force
major who had been forced to resign because he was an alleged sex
offender. The exact nature of the alleged offense was not detailed. In
any case, the Air Force rationale was that the major's actions created
a security risk, leaving him subject to blackmail.

The White House was desperate to keep the whole story under
wraps. Jenkins was whisked off to a hospital for treatment of "hyper-
tension" or "nervous exhaustion"—LBJ and friends couldn't quite get
their stories straight. The real reason for the confinement was to keep
Jenkins away from the media. Two Democratic lawyers, Abe Fortas

(later a justice of the Supreme Court) and Clark Clifford (later secretary of defense), made the rounds of Washington newspapers urging the editors not to publish the story. The editors complied, but their motivation, I believe, was more political than humanitarian. When Dean Burch learned of the White House shuffle and arm-twisting, he persuaded Barry to let us pass along at least a brief statement to the effect that "The White House is desperately trying to suppress a major news story affecting the national security." National security trumped personal pain.

LBJ's reaction to all of this—unknown to us at the time, of course—is well documented in Michael Beschloss's 2001 *Reaching for Glory,* a presentation of secret White House tapes from 1964 and 1965. The White House damage-control team, Fortas, Clifford, Moyers, and the president, was trying to put some, any, positive spin on the problem, in case their efforts to keep the story out of the news failed. They could say that Jenkins was drunk, or that the policemen who had observed and arrested him had been bribed or were lying. They could suggest that it was all a set-up by the Goldwater campaign. As for any "alleged" previous arrest, Walter Jenkins is a common name.

Beschloss summarized an interesting phone conversation between LBJ and Fortas that took place October 14, a week after the alleged offense occurred and the same day the story broke on UPI: "LBJ is anxious for Fortas to seize the contents of Jenkins's private safe and files, which include material that Johnson fears could be used to damage him. He worries that if Fortas does not grab it first, the FBI might impound it."

He need not have worried, I suspect. FBI chief J. Edgar Hoover sent flowers and a get-well note to Jenkins. LBJ (fully aware of rumors about Hoover's own sexuality) complained to Cartha ("Deke") De-Loach, the FBI assistant director, "I think its very unfortunate." Someone put out the story that the flowers had been dispatched by an overly efficient secretary in Hoover's office, unaware of any connection between the hospitalization and arrest.

On October 15, the White House announced that Jenkins had re-signed. Clark Clifford suggested that LBJ's position should be, "You just don't have any facts about it. You've been away, you got it by phone, you just don't know what this is."

Over precisely the same period, October 14–16, a quick succession of international incidents put the commander-in-chief smack in the public eye and drove the Jenkins story into obscurity: Nikita Khrushchev was ousted as leader of the Soviet Union; British elections ended the thirteen-year reign of the Conservative Party; and Communist China exploded its first nuclear bomb. We learned that the Democratic National Committee had planned to buy fifteen minutes on NBC on October 17 for "presidential comment" on the events of the week, but that LBJ instead demanded free time on all networks—an estimated value of $500,000—to address the nation on a matter of "national significance." The networks promoted the broadcast throughout the day, building a vast audience. However, the broadcast offered no important information not already published in the newspapers and offered no new proposals for dealing with Red China or the Soviet Union. LBJ did not even mention the names of the new leaders in the Kremlin.

Dean Burch asked the networks for equal time for Goldwater to address the issues. There was a precedent for this request: Just six days before the 1956 election, all three networks had granted Democratic candidate Adlai Stevenson equal time to respond to President Eisenhower's comments on the Suez crisis. But Burch's request was denied. Dean appealed to the FCC on October 19, but to no avail. (For the record, the 1956 FCC likewise ruled that Stevenson was not entitled to equal time; but the determination was not made until five days after his comments had already been broadcast.)

Dean would subsequently lodge an appeal with the Court of Appeals for the District of Columbia and lose in a 3–3 tie. But the FCC's refusal to grant equal time gave us a good excuse to make a direct request for funds to buy more TV time. NBC broke ranks a bit and granted us fifteen minutes. On camera, Dean reiterated the points he had made earlier to the networks and the FCC and ended the program with a brief appeal: "It's a sad state of affairs when *candidate* Johnson is given free time on three TV networks and four radio networks and Barry Goldwater is denied equal time to answer. . . . That's *wrong*—and every American *knows* it's wrong. But Barry Goldwater can't be kept off the air—not if you help. Send your contributions to: Barry Goldwater, Box 1964, Washington, D.C." The Democrats cried foul and demanded equal time from NBC, but the network would not agree to this.

The number of homes tuned in to the broadcast—3 million—was just a fraction of the 27 million (some 60 million viewers) reached by LBJ the day before. Still, it was enough to trigger an amazing response. The money began pouring in—by the end of the week, we had received 3,700 telegrams and 82,000 letters. It took sixty-five people working eighteen-hour days to open the envelopes and log the contents—at least $850,000, more than 7 percent of total receipts for the entire campaign. The money was immediately put to work. Barry was able to purchase a half-hour of TV time on ABC, Wednesday, October 21, to say some of the things he would have said if granted equal access.

This was a fantastic response, but it was from Barry's faithful followers. Louis Harris reported that despite any negative impact of Jenkins's resignation, the events of the week before had added two points to LBJ's standing with probable voters. "It is not so much that the American people are unmoved by the Jenkins episode," Harris wrote. "Rather, the question of which candidate shall be in charge of foreign policy during the next four years clearly has superseded every other issue in the campaign."

Back in July, exploitation of racial discord had been put off-limits by the White House agreement. The summer riots, however, gave Barry's poll numbers a temporary boost: He gained five points and LBJ lost

three. To capitalize on this without violating the agreement, our candidate turned to the general topic of "morality," hoping this would
have some resonance with the voters. Replaying a theme of his convention acceptance speech, Barry began charging that a lack of national leadership had "turned our streets into jungles . . . [and]
brought our public and private morals into the lowest state of our history," pointing to climbing divorce rates, juvenile delinquency, and
street violence. "When morals collapse," he said, "they don't collapse
upward." It was one of his more successful pitches.

The campaign launched a series of ads and handouts focused on
graft, crime, influence-peddling, and corruption. The text for newspaper ads read, in part:

> Americans everywhere are indignant about the moral decay in
> Washington and nobody should accept corruption in positions of
> public trust as a way of life. All it takes to clean it up is an adminis-
> tration that really wants it cleaned up—an administration with the
> moral courage to fire the influence peddlers and graft takers no
> matter whose friends they may be.
>
> Rioting runs rife in our cities, crimes continue to increase at an
> alarming rate and our parks and streets have become unsafe.
> . . . Vice, influence peddling and graft among high political offi-
> cials sets the worst possible example for our youth.
>
> What has happened to law and order in America today? My op-
> ponent refuses to debate the question—perhaps he prefers not to,
> in light of recent rioting and the terrifying increase of crime. Our
> parks and streets are unsafe. Our crime rate is rising five times as
> fast as the population.

For TV, spots included a fast-paced five-minute version that
opened with the announcer declaiming "Graft! Swindles! Juvenile
delinquency! Crime! Riots!" punctuated by blaring horns, drums,
cymbals—and the sound of breaking glass. On camera, Barry re-

peated some of the points presented in the newspaper ads and added, "Crime grows faster than the population, while those who *break* the law are accorded more consideration than those who try to *enforce* the law."

Barry addressed the topic head-on at a mid-October speech at the Mormon Tabernacle in Salt Lake City. It may have been the highest-rated nonpresidential televised political address ever. He charged that "the moral fiber of the American people is beset by rot and decay"; noted that the Democratic platform, "written to the exact specifications of Lyndon Johnson," had no mention of God; and decried the "recent wave of rioting." "With your help and God's blessing," he said, "I pledge my every effort to a reconstruction of reverence and moral strength, those great pillars of human happiness in our land."

Clif White saw an opportunity to make an even greater impact with a made-for-TV documentary that would not just talk about collapsing morals but actually show them tumbling. He sent Barry a note suggesting that his Citizens for Goldwater-Miller group undertake production, and Barry—out on the campaign trail—responded, "Agree completely with you on morality issue. Believe it is the most effective we have come up with. Also agree with your program. Please get it launched immediately."

Produced by Citizens PR-man Rus Walton and a team from Hollywood, and narrated by Raymond Massey, the program was called *Choice*. The recurring theme was that the nation's morals had gone down the drain since the death of "the young inspiring leader" who dreamt of an "honest, decent, law-abiding America" and now "is gone." It was filled with images of immorality (women in topless bathing suits), depravity (drunken college students on a spree), and antisocial behavior (blacks rioting and looting in the streets). Several sequences showed a speeding Lincoln Continental, the unidentifiable driver tossing out beer cans as he careened down a road. Viewers would know that this was meant to be LBJ; in the spring, he had given a group of reporters a 90 m.p.h. tour of his Texas ranch, sipping beer all the while. (*Time* reported that when a passenger in the car "gasped at how fast Johnson was driving," he "took one hand from the wheel, removed his five-gallon hat and flopped it on the dashboard to cover the speedometer." *Time* added, "Later, White House Press Secretary George Reedy—in a statement almost as foolhardy as the president's driving—tried to deny that Johnson had exceeded Texas' 70 m.p.h. speed limit."

According to the film's producers, the goal of *Choice* was "to portray and remind the people of something they already know exists, and that is the moral crisis in America, the rising crime rate, rising juvenile delinquency, narcotics, pornography, filthy magazines." The American people, they added, "will see all this on television, and there is only one way they can go, and that is with Goldwater." This was powerful stuff. The broadcast was scheduled for October 22; about a week before that, I canceled my plans to participate in a trip to Gettysburg to give Ike a birthday cake and fiddled with the budget to find the money to purchase the air time. (Dean and two other staffers went ahead and made the presentation to Ike.) We sent out a promotional telegram to Goldwater supporters around the country that said, in part:

Choice, the documentary film sponsored by Mothers for Moral America, will be shown on NBC-TV, Thursday, October 22. It will pre-empt the Loretta Young one–half hour show in your viewing area. . . . Please make your greatest effort to build a viewing audience, and get additional telephoners to work. We suggest you use the following message: hello, I'm (caller's name.) I thought you, as a responsible citizen, would like to know about a special documentary film. . . . It deals with a situation that endangers the future of our country.

However, the program never ran. The Democratic National Committee knew what was coming. The stenographer who recorded a planning session in September was a White House spy, dutifully recording everything Rus Walton said when he told his associates that he wanted to arouse "raw, naked emotions," make the voters "mad, make their stomachs turn," and "play on the prejudices" of small towns and rural areas against the "big city." The Democrats begged, borrowed, or stole a print—there were plenty of copies floating around, pre-positioned for local showing or rebroadcast—and Dick Tuck, a man known to some as the "merry prankster," took the purloined copy and showed it to a group of journalists, triggering an avalanche of adverse public comment. DNC chair John Bailey called it "the sickest political program to be conceived since television became a factor in American politics." NBC requested about sixty seconds of cuts, including "front shots of a woman in a topless bathing suit, views of pornographic book covers, strip-teasers in the final phases of their performances and a man clad only in a fig leaf." The network did not consider this censorship but just a necessary precaution to excise "material that might be defamatory or morally improper for family viewing."

Clif and friends postponed the broadcast and planned to call in all outstanding copies for editing to conform with the changes NBC had requested. Goldwater saw the show (for the first time) a bit later in the day and said, "It can't be used." Period. The next day, he elaborated: "It's nothing but a racist film." *Choice* gave equal time to black and white miscreants, but blacks were in the more violent shots. Barry had made the correct choice. One might wonder why NBC requested edits focused only on lewd and not racist images.

It was bizarre, but some of our critics, then and up to the present day, have used this incident as an example of disorganization within the Goldwater camp. There was some disagreement among us, perhaps, but the decision reflected Barry's unwillingness to compromise his sense of humanity. If there was internal chaos, it was not of his doing.

The day *Choice* had been scheduled to run, our photographer Don Dornan had a run-in with LBJ in a corridor at the Waldorf-Astoria. The president and his wife came around a corner, the photographer instinct cut in, and Dornan took a quick photo. "Johnson turned and grumbled something at me," he reported. He didn't hear what was said, but as LBJ was getting into an elevator, he "whispered something to a secret service agent, who then came over and politely asked me to identify myself." Dornan explained who he was, whereupon the agent said the president had ordered him to give Dornan "a good chewing out" and to make sure Dornan understood that "the president was never photographed from the right side" and didn't like to be so abruptly confronted. Dornan apologized, and the agent offered the thought that Goldwater was "one hell of a great guy. . . . Maybe I'll be lucky enough to be working for him, someday."

Our TV plan for the last couple of weeks before election Tuesday included one fifteen-minute show, five thirty-minute visits with the candidate or his surrogates, and one ninety-minute program that was billed in the *New York Times* as a "golden shower for Goldwater," featuring Hollywood entertainers and Dick Nixon. This was a singularly inappropriate designation, but it was only later that I learned that "golden shower" was the street term for a far-out sexual fetish. If the *Times* article was a set-up by a saboteur or joker, we were too unschooled in the fine points of sexual deviancy to notice. Now I suspect that someone was enjoying a hearty laugh at Barry's expense.

We had twenty-six five-minute spots inserted into some of the most popular shows on televison, ranging from *As the World Turns* to *You Don't Say.* (Social historians might be interested to know that some of the others were *Today, Password, Edge of Night, The Entertainers, The Secret Storm, To Tell the Truth, The Danny Kaye Show, The Lawrence Welk Show, The Ed Sullivan Show, I've Got a Secret, Jeopardy, Say When, The Jackie Gleason Show, The Red Skelton Show, Candid Camera,* and *What's My Line?*)

One five-minute booking was on CBS for 9:00 P.M., Thursday, October 15. The Democrats wanted to preempt us to run a thirty-minute program in that time slot. LBJ personally tried to convince his good friend, CBS head Frank Stanton, to order us to move to a different time slot. Stanton equivocated. I told our agency not to relinquish the time. This was a bit of tit-for-tat: When we had tried to book thirty minutes for live coverage of a rally on September 29, the Democrats had refused to move a one minute spot to another slot. We held on to the October booking.

The final push could have been much greater: We had the money to do more TV ads, but we did not book the time. On this, there has been some confusion in all of the accounts that have been published thus far. It is true that, for a time, our projected expenditures were outrunning our fund-raising, and Ralph's Rules, described earlier, had often prevented us from doing all we could in TV advertising. But it is not true, as has often been reported, that Ralph's Rules prevented us from buying TV and radio time in the critical final week of the campaign. By that point, money was pouring in from TV appeals and our last-minute mailings.

Instead, our broadcast budget simply went unused. As we were about to enter the homestretch, Barry asked, "How are we doing?" I told him I was about to make a big buy to "push us over the top." Showing him a revised broadcast schedule, I assured him, "We have the money, no problem."

He thought for a minute, then put his hand on mine and said, "Don't spend it, Bill. Leave some money in the bank to keep the party alive after the election." He knew that no amount of last-minute spending would make any difference in an election where so many people had long since decided, and of course he was right. We booked no additional spots. We scrapped plans for a $400,000 telethon on election eve. Thus, perhaps $1 million was not wasted on the past but passed along for the future. We canceled one last preelection poll—we didn't need to pay for any more bad news—but we did schedule several post-election surveys. The point, by then, was to learn, for the future.

The best TV speech of the campaign—perhaps of any campaign—came on October 27, when Ronald Reagan stepped onto the national political stage. His appearance was not scheduled or paid for by the Goldwater campaign, but by a group of his friends and supporters in California led by Henry Salvatori.

It almost didn't happen because of irrelevant objections by Kitchel and Baroody. They heard the tape and told Barry that the speech was unacceptable—it would open the Social Security wound anew. They proposed using the booked time slot for a rerun of the useless "Conversation at Gettysburg." Barry called Reagan to ask him to cancel; Reagan said it wasn't up to him, since some other fellows were paying for the time out of their own pockets. Besides, he asked, what was wrong with the speech? Barry said he didn't know and would go listen to the tape.

The offending paragraphs actually articulated the Social Security debate far better than Barry ever had:

> We're against those entrusted with this program when they practice deception regarding its fiscal shortcomings, when they charge that any criticism of the program means that we want to end payments to those people who depend on them for a livelihood. They've called it "insurance" to us in a hundred million pieces of literature. But then they appeared before the Supreme Court and they testified it was a welfare program. . . .
>
> A young man, 21 years of age, working at an average salary—his Social Security contribution would, in the open market, buy him an insurance policy that would guarantee 220 dollars a month at age 65. The government promises 127. . . . Now are we so lacking in business sense that we can't put this program on a sound basis?
>
> Barry Goldwater thinks we can.
>
> At the same time, can't we introduce voluntary features that would permit a citizen who can do better on his own to be excused upon presentation of evidence that he had made provision for the non-earning years?

When the tape was finished, Barry looked at Kitchel and Baroody and said, "What the hell's wrong with that?"

But Kitchel and Baroody would not give up. I believe that they had been goaded by our ad agency, which had already complained to me of "an obvious attempt to circumvent" their contract with TV for Goldwater-Miller by a newly created Reagan-Goldwater TV Committee as sponsor for the broadcast. This pulled their right to claim a commission of perhaps $23,000. Within three hours of air time, Kitchel and Baroody were still trying to substitute a Goldwater rerun. However, as Reagan had intimated, the spot was not being paid for out of our campaign budget. The Californians who were funding it insisted that if Reagan didn't get the time, no one would.

The speech was called "A Time for Choosing." It began:

PROGRAM ANNOUNCER: Ladies and gentlemen, we take pride in presenting a thoughtful address by Ronald Reagan. Mr. Reagan?

REAGAN: Thank you. Thank you very much. Thank you and good evening. The sponsor has been identified, but unlike most television programs, the performer hasn't been provided with a script. As a matter of fact, I have been permitted to choose my own words and discuss my own ideas regarding the choice that we face in the next few weeks.

Reagan continued on for another 5,000 words. Here are some of the highlights of the now-famous speech:

This is the issue of this election: Whether we believe in our capacity for self-government or whether we abandon the American revolution and confess that a little intellectual elite in a far-distant capitol can plan our lives for us better than we can plan them ourselves.

No government ever voluntarily reduces itself in size. So government programs, once launched, never disappear. Actually, a government bureau is the nearest thing to eternal life we'll ever see on this earth.

We were told a few days ago by the President, we must accept a greater government activity in the affairs of the people. . . . [One Democrat] voice says, "The profit motive has become outmoded. It must be replaced by the incentives of the welfare state." Or, "Our traditional system of individual freedom is incapable of solving the complex problems of the 20th century." . . . Another articulate spokesman defines liberalism as "meeting the material needs of the masses through the full power of centralized government."

Well, I, for one, resent it when a representative of the people refers to you and me, the free men and women of this country, as "the masses." [As to] "the full power of centralized government"—this was the very thing the Founding Fathers sought to minimize.

We're now going to solve the dropout problem, juvenile delinquency, by reinstituting something like the old CCC camps [Civilian Conservation Corps], [but] we're going to spend each year just on room and board for each young person we help 4,700 dollars a year. We can send them to Harvard for 2,700.

You and I have a rendezvous with destiny. We'll preserve for our children this, the last best hope of man on earth, or we'll sentence them to take the last step into a thousand years of darkness.

This was an updated version of a speech Reagan had been making for a long time as part of his representation of General Electric. The reaction—no pun intended—was electrifying. A letter from Tampa resident Mrs. Fred E. Eberlin exemplifies the type of feedback we received. She wrote:

We've always been Republicans but have been seriously considering voting for Johnson. After watching Ronald Regan's [*sic*] speech last night we have returned to the fold. His speech was excellent—jam packed with facts. . . . We've come to the conclusion that Goldwater has the right ideas but doesn't know how to express himself. What's the matter with his speech writers? . . . After some of Goldwater's speeches my husband and I have looked at each other and said, "So what—he really didn't say anything."

Deak Price, Goldwater TV chairman for Tampa-St. Petersburg-Clearwater, sent a telegram: "The election is yours for the asking—you have the film so use it. Show it day and night on every spot you can beg, borrow or steal, if no spots available then put it on CBS tonight [Thursday, October 29] instead of Goldwater . . . since he is not going to change any votes at this late date but the Reagan film will."

Price offered the results of limited spot phone-polling after the program had been broadcast: Thirty-six percent of respondents said they had been in favor of LBJ before seeing the program, and 32 percent had been in favor of Goldwater; 32 percent had been undecided. After the show, 33 percent were for LBJ and 51 percent for Goldwater; 16 percent were still undecided. "The undecided," Price noted, "were favorably impressed but still were concerned about Social Security."

"A Time for Choosing" launched Reagan's political career; the first "Reagan for President" club was established soon after, and he was elected governor of California in 1966 with a plurality of 1 million votes. If the speech had been introduced earlier in our campaign, might it have made a significant difference in the outcome? It is a question that I can't answer, but something for more skilled political minds to ponder.

In the wake of probable voting fraud in the 1960 election, the RNC developed a ballot security program. Volunteers at most, if not all, of the nation's 176,500 voting precincts were trained to spot irregularities in procedures or equipment and to make appropriate challenges. A more intense effort, Operation Eagle Eye, was focused on thirty large cities where experience had earlier shown that problems were most likely.

Eagle Eye volunteers mailed out some 1.5 million pieces of first-class mail to the entire voter registration lists in certain precincts where voting fraud had earlier been suspected or proven. The envelopes included a local return address and postal instructions to "Return to Sender." This procedure provided a great start for uncovering fraudulent registrants. Workers followed up at all "undeliverable" addresses to document whether the registrant was or was not at that address (and, frequently enough, to document whether the address even existed).

By October 29, almost 3,000 names had been excised from the rolls in Chicago alone. DNC chair Bailey called it "a program of voter intimidation, . . . a serious threat to democracy as well as to a Democratic victory on November 3."

Barry began the final campaign swing—and asked me to go along—during the last week of October. Also joining us was Raymond Massey, for whom my father had once been an investment adviser (and whose son was a prep-school classmate of mine). We began with another capacity crowd at Madison Square Garden and ended at sunset in Fredonia, Arizona, on November 2. In between, we made eighteen stops in seven days: in Tennessee, Ohio, Iowa, Wisconsin, Illinois, Pennsylvania, Wyoming (where the local Teen Age Republicans handed Barry a bag full of pennies—16,000 of them, weighing almost 90 pounds), Nevada, Arizona, California, Arizona again, Texas, South Carolina, back to California, and then for one last time, Arizona.

Barry delighted in frequently taking the controls of the campaign Boeing 727, but his skills were a bit rusty—if triple-bounce landings signify anything. One time, Barry asked me (with a knowing smile),

"How was the landing?" I smiled wanly, stomach churning, and said, "Oh, Great!" Another time, Barry put the plane down so hard that I thought we had crashed. There was a small consolation: Some of the more hostile reporters riding in the back of the plane were equally terrified.

In his October 30 speech in Las Vegas, four days before the election, Barry reported on a recent Harris poll that showed how many Americans were on his side on a range of issues:

- 94 percent believed that security regulations over government employees should be tightened (likely a result of the Walter Jenkins incident);
- 88 percent agreed that prayer in schools should be reinstated;
- 61 percent believed that Goldwater wanted to curb extremist groups;
- 60 percent felt that government power should be trimmed;
- 60 percent agreed with the proposition that welfare and relief tend to make people lazy;
- 50 percent believed Barry would do a better job than Johnson on the issue of morality and corruption in government.

One might think that one could take numbers like that to the electoral bank. Unaccountably, 60 percent of these same respondents still favored LBJ over Goldwater. Here was evidence that most voters were leaning well to the right of center—but not toward Barry the bomb thrower, the Grinch who wanted to steal Social Security.

The same day he gave that speech, an editorial in the *New York Daily News* offered—sad to say—a cogent summary of the mood of the electorate:

Goldwater is right in most of his positions on governing the U.S.— keeping the country prosperous, regaining national prestige, and rolling back Communism. We do not like Johnson's extreme welfare statism, his pie-in-the-sky promises, his sanctimonious excuses for such as Walter Jenkins, or his flabby attitude toward Communism. Also we detest beyond words the campaign of vilification which Johnson's backers and flunkies have mounted against Goldwater. But the Goldwater campaign has been so clumsily conducted and the Senator has made so many unfortunate remarks in public that one wonders how capable a President he would be.

Out on this final leg of the campaign trail, Barry may have just been going through the motions, but if so, he did it well, and the crowds that turned out were as enthusiastic as ever. At the airport in Columbia, South Carolina, he was treated to a roaring, shouting, cheering outpouring of support and affection by more than 50,000 people. On the way into town his motorcade was blocked by a friendly throng of perhaps 1,000 (including a goodly sampling of costumed Halloween revelers), who demanded a speech. Someone handed Barry a bullhorn, and standing in his open convertible, he gladly obliged. He was welcomed to the Columbia Township Auditorium by a capacity crowd of 3,500 people enthusiastically singing "Dixie."

This jog to Columbia was for a televised rally with Raymond Massey, Senator Strom Thurmond, and ex-governor James F. Byrnes. Barry delivered what had become, with the help of Henry Jaffa and William F. Rehnquist—a longtime friend and supporter—his civil rights vision statement. Basically, he said he believed that compulsory integration was as bad as compulsory segregation, that freedom of association meant also the freedom not to associate, and that schoolchildren should not be transferred to schools outside their neighborhoods to correct racial imbalance in classrooms. It was a message that was as well received in northern cities as it was in the South.

The Columbia event was broadcast live on eighty-five stations throughout fourteen southern states. It was not a very useful program, however, for two reasons: One was that Byrnes hogged the prime-time portion of the show with a rambling introduction, putting

Barry off until the very end of the slot (and driving me to such dis-traction—as I ticked away the loss of thousands of Goldwater dol-lars—that I almost went up and grabbed the microphone); the other was that someone back at headquarters had inadvertently scheduled a national rebroadcast of Reagan's "Time for Choosing" in the same time period, which siphoned off the audience. It was another exam-ple of poor preparation and coordination, and it sent almost $100,000 down the drain.

The final substantive speech was delivered in San Francisco the day before the election. In what I thought at the time and believe to this day was a brilliant, unprecedented move, Barry repeated, almost word for word, the speech he had made in his first official campaign appearance in Prescott back on September 3. He would end the draft. He would oversee a prudent, slow, but steady withdrawal of "the central government from its many unwarranted interventions in our private economic lives." He would help the private sector to flourish, creating jobs. He would call for across-the-board tax cuts, stimulating growth in the economy with accompanying growth in tax revenues.

And he reaffirmed his core beliefs:

That each man is responsible for his own actions.
That each man is the best judge of his own well-being.
That each man has an individual conscience to serve and a moral code to uphold.
That each man is a brother to every other man.

In closing, he revealed to his audience that "Every word I have just spoken to you is from the very first speech of this presidential cam-paign. The issues have not changed. I have not changed. The chal-lenge and the choice have not changed. I have repeated the first speech of this campaign . . . as a way to tell you, and to pledge to you, that I will never say to you on a Monday one thing, and then change it on Tuesday just for political advantage."

It may have been a brilliant move, but most of the voters had stopped paying attention just after Labor Day—and many had stopped even before that.

Our focus—the focus of the nation—had been on LBJ, but his often-overlooked running mate, Hubert Humphrey, had been busy on his own campaign trail. On Halloween, he told an audience in South Carolina that "We must crush for all time the forces of bitterness and rancor and hate that have clustered around the Goldwater banner in this campaign." He said that extremists flocked to Goldwater because "by every standard of American life, Goldwater is a radical who seeks to destroy the social and economic achievements of the past generation."

A few days later, on Election Day itself, I believe that Hubert Humphrey broke the law by making a political broadcast on NBC. This former professor of political science and mayor of Minneapolis must not have been aware that many states forbade political broadcasts on Election Day, including his home state of Minnesota.

After the wrap-up appearance at sunset in Fredonia, in which Barry thanked a lot of people but said nothing memorable, he gave me a weary smile and said, "Well, Bill, how are we going to do tomorrow?"

Gallup and Harris both had it 64 percent for LBJ, 36 percent for Goldwater, but I, ever the cheerleader, said, "Barry, it's in the bag. The silent majority will turn out in force!"

We then went down to spend Election Day in Phoenix and await the returns. It was not a long wait. NBC called the election for LBJ more than four hours before the polls closed in California.

Just after Goldwater's nomination, James A. Farley, postmaster general in the Roosevelt administration and therefore a Democrat whose opinion might safely be disregarded, had predicted that Goldwater would only carry six states. His view was challenged by Hamilton

Fish—a former Republican congressman, bête noir of FDR, father of my Harvard roommate, and a man with impeccable political and social credentials. In a July 20 letter to the *New York Times,* Fish opined that Farley "has been spending too much time traveling on business in Europe, where he must have absorbed some unfriendly news items in the English, French, and other European papers. . . . Every radical, left-winger, Socialist and Communist," he wrote, "is against Senator Goldwater's courageous effort to stop the march of state socialism. . . . This may well be the last chance for voters." Fish offered a prediction: "In the last 50 years we have had three wars under three different Democratic Presidents, and if President Johnson—backed by the ardent internationalists of the East—is re-elected, we are headed for another war . . .

"I am disturbed," he concluded, "by the mealy-mouth statements on appeasement, or compromising with liberty, either from Democrats or Republicans. When this issue is presented clearly to the American people, Goldwater will carry *all* but six states."

On November 3, Barry Goldwater carried six states: Alabama, Arizona, Georgia, Louisiana, Mississippi, and South Carolina. As for the popular vote, the final tally put Johnson at 42 million, with Goldwater, 15 million votes behind, at 27 million. It was 64 to 36 percent.

PART III

Goldwater was not the end, but the beginning.

CHARLES MALIK,
former president of the United Nations
General Assembly, December 1964
[Personal letter to author]

CHAPTER 18

After the Ball

Barry, visibly stunned, went to bed. He did not concede until the next morning.

The man who, in his heart of hearts, really didn't expect to win, came off as a sore loser. "Twenty-seven million votes is a lot of votes," he said with a touch of defiance, reacting in his normal tell-it-like-it-is fashion. Even though he expected to lose, he wasn't prepared for the magnitude of the loss. He was upset and embarrassed. And I think, too, that he may have started regretting some of his choices during the campaign.

To many observers, the telegram he sent to LBJ was not a concession, but a continuation of the campaign:

Congratulations on your victory. I will help you in any way I can toward achieving a growing and better America and a secure and dignified peace. The role of the Republican Party will remain in that temper, but it also remains the party of opposition when opposition is called for. There is much to be done with Vietnam, Cuba, problems of law and order in this country and a productive economy. Communism remains our number one obstacle to peace, and I know that all Americans will join with you in honest solutions to these problems.

The pundits quickly piled on. On November 5, Jimmy Breslin took a swipe in the *Herald Tribune:* "Among the many things Barry Goldwater knows nothing of is the way men are supposed to act when they lose the Presidency of the United States." On the same day, James Reston wrote, for the *New York Times:* "Barry Goldwater not only lost the Presidential election yesterday but the conservative cause as well. He has wrecked his party for a long time to come and is not even likely to control the wreckage."

In a final campaign press conference, Barry said, "I say to the president, as a fellow politician, that he did a wonderful job . . . and I have to congratulate him on it. . . . I want to thank all of you across this nation who turned out in those numbers to support my candidacy and that of Bill Miller and the Republican Party. I don't think that I have ever seen more dedicated people in my life who worked as long and produced the results that they did."

Privately, he gave the media a large share of the blame for his loss. Publicly—for a change—he chose his words with care: "I want to thank and again tell all of you fellows in the press, radio and TV that regardless of how you feel toward me I have a friendly warm feeling towards all of you, and I hope to see you again somewhere down the pike." It may seem hard to believe, but most of the traveling press—especially those who had been with Barry throughout the campaign—liked the man, if not his politics. I think, of the fifty-three reporters on board for the last big swing, only three were really belligerent. Barry's big problem was not with reporters, but with editors. Of the major newspapers in the country, only a handful came out in support of his candidacy: the *Los Angeles Times,* the *Chicago Tribune,* the *St. Louis Globe Democrat,* the *San Diego Union,* and the *Cincinnati Enquirer.*

James Reston, Bob Novak, Theodore White, and countless others had us down for the count: They said the party was in tatters, its leadership in the sewer. The tone had been set by *The Saturday Evening Post,* when it endorsed LBJ back in September:

It was clear, from poll after poll, that the rank and file of Republican voters overwhelmingly preferred other leaders to Goldwater. It was equally clear that the fanatical Goldwater bias of a majority of convention delegates revealed the capture of the Republican Party by a new breed of so-called "leaders" whose selection had been steam-rollered by extremist, well-heeled types. The men who have most deserved to lead the Republican Party, by virtue of their long, distinguished and responsible service to it, and to the country, have been made to feel unwelcome, hissed and hated in it, as they were repudiated by it. A crushing defeat for Goldwater will drive the fanatic saboteurs of the Republican Party back into the woodwork whence they came. It will provide the opportunity for the party's true leaders to build anew from the wreckage that these heedless, reckless, ill-mannered and arrogant men are sure to leave.

At that point and for some time to come, I was part of that "heedless, reckless, ill-mannered and arrogant" leadership, and we saw things a bit differently. Two of my fellow saboteurs offered comments in the December 1, 1964, edition of *National Review:* George H.W. Bush wrote, "I am convinced that conservatism was not beaten here on November 3. . . . The GOP must remain the conservatives' hope." Ronald Reagan added, "All of the landslide majority did not vote against the conservative philosophy, they voted against a false image our Liberal opponents successfully mounted. . . . I'll add a postscript—I don't think we should turn the high command over to leaders who were traitors during the battle just ended."

Reagan's comment illuminated the main problem within the party. Those who were part of the Rockefeller-Scranton-Romney crowd were not happy with the new conservative tilt. They did not understand the sea change—that the center had moved away from Philadelphia, New York, and Boston; that power in the South and West was shifting to Republicans; and that more people had contributed financially to our

campaign than had ever given before to any presidential campaign—
three times as many, actually, as gave money to the Democrats.

A couple of days after the election, I stood alone in the shambles that
had been RNC headquarters. The staff had melted away. The floor
was littered with stacks of unopened mail, great piles of campaign literature, a mountain of those gold-elephant-with-glasses buttons.
Phones were ringing off the hook; I answered a few: mostly creditors,
screaming for their money. I tried to be reassuring. "Send in a letter,"
I said. This probably reassured no one.

My secretary and my brother Harry came down from New York,
and over the next month we sorted through thousands of bits of un-
finished business. There were bills to pay, and there was useless junk
to be hauled away.

Jerry Milbank joined me for the political clean-up. We called Dick
Nixon to thank him for his tireless help. He said, "Makes you sick that
fellows like you worked so hard, and they have to lose, doggone it.
Well, there'll be another day. You fellows deserve tremendous credit,
believe me, for coming out from a losing campaign with a surplus,
gosh it's terrific."

I replied that we had enough money to pay bills through the end
of the year, with maybe a little left over, and offered any help that
Jerry and I might be able to provide for "any plans" he might have.

"Let me say this," he said. "We have to win the House, then we get
the investigative power, we can tear these people to pieces. This Johnson is crooked. He's as vulnerable as he can be, but you see you've
gotta have that power. I'd like to play a part in that, I think we all can.
I'll do as much as people ask me to."

Thanks to Barry's good sense in restraining the media buy, we
ended with a surplus of $1 million. The Republican National Finance
Committee (RNFC)—which covered the national, senatorial, and
congressional committees—ended the year with $500,000 in the bank
and all bills paid. The National TV for Goldwater-Miller Committee

had another $500,000. Not surprisingly, news of the surplus triggered a flood of requests to cover bills unpaid by local organizations: The Waldorf-Astoria was looking for payment for rooms rented for journalists by a New York group; a barber claimed he had given Barry a haircut and had not been paid. We took the logical and appropriate position that we couldn't pay bills other than those for which we contracted. A creditor's recourse was with the agent or agency that requested the services.

We also collected complaints from losing congressional candidates who felt that if only we had sent them just a few dollars more, or covered just a few additional spots, they might have won. They overlooked (or did not understand) the fact that broadcast monies had to be committed—and paid—two or three days in advance of broadcast. This had nothing to do with Ralph's Rules, it was just the way the business worked, and *all* of our surplus funds had come in after the window of opportunity for local placements had passed, many of them even after the campaign had ended.

I signed Ernst & Ernst for an audit because I wanted to account for every penny. In all, the Republicans had spent $17,200,000 on national-level campaigns, mostly for the presidency. Of that, the RNFC supervised the expenditure of $14,416,324. Our numbers were precise—and, for the first time in U.S. election history, I believe, we submitted to a completely verified national audit, not just certification of a balance sheet.

About half of these expenditures, a bit more than $7.3 million, went for "publicity," and the overwhelming share of that, $5,606,635, was for radio and TV time and production. Other major items included salaries, $1,586,672; postage and express, $955,827; travel, $909,632 (plus $807,997 for chartered airplanes and railroad cars); printing and reproduction $555,252; telephone service, $389,113. The smallest expense: $1,505 for automobile maintenance.

The audit covered the actual campaign; for a complete picture, one must add the data from 1962 until the convention, when some

300,000 individual contributors sent in $5.6 million. We spent $4.75 million on the primaries; I understand that Rockefeller may have spent $5 million—of which all but $100,000 came from the Rockefeller family. Scranton spent $827,035 in reportable funds, most in the month before the convention; Harold Stassen, something above $70,000; the Lodge campaign, $100,000. Supporters of Dick Nixon spent $72,000. The record for bare-bones campaigning in any year must go to Maggie Smith; she claimed travel expenses only, $85 for a trip to Illinois and $250 in New Hampshire. Friends spent perhaps $10,000 in her support.

In the interest of full disclosure (and to illustrate the sort of thing a campaign treasurer must put up with), I note two bills that were paid after the audit, and thus do not show up in the totals:

I was presented with a $375 bill for "1 Gambler Suit: Grey Prince Albert coat, pants, vest, shirt front ascot and hat" and "1 Donkey costume: head and body." They appear to have been rented for the convention by a man ostensibly from the Goldwater for President Committee—but unknown to me—named "Donald B. Sly," and never returned. Second, Barry was sued by a dress designer who claimed not to have been paid the full amount due for dresses worn by the "Goldwater Girls" at a California rally. The *New York Times* published a story about it on April 30: "Jerry DeLee of Beverly Hills said in his suit yesterday that he had designed the dresses for the Arizona Republican at a cost of $1040, but had been paid only $400." It fell to me, at the suggestion of my brother Harry, "to put out the fire." There had been a misunderstanding. The fire was doused with a bank draft.

Another item not covered in the audit was the boost we had from the City of San Francisco, which paid the physical cost of the Republican convention ($664,750) with donations, a tax on hotel rooms, and the sale of advertising for the convention program. Our out-of-pocket convention expenses stood at $384,000.

For the sake of comparison, it has been estimated that the Democrats spent some $2 million on their convention, over and above any contribution from Atlantic City. However, the exact amount is unknown; the Democratic Party never released the information to the public. As Herbert Alexander of the Citizen's Research Foundation reported in 1965: "Democratic reluctance to account for convention funds contrasts sharply with Republican openness on the subject."

Alexander's report highlighted a mild paradox: Even though Republicans were not happy with the media, we nonetheless were open about our finances. In contrast, Alexander wrote, "the Democrats, enjoying generally good press relations, were less than candid about their financial operations—and the press did not generally press hard for answers to questions about national party and campaign finances."

For example, Democrats sold ninety-three ads in the convention program at $15,000 a page, clearing perhaps $1 million. Perhaps. The Federal Corrupt Practices Act, which prohibited direct political contributions by corporations, may have had something to do with the secrecy. The courts had held that ads in convention programs were okay, but the use of any of that money for nonconvention purposes was at best legally ambiguous. So—how did the Democrats spend the money? They never said.

We commissioned two postelection surveys: one by Opinion Research on "Trends in Public Opinion," the other a more narrowly focused study of conservative voters in Fairfield County, Connecticut.

Among other topics, "Trends" probed the level of public awareness of various groups. During the campaign, we made a big effort to emphasize Hubert Humphrey's ties to Americans for Democratic Action (ADA)—a group we saw as among the most extreme of the liberal forces. We were encouraged by polling back in September, when Opinion Research had tested the premise, "The ADA has endorsed recognition of Red China and abolishing the House Un-American Activities Committee," and posed the question: "Do you think a man supporting such views should or should not hold high office such as

Vice President or President?" The opposition was, statistically speaking, tremendous: 41 percent said "should not." Even among Democrats, 25 percent said "should not." Our game plan was affirmed.

But trying to link Humphrey with the ADA turned out to be a waste of time and money. Most Americans knew very little and cared less about the ADA. Only 48 percent of those polled in the "Trends" survey had ever heard of the organization, and of those who had, only 9 percent said they had a "highly unfavorable" opinion, versus 13 percent who said "highly favorable."

Of greater utility, the survey summarized issues upon which we might capitalize for the next election: public concern over rising prices, government spending, the Johnson administration's lack of candor and failure to consider the wishes of the electorate, fear of big government in general, and fear of war in particular. The most interesting—but not surprising—finding was that the public knew little about their local politicians. Even if they knew the name of their congressman (57 percent did), an overwhelming majority, 86 percent, did not know of anything he or she had done for the district, and 70 percent had no idea as to when their representative would be up for reelection. This part of the survey told us that there was lots of work to be done.

The Fairfield County study surveyed people pre-identified as Goldwater supporters and centered on Ronald Reagan's thirty-minute "A Time for Choosing" speech that had been broadcast on national TV. In Fairfield County, it had been heard or read by 90.8 percent of those surveyed. From the results, we were able to deduce that:

Conservative and constitutional government was desired and possible.

Conservatives needed to offer positive alternatives to liberal programs.

There were so many different organizations seeking funds in the name of the "conservative movement" that people were confused.

Liberals were seen as more "organized and cohesive" than conservatives, both inside and outside of government; the conservatives should have direct counterparts to such liberal groups as the Committee on Public Education and the ADA.

A large percentage of conservative voters (96 percent of those surveyed) would be willing to contribute to and support a "nationwide clearinghouse" to monitor and, as feasible, coordinate the efforts of "reputable" conservative groups throughout the land.

Broadcasts similar to the Reagan program would be a very effective educational tool.

Clearly, the respondents were not aware of the general range of conservative efforts—which meant that we had not been doing a very good job. I thought we should use some leftover campaign funds for a voter-education program, perhaps supporting Republican candidates for Congress. In March 1965, we began a five-minute weekly radio show, distributed to about 160 broadcasters.

Steve Shadegg also did a postelection poll, surveying the 1,308 people who had been delegates to the convention. Of those responding, 79 percent had supported Barry, and almost 70 percent admitted that they had been supporters before he even announced his candidacy in January, thus validating Clif White's basic strategy of identifying and wooing potential delegates. Sixty-four percent said they were conservative, 34 percent moderate, and a trace said they were liberal.

Eighty-two percent of respondents were unhappy with the campaign, but 70 percent believed Goldwater's personal appearances had been effective. Since only 80 percent had actually heard the candidate in person, that was a remarkably high approval rating. However, although 99 percent had seen one or more of the TV programs, only 55 percent thought they were effective. "Conversation at Gettysburg" had the lowest rating, 20 percent. The "honest politician" broadcast was deemed "effective and convincing" by 72 percent.

Respondents confirmed that the most damaging charges of the opposition had been the ones we already suspected: that Goldwater was "trigger happy," that he would abolish Social Security, that he was "reckless and irresponsible," and that he would sell the TVA.

Former West Virginia Governor Cecil Underwood spoke for many when he added a note to his response to the survey, "I am at a loss to understand why Goldwater sidetracked all the first team which had helped him win the nomination. . . . Beginning with his acceptance speech he was on the defensive and losing ground. . . . He never did get around to spelling out the conservative philosophy for which all of the country waited." Sixty-nine percent of the respondents to Shadegg's poll seemed to agree.

In another postelection survey, the Congressional Campaign Committee collected views from losing Republican candidates. What were their biggest problems? What could we have done better to help them? The major complaints were that they did not have enough money and that they had gotten a late start. And Dean Burch told a January 1965 meeting of the RNFC, "You cannot campaign three months out of every four years. The time to start winning elections is not at the convention, but several years ahead of time." The RNC, he said, should conduct regular surveys in key states to determine the weaknesses of opponents and the strengths of Republican candidates based on what people at home say—not some judgment made in Washington. The state of Texas had more field operatives than the RNC. That had to change.

We also needed to continue and strengthen our focus on youth. As Fulton Lewis III, an executive with the Teen Age Republicans, reported, "We know that 92% of those who make a commitment to a political party during their pre-voting years will retain that commitment throughout their voting years."

Getting that commitment meant fighting off all sorts of cultural biases. The Congressional Campaign Committee discovered a possibly unconscious (to be charitable)—but nonetheless unconscionable—

effort to indoctrinate the youth of America in the liberal canon. The 1965 "Otis Quick-Scoring Mental Ability Test," published by Harcourt, Brace & World and sent out to more than 500,000 high school students each year, contained a number of suspect multiple-choice questions. For instance:

Q—A club that accepts only very rich members is said to be—
   a) Snobbish
   b) Exclusive
   c) Conservative
   d) Republican
   e) Un-American

The correct answer, of course, is "exclusive"—but the not-too-subtle assumption is that conservatives and Republicans are a group of very rich un-American snobs. When challenged on this, the director of the company's test department, Roger T. Lennon, responded that, in designing multiple-choice questions, the author "seeks to present the examinee with choices which will have some plausibility in the context," but added: "The notion that any political overtones are to be read into any of the choices is, of course, too fatuous even to comment on."

This, too, told us there was lots of work to be done.

CHAPTER 19

Regroup and Recover

WHILE JERRY AND I WERE wading through the minutiae of the immediate past, Dean Burch and Barry joined us to discuss the future. Jerry and I offered to be the guardians at the gate, to keep the flame alive, and Barry was more open, I think, than he had been at any time during the campaign. "We made all of the mistakes in the book," he said, "but that's behind us. Millions of Republicans lost faith in us because the damn fool Rockefeller and his tribe cast seeds of doubt." He added, "LBJ never laid a glove on me compared to the destruction of these men. . . . Our job should have been to win the battle of image. . . . We lost."

In the end, the Goldwater of *The Conscience of a Conservative,* the Goldwater who had excited so much attention and support, had stumbled. But Barry didn't coast through the campaign; he had worked very hard. As I've already noted—many of those things that some of us saw as tactical errors or unwitting blunders were things that he did on purpose, believing that voters would see him as an "honest guy" who wasn't afraid to tackle big issues—as a man who would be an honest president, and worthy of their vote.

He may even have been right. As Tom Benham had said, Barry might have won, if only the election were to be held in April. In another postelection poll, Opinion Research reported that almost three times as many voters shifted their August preferences from LBJ to

Goldwater as went the other way. Twice as many of the August 1 "un-decideds" voted for Goldwater as for Johnson. The problem was that only 20 percent of the voters were undecided on August 1.

In December, key Goldwater Republicans met with Barry and Dean Burch to discuss the leadership of the RNC. Wayne Hood urged Dean to resign as chairman so that he could take over. Ralph Cordiner reported that "the Augusta crowd" (by which he meant Eisenhower, George Humphrey, and cofounder of the Augusta Golf Course in Georgia, Cliff Roberts) might be ready to nominate someone else as RNC chair. Ralph—along with Jerry Milbank, Peter O'Donnell, Stets Coleman, John Grenier, and me—wanted to keep Dean as chairman. Dean asked us directly for our support, and we pledged to fight for him all the way.

Barry agreed—or so we thought—and we were off and running. We set January 21, 1965, for the next meeting of the Republican National Committee, hoping that by then we might have recovered a bit from our family squabbles. Jerry and I set to work lining up votes for Dean, charged up with faith in our cause.

We didn't know it, but Eisenhower and Nixon already had suggested that Barry consider other candidates—and, in any event, Dean had decided he wanted to go home. Stets called me and said that we had been sold out, that Dean was out and Ohio state chairman Ray Bliss was in. Peter O'Donnell could hardly believe it; he asked me to call Dean to see if it was true. Dean said "absolutely not." But the next day, we read in the newspapers that Barry was supporting Ray Bliss and that Dean was resigning. At the RNC meeting, Barry went around the floor advocating Bliss and quite viciously knocking support of anyone else. When O'Donnell and Grenier told Barry that they were going to make a push for Wayne Hood, he said, basically, "Okay, but don't bother me until you can show me the votes."

I suppose we might have been able to line up enough votes for a simple majority, but it would have been a Pyrrhic victory. We would have gained, as a practical matter, nothing. Bliss it was.

We indeed had been sold out. Over lunch a year later, Dean apologized. He said he and Barry realized—too late—how presumptuous they had been to pick a successor and ram it down our throats. Dean admitted that the real reason he had resigned was to escape the flak from the media, of which so much was directed at him. Life back in Arizona was, well, sweet. He did allow that Bliss might not have been a wise choice: it was probably not "the best thing for the party" to have a national chairman who chose to stay out of sight and spend all of his time behind closed doors.

There was considerable soul-searching within the RNC—reassessment of policy, strategy, party organization—much of which was constructive. Dean Burch was chairman for another five months, and Barry Goldwater was still, for the time being, the titular head of the party. There were lessons to be learned and shared. There also were wounds to be healed, but most involved public perceptions and rejected suitors, not reality on the ground. The grassroots, "dominated by the activists who had been most enthusiastic about Goldwater and his brand of conservatism," remained undisturbed.

In a wound-healing mode, Melvin Laird proposed a new Republican Coordinating Committee, with membership to include Eisenhower, all past Republican presidential nominees (Alf Landon through Goldwater), the House and Senate Republican leadership, five governors (including Romney, Rockefeller, and Scranton), and four representatives from the RNC, with the RNC chairman as presiding officer. Unity was the goal, and I do believe that Laird, at least, was sincere. Ray Bliss told me that the real value rested on the concept that if people knew they would have to be working together on a regular basis, they might not be so quick to criticize each other in public. The first meeting was held in March while Dean was still chairman, and there was another in the fall. The participants had trouble agreeing on basics like punctuation and grammar, and after issuing some bland declarations the committee went dormant. In 1973 it was temporarily revived by then–RNC chairman George H.W. Bush to deal with the crisis in the Nixon White House. President Ford tried to reintroduce the concept following his 1976 defeat by Jimmy Carter, but there was not much interest.

Some of us were not ready to entrust the RNC with the future of Republican conservatism. On November 23, 1964, Charles Edison (former secretary of the Navy, former governor of New Jersey, and son of inventor Thomas Alva Edison) invited me to join him and "several other gentlemen at a small, informal, and off-the-record dinner meeting" with Congressmen John Ashbrook of Ohio and Donald Bruce of Indiana. "I am sure," Edison wrote, "that what these two young congressmen will present to us on that evening will be of substantial interest and importance." As with Clif White's cryptic invitation of two years earlier, I already knew what this was about.

We—that is, the Draft Goldwater veterans and a few additions—were about to launch a new conservative group. I knew about it because we had held the first exploratory meeting in my Wall Street office just two days after the election. The "several other gentlemen" would include Jerry Milbank, Roger and Gerrish Milliken, Bill Buckley, Brent Bozell, Bob Bauman (president of the Young Americans for Freedom), *National Review* writer Frank Meyer, Peter O'Donnell, and Marvin Leibman (who had proposed such a group some years earlier). While I was to be involved in the initial formative moves, my position at the RNC prevented me from taking an active role in leadership. But I could offer support.

Don Bruce set the stage: The majority of people, he said, were inclined to be conservative; they agreed with Barry's positions as long as his name was not attached. They agreed on issues, not personalities. What went wrong? "We have not well enunciated our philosophy; have not done our homework," he said. He pointed to the urgency of building up our contacts with newspapers, radio stations, and TV. "We won the convention on January 3, when O'Donnell and friends got

Barry to declare," he said. "But then the amateurs like Kitchel did everything to undo our victory and considered it their victory." We won at the convention but had to campaign in a vacuum, sabotaged by the professors—Baroody and friends, men with no political experience—while shrewd political pros were frozen out.

"We must have our own organization," Bruce continued, "to act as a clearinghouse. Provide talking points, news sheets, backgrounders, for columnists and commentators, to explain and make palatable 'conservatism' to the man in the street." Perhaps carried away with enthusiasm, he exclaimed: "We must save America from national suicide!"

The name we chose for our group was "American Conservative Union" (ACU), although I said I would prefer "Federation"—a libertarian word—to the collectivist "Union." That may seem a distinction without a difference, but "communism" is a collectivist word, too.

We saw the ACU as a counterweight for the liberal Americans for Democratic Action (ADA), organized in 1947 as "an organization of Liberals, banded together to help all mankind work toward freedom, justice, and peace." (Noting the tremendous influence of the ADA in the political arena, we paraphrased this mission statement as "an organization of Liberals banded together to help *other* Liberals achieve positions of power and influence in government, the press, radio and TV, and private foundations to work for a socialist America.")

The ACU mission was easily stated: to consolidate the overall strength of the American conservative movement through unified leadership and action, mold public opinion, and stimulate and direct responsible political action. The group would struggle a bit—finances were a problem—but by 1966, Chairman Ashbrook and Political Action Chairman Rusher had begun a grassroots mobilization effort, "Action Now," which used the Goldwater petitions and lists of contributors to reach as many of the 27 million Goldwater voters as possible. As the movement grew, ACU was joined (and somewhat overshadowed) by its philosophical cousins the Heritage Foundation, founded in 1973 by Paul Weyrich, and the Cato Institute, founded in 1977, but it remains the nation's oldest conservative grassroots organization.

In June 1965, Barry created a group of his own, the Free Society Association (FSA), with Denny Kitchel in charge. It was founded on the premise that the two major parties offered voters no "real political choice," and with the goal, as a nonpolitical entity, to revitalize the two-party system. The management vowed that the group would not endorse candidates or engage in political action. The *New York Times* reported that my new RNC boss, Ray Bliss, complained that all such "splinter groups" were destructive of "party unity." A bit selfishly, Ray also warned that the FSA would siphon off funds from party coffers.

Goldwater responded to Ray's criticism in his newspaper column: "How can research into the principles of a free society, and application of those principles to the problems of the day, hurt the Republican party? How can such research splinter the party?" He added, "Shortly after the formation of the Free Society Association was announced, an actual Republican splinter group, calling itself Republicans for Progress, issued its first public newsletter. It is roughly dedicated to the proposition that the best way to be a Republican is to be a frugal or efficient Democrat, to follow the same philosophy, advocate the same bureaucratic solutions, but promise to do it better or for a few cents less."

Not to be outdone, Pennsylvania Senator Hugh Scott gave a fighting keynote address to "the first annual convention" of another group, the California Republicans League. Scott blasted the Free Society Association and other "splinter" groups. "All of these ultra-conservative 'out' groups are seeking to raise more money than the Republican Party can hope to get. They plan to use this money for their own independent objectives. . . . These splinter groups are organizing people as a lever against today's party; their goal is to take the party over—and if it will not capitulate, to rob it of a significant part of its strength." Of course, the California Republicans League was in no way a party to party-splintering.

The FSA did not survive much past the next presidential election. The management seemed to lack vision, and efforts did not go far beyond sending out a newsletter.

The vital topic of raising money had been Topic A when, three weeks after the election, Frank Kovac, Jerry, and I sat down to review the lack of a permanent fund-raising organization to bridge the gap between elections. Thus was born the RNC Finance Executive Committee. Our first effort was a financial disaster.

The Democrats had a superb noncampaign fund-raising program, the "President's Club." The $1,000 entry fee entitled donors to such privileges as invitation-only functions at which the president himself might shake a few hands. The President's Club was wildly successful, with some 3,800 members in New York City alone. The Republican version was the National Republican Associates, created before the 1960 election to encourage regular supporters to donate extra money to build a contingency fund to cover unexpected needs.

In late March 1965, in an effort at revitalization and on behalf of the Finance Executive Committee, I signed a solicitation letter that was sent to 1,700 recent contributors to the National Republican Associates. The early (and almost the only) returns amounted to $60,000. This was not very impressive, although we knew that some of those contributors had already put a lot of money into the recent campaign and might have been temporarily tapped out.

But while the solicitation didn't bring in much money, it served as an opinion poll of sorts, provoking comment from disgruntled Republicans who chose not to contribute. They were unhappy with the new RNC chairman, unhappy with his reported salary of "double" Burch's (it was actually the same, $30,000, which was $5,000 less than he had been earning as Ohio state chairman). They were unhappy with the makeup of the Republican Coordinating Committee, and unhappy with what they saw as a repudiation of Goldwater's principles. Typical comments: "Mr. Bliss did not support Mr. Goldwater. I cannot support Mr. Bliss." "I can understand the losers' strategy of wrecking the party to take control of what is left. So I have left." The brewer Joseph Coors wrote, "Only when the Republican Party unites solidly behind a good sound conservative program will I contribute again and feel the cause worthwhile." (In 1973, he contributed $250,000 to the start-up of the Heritage Foundation.)

Many of the complainants objected to contributing to, as one put it, the "Eastern me-too Republicans who are still in the 'driver's seat,' the very ones who helped bring about the defeat of Senator Goldwater." One stated, "I have no intention of making further contributions to the Republican Party. This is not basically in a spirit of reprisal that I feel this way, although I do think it is impudent of those who have behaved as they did in the last campaign, to expect conservative support." He wanted to be kept informed, however, "because if it should turn out that after all, contrary to present appearances, . . . conservatives retain control, I should be anxious to renew my support."

However, the complainants had missed something important: Eleven of the twenty-one people listed as members of the Finance Executive Committee on the solicitation letterhead had been part of Draft Goldwater or had come aboard during the primary campaign: Stets Coleman, Cliff Folger, John P. Fraim, Dan Gainey, Frank Kovac, Fred LaRue, Jerry Milbank, Roger Milliken, Peter O'Donnell, Gordon Reed, and me.

New York Times columnist James Reston missed this too—or misunderstood. On November 3, 1965, he wrote, "The outlook for the Republican party . . . and for a healthier balance between the two major parties in America is not good. In some ways it is worse. For the conservative cause in the Republican Party is now in the hands of a more articulate and sophisticated generation, whose capacity to split the Republican Party is even greater than it was under Goldwater." I was not sure how our group—with virtually the same members as it had two years earlier—had become so fearsome, but I took it as a compliment.

Six months after the election, Barry's campaign suggestion to take the war to North Vietnam—deplored far and wide as warmongering—was being carried out by the Johnson administration. Tom Wicker of the *New York Times* acknowledged that "bombing targets in North Vietnam were pinpointed as long ago as October but the planes were not sent for months, until the American elections were past." And General Eisenhower told a press conference on May 13, 1965, "Barry Goldwater was talking about this kind of a military campaign even before he got the nomination. Probably at that moment it was untimely and shocking to the American people. But many of the things he recommended are now being done." "Time," the general noted, "changes everything."

In our own postelection musings, Jerry Milbank and I decided we would never win the media war until conservatives had their own captive outlets. In a misguided effort to broaden our reach, after a fifteen-minute negotiation with the owner of 3M Corporation and with the help of Jack Fraim and some other Goldwater veterans as investors, we bought the Mutual Broadcasting System (MBS) for $1 million. I scribbled out the details on the back of an envelope—my electric bill—and an executive of 3M and I signed it. We left it to the lawyers to make it neat, later.

Our plan for MBS was to improve on the type of discourse then delivered by Fulton Lewis, Jr., and later perfected by Rush Limbaugh. The plan was flawed, however, because the 500 or so affiliated radio stations under Mutual's umbrella were independent entities, not owned by MBS. Some provided programming that could be used by the others—"mutual" was an operative concept—but trying to get them all pulling on the same oar was simply impractical. As an investment, however, this wasn't a bad deal. Jack Fraim and the investors turned a handsome profit when the Amway Corporation bought the network in 1977.

I settled back into the rhythms of Wall Street. Business was good—in fact, better than ever. Middendorf, Colgate, put together ten of the largest insurance company mergers to that point in history: the merger of

Phoenix Insurance Company with the Travelers, for one, the merger of
Maryland Casualty with American General, and the purchase of The
Hartford Insurance Company by ITT, under the control of the prototyp-
ical conglomerate-builder, Harold Geneen. The last was a billion-dollar
transaction, back when a billion still meant something. Geneen didn't
worry about core competencies or synergy or a "good fit"; he looked for
a good business. He believed that companies that did well on their own
would, as part of a greater whole, protect the parent from cycles or down-
turns in one business segment or another. During his tenure, from 1959
to 1977, Geneen added about 300 companies to the ITT portfolio, taking annual sales from $765 million to nearly $28 billion.

Our services earned substantial fees, and at the time, Middendorf,
Colgate was one of the most profitable of its size in Wall Street. But at
thirty-nine, I missed the excitement of the political stage, despite
some continuing but minimal involvement as RNC treasurer. I soon
would become more involved again—courtesy of Dick Nixon.

When Nixon moved east in 1963, he had taken a position with the
prestigious law firm of Mudge, Stern, Baldwin, and Todd, which had its
offices in the same neighborhood as Middendorf, Colgate. We sometimes used the firm's legal services, and I got to know Nixon a bit. At first
it was no more than a nodding acquaintance. Later, when we worked together in the Goldwater campaign, I came to know him rather well.

Nixon was an awkward, insecure guy who came up the hard way.
He was born poor and never made much money when working for
the government, but the royalties from his book *Six Crises* weren't
bad, and he became rather well-off when he joined the law firm,
bringing along some high-dollar clients. He bought an apartment in
the same building in which Rockefeller lived.

Nixon's involvement in politics always seemed something of a
paradox. He was a loner by inclination, and he had thrust himself
into the public arena with very mixed emotions. (He once told Peter
O'Donnell, "Politics is a great conspiracy." How little did we know!)
Despite the debacle of 1964 (or more likely because of it), Nixon

never stopped working for the party—or for himself: Newspaper columnist Andrew Tully—not a fan—wrote:

> Dick Nixon is wandering around the country like a salesman, running for president but refusing to admit it, and to the professional politician watcher he is unimpressive.
>
> He is too much the new Dick Nixon. The Old Dick Nixon was infinitely to be preferred. . . . he at least had a personality.
>
> Dick Nixon, circa 1965, is not so much a politician as he is a lodge-joiner.

There was some truth in this: I think he joined every club that would accept him. (This predilection led to an embarrassment for both of us later, when, as president, Nixon asked me to nominate him for membership in the American Antiquarian Society. I did, and they turned him down! I don't think the membership committee for one moment thought that Richard Nixon was deeply interested in early American history.)

Nixon wasn't the only politician looking to the future. In 1966, Barry Goldwater commissioned a private poll to assess his chances for a 1968 Senate run. Barry was encouraged by the results, although not overconfident. "I am conducting what I might call a low-key campaign," he wrote me, "speaking daily with groups of all ages and communities all around the State." It didn't sound all that low-key to me, but I didn't say so.

George H.W. Bush also decided to make another run for office. Although he had lost his 1964 bid for the Senate—nosed out by Ralph Yarborough, who rode to victory on LBJ's coattails—he nonetheless pulled in more votes than any Republican had ever received in Texas. Now he was shooting for Congress from the 7th District, Houston (which, he wrote me, "appears to be the only district in Texas where the word 'Republican' doesn't hurt too much"). To prove he was serious, he even resigned from his job at the oil company he had founded,

Zapata, and sold his shares for a sum considerably lower than the value they reached a few years later. That's dedication—he won.

Finally, front and center was George Romney. The Michigan governor was up for reelection in November, but he and his team clearly had set their sights on bigger game. As *New York Times* columnist David Broder noted in February: "The Governor's political advisors simply do not believe that anyone is going to 'lock up' the 1968 Republican nomination by advance work, as F. Clifton White and his colleagues did for Barry Goldwater in 1964. As the Governor's advisors see it, the Goldwater experience conditioned all Republicans—liberals and conservatives, Congressmen, governors and party workers—to recognize the practicalities of politics and support a man who looks like a winner."

Broder quoted one of those anonymous political advisors as saying: "Dick Nixon is in for a terrible shock. Those Congressmen he is busy campaigning for owe him something, all right, but those guys are still just white around the gills from the shock of seeing so many of their friends beaten in 1964. They don't want to go through the mill again. Nixon is trying to take the remnants of the Goldwater team and give it some responsibility but it won't work."

We former members of Draft Goldwater were those remnants, and despite the shattering loss at the polls, we continued to enjoy the loyalty of a large number of probable convention delegates. The leaders at the top may change, but the grassroots locals, the precinct and district workers, endure. We also understood how to "to recognize the practicalities of politics and support a man who looks like a winner." To that point, we had not cast our lot with Nixon—but we had been giving it some serious thought.

Over lunch on November 10, 1965, Dean Burch, Jerry Milbank, and I agreed that Nixon was probably the front-runner for the 1968 nomination. His efforts for Barry and others had earned a lot of goodwill throughout the party and merited consideration, although other credible players might emerge after the 1966 midterm elections, heavy with gubernatorial contests. Our consensus, as recorded in my notes of the meeting, was that: "Nixon is all we have at the present time and makes good speeches to boot. He suffers only from a lack of television personality and the fact that he has been licked a couple of times in other elections."

According to a poll taken a few months later, Nixon was indeed the front-runner with 27 percent of Republican voters. Romney was at 14 percent, and Goldwater ran a close third at 13 percent. Dirksen pulled 12 percent, then came Scranton, Rockefeller, Reagan, and New York Mayor John Lindsay at 7, 6, 5, and 4 percent, respectively. Twelve percent were undecided.

In February 1966, Peter O'Donnell, Jerry Milbank, and I agreed that siding with Nixon was a reasonable choice, and toward the end of April, five Goldwater veterans spent a weekend at Peter's Dallas office: Peter, John Grenier, Fred LaRue, Fred Agnich, and me. Our purpose was to launch "Project X." The label was more in fun than an effort at secrecy, but our goal was serious: to determine whether Dick Nixon was the best hope to win back the presidency, and if not, to decide who was. We felt it was time to offer our support to a presidential candidate for 1968.

LaRue, who had just attended a strategy session in Chicago with Nixon and some of his advisers, offered a cogent bit of intelligence: Nixon was spooked by the thought of having too many Goldwater supporters. Nevertheless, we knew we had a few things to offer. First and foremost, we could deliver delegates. By our best estimate at that time, we had a line on perhaps 500 of them. We could also raise cash. Moreover, though we'd been burned by our experiences on the campaign trail, we felt we could deliver some reasonably good advice. But we had to consider two key questions: Would we be comfortable working with Nixon, and would he accept our assistance?

Nixon answered the second question himself, without being asked. In June, he invited Jerry Milbank and me to join him for lunch and some friendly probing. Dick was in a most expansive mood, even drifting into something resembling humor. The current issue of *Time* magazine had an extraordinarily favorable write-up about Bill Buckley, and Nixon joked, "Maybe all along he's just been a Trojan horse for the liberal left. . . . assigned to infiltrate and sabotage by becoming a spokesman for the right."

We knew the real reason for the lunch, and both of us thought he was pandering, consciously or not, by constantly referring to "we conservatives." I could picture him in different settings, each with a handy "we": moderates, war veterans, fathers of two daughters. But when we got down to business, he was very direct: "Look, I gave my all for you guys, gave it everything I had, and I want you to give some thought to turning those delegates loose to support me in '68."

It was our turn to probe. How did he feel about our team? (Favorable, with especially positive comments about O'Donnell and LaRue.) What did he think about, and what were his connections with, the RNC? (Not much, and limited; this may have been the most honest comment he offered.) His plans for the immediate future? (More whirlwind trips, fund-raising, and being a good Republican.)

It was like an employment interview, and, like a good interviewer, I took notes: "Overall impression . . . a man of great energy, but not particularly prepossessing, a man of great devotion to the party, but perhaps motivated a touch by self-interest, a man so much on the run . . . perhaps to obscure a shallowness that would show up if he slowed down and could be analyzed."

A meeting of the RNC was coming up three days later, and Dick asked me to take some soundings. I found that he was riding pretty high with the South and Midwest but that Romney, backed by the Rockefeller-Scranton crowd, was coming on strong in the Northeast. I also found that everyone was fairly optimistic about the midterm elections except for Ray Bliss, our overly cautious director, who warned that we were becoming "overconfident" and should "run scared." The meeting went largely unnoticed in the press. The *Wall Street Journal* of June 30, 1966, explained, "Bliss distrusts the press, refuses to speak out on issues, ducks troublesome decisions. . . . If Lyndon Johnson ever starts

giving thanks for small favors, he might manage a short note of gratitude to the Republican high command for its public relations policies."

The general consensus was that Bliss was a good "nuts-and-bolts"
manager. It was his favorite self-description, and I suppose the press
meant it more as faint praise than as a pejorative. Anyway, "nuts and
bolts" wasn't all bad. I did have reservations when Dean Burch was replaced by Ray: Dean was a friend, a coworker in the Goldwater vine-
yard, and an effective manager. I thought he should have stayed on to
help heal whatever wounds the party had received, and that dumping
him was an unnecessary repudiation of party leadership.

Still, Ray Bliss proved to be a solid, if somewhat stolid, performer.
Up close and personal, I thought he was in fact doing a decent job, although he spent too much time in Ohio with his insurance business,
leaving much of the "nuts and bolts" to others. But under Ray's leadership we had set up four campaign manager schools, three-day sessions covering topics ranging from how to pick a candidate to how to
position a billboard. Some 400 volunteers from state and local levels
attended. We also financed training for candidates, public relations
directors, and campaign finance managers, and we expanded the
five-minute weekly radio program from 160 stations to 1,000.

On the downside, when the head of our Goldwater for President
TV Committee, John B. Kilroy, offered to take the idea of doing the
five-minute broadcasts to television, Bliss, operating in the "not invented here" mode (or perhaps eager to assert his new authority),
worried that an independently produced program might convey "an
unacceptable image of the party." Barry Goldwater played negotiator
and engineered an agreement to ensure that the RNC and the Senate
and House campaign committees would have full control of content.
In the end, however, nothing came of it.

Our fund-raising continued to have a solid focus on small donors:
In the twenty-four months between the 1964 and 1966 elections, we received an average of $10 each from more than 1 million contributors.

The Democrats had been paying attention and tried to set up a small-donor base of their own. They do not seem to have been very successful. As noted in the *Washington Star:* "In recent years, the Democrats have received almost 80 per cent of their funds from donors over $100—most of them $1000 givers. An effort last year to stimulate small contributions through a contest was a dismal failure. So few people entered that winners at the state level have not even been announced."

Not to put too fine a point on it—but the Republicans, "destroyed" by the Goldwater campaign, came back strong in the 1966 elections, thanks in large part to an increased focus on conservative issues. A report in the *New York Times,* headlined "Congress Is Found Turning to Right," presented data collected by the nonpartisan Americans for Constitutional Action that showed higher approval ratings on conservative positions compared with a year earlier. The change was attributed to "a growing awareness of voting records by constituents and strong conservative opposition in the forthcoming election."

How strong? We picked up 700 seats in state legislatures, more than erasing the 529-seat loss of 1964. Where we had lost 37 House seats in 1964, we made a net gain of 47 in 1966, plus three Senate seats and eight governorships. With the governorships, the Republican Party now controlled 25 out of 50 statehouses, but it almost was 26. In Georgia, the race for governor was so close that it ended up in the U.S. Supreme Court, which allowed the state legislature to pick the winner. Bo Callaway had won the popular vote, but not a majority (thanks to a third-party spoiler), and the legislature selected the segregationist Democrat Lester Maddox as governor. (This is not too surprising, since Georgia did not elect a single Republican governor between Reconstruction and 2002.)

The postelection issues of *Time* and *Newsweek* both featured the same six beaming Republican winners on their covers: Governors Rockefeller, Romney, and Reagan, and senators-elect Mark Hatfield of Oregon, Charles Percy of Illinois, and Edward Brooke of Massachusetts.

CHAPTER 20

Nixon

THE REAL WINNER OF THE 1966 election was Dick Nixon. From the beginning of 1965 until midterm election eve, Nixon helped Republicans raise some $6.5 million, visited thirty-five states, and spoke on behalf of some 100 candidates, building the grass roots by planting seeds. He went into the tough districts—Chicago and Miami, for example—as well as the secure ones. A statistician at the *New York Times* concluded that "a GOP House candidate for whom Nixon did not campaign stood only a 45 percent chance of winning while a man he embraced stood a 67 percent chance."

Nixon's competition on the campaign trail included LBJ, Hubert Humphrey, and the Senators Kennedy. Robert Kennedy was followed by twenty or more reporters; Nixon's entourage was usually two, maybe four. But as the *Chicago Tribune* would later muse, "Bobby made a big hit with the teenagers. Richard Nixon put himself across with adults."

In a small irony, our nuts-and-bolts manager refused to provide this highly influential campaigner with any travel funds because he wanted to avoid any appearance of favoritism. Nixon drew funds from the Congressional Campaign Committee and the pockets of a few close supporters: Maurice Stans, Connecticut Governor John Lodge, Peter Flanagan, Henry Salvatori, Jerry Milbank, and yours truly.

At the beginning of the year, the January 19 syndicated newspaper column written by Robert S. Allen and Paul Scott asserted that the

RNC was "missing some $700,000." Of course, there was no truth in the statement, and I had an audit to prove it. When I suggested that the columnists had made "a false and serious charge," they expressed regret, blamed "a reliable source within the National Committee," and issued a correction. I always thought that good reporters were supposed to check information with two sources, or at least have the common sense (or courtesy) to come to the ultimate source—in this case, me. Allen and Scott had also been the authors of an April 10, 1965, report that Bliss was being paid a salary twice that of Dean Burch. When challenged, they had issued a retraction then, too. Is it so surprising that conservatives are suspicious of the media?

On the other side of this coin, CBS executive Frank Shakespeare had been offering excellent advice and assistance to our effort since 1963. "Whenever you see an attack or misrepresentation," he told me, "immediately ask for a transcript, and then get in touch with the top man at the network. Not the show producer. The top man." He suggested that a carefully worded letter, not indulging in vitriol or accusation but merely stating how we felt our position or action had been misrepresented, could help put things in perspective. At the least, it would let the network know we were watching.

Our use of TV became properly sophisticated when Frank later took a leave of absence from CBS to more directly support our efforts during the 1968 campaign. He conceived and produced *The Nixon Answer,* a series of half-hour and hour-long shows tailored to regional audiences in a sort of town meeting format. In essence, a relaxed and cheerful Nixon began the presidential campaign long before the convention. Would that Goldwater could have done so, four years earlier.

Barry, meanwhile, had decided to support Nixon and was upset about Romney's rise in popularity. Romney's candidacy had received a huge boost from his reelection: Polls quickly put him as the Republican front-runner, while Nixon and Percy were tied for second. Ronald Reagan was coming in fourth. The Harris poll of November

1966 had Romney over Johnson 54 to 46. Old pro Len Hall signed on as Romney's campaign manager.

Barry was not thrilled and wrote to remind me of Romney's "vivid apostasy" after the 1964 election:

> "When you finish boiling down what [he] did, it was . . . a repudiation of the entire Republican Convention of 1964. . . . His problem is . . . whether a man can, for his own selfish, political means, kick the Republican Party down the rat hole, and if I am any judge of Republican feeling, they are not going to accept this case.
>
> Also, besides, . . . just where in the hell does he stand on Vietnam?
>
> When he starts to level with the American people . . . then I think we can more studiously appraise Romney as a candidate but, up to now, I am backing Nixon and can't back anyone else."

Barry's feelings also boiled over in a strong letter to Romney, who was quick to respond—with a twelve-page, single-spaced defense. With the internecine warfare of 1964 a vivid memory, I exercised my position as an official of the RNC and did a bit of shuttle diplomacy, meeting Romney in his office in Lansing on March 17, 1967. I was prepared to endure a lecture on the true meaning of Republicanism—Romney often turned any conversation into a lecture—but he said, in essence, "Okay, I'm willing to back off . . . but what about Goldwater?" So I called Barry, who agreed to drop the whole subject.

On the first of January, 1967, Nixon's law firm merged with Caldwell, Trimble and Mitchell, bond specialists, and the name was changed to Nixon, Mudge, Rose, Guthrie, Alexander, and Mitchell. The last named, of course, was John Mitchell, a real professional in the field of municipal bonds—maybe the best ever, never mind his later Watergate troubles. Mitchell's firm did legal work for Middendorf, Colgate and many other Wall Street firms.

The nascent Nixon for President movement moved forward a week later with a two-day planning session in the Waldorf Towers suite once occupied by Herbert Hoover. Project X contributed three of the eight attendees: Jerry Milbank, Peter O'Donnell, and Fred LaRue. As an official of the RNC, under orders from Mr. Nuts & Bolts, I now had to remain on the outside. Others were California Lieutenant Governor Bob Finch, stockbroker Peter Flanagan, Nixon law partner Tom Evans, political PR expert William Safire, and Nixon. Taking into account the chits Nixon had been collecting, the Project X figure of 500 possible delegates was reevaluated and set at 603. All present agreed that it was time to go public (although Nixon would not yet be an "announced" candidate), and they decided to open a Washington office. It was occupied in March by a "Nixon for President Committee," initially headed by San Diego obstetrician Gaylord B. Parkinson. As GOP state chairman for California, Parky championed the so-called 11th Commandment—"Thou Shalt Not Speak Ill of Other Republicans"— which became a keystone of Reagan's political philosophy.

To hone his international reputation before the heavy campaigning began, Nixon himself went on a six-month "political moratorium" that included an extended overseas fact-finding tour: He went to Bucharest, Prague, London, Paris, Berlin, Rome (where he met with the pope), and Moscow (where Soviet officials declined an invitation to meet). The main topic of interest everywhere was Vietnam, followed by East-West tensions and Chinese hostility.

Back in November 1966, when Rockefeller was asked if he planned to honor an earlier pledge not to seek the presidency again, he had said, in essence, "Yes, sir . . . unequivocally."

"Unequivocally" seems to have meant "not in public." In November 1967, Peter O'Donnell reported that a fellow in Texas had been offered $30,000 to work for Rockefeller as one of ten regional vice chairmen—and if Rockefeller got the nomination, Rockefeller would see that the Texas Republicans received $30,000 a year for ten years.

The Democrats—to borrow a phrase from a Rowland Evans and Robert Novak column—were showing "blind faith in the political luck of Lyndon Johnson." Incredibly, the Democratic National Committee was not even pushing voter registration, especially if it involved sending money to state-level committees. My counterpart as treasurer, a young fellow named John Criswell, was under orders from the White House to run things with a minimum of fuss and money—especially the latter. According to Evans and Novak, the Democrats' complacency rested on one assumption: "supreme confidence that the Republicans will pass over Gov. Nelson Rockefeller, whom they fear, and instead nominate Richard M. Nixon."

Heading toward 1968, Romney was still a leading contender, but not for long. He suffered from the Goldwater malady: He was successful when dealing with local media on local issues, but thrown off by the skeptical, competitive, and often hostile questioning of the national media. Like Goldwater, Romney could not resist answering a question, even if he made up the answer as he went along.

The beginning of the end for him was September 3, 1967, during the broadcast of an interview on a Detroit TV station. When asked about inconsistencies in his stated positions on Vietnam, Romney answered: "Well, you know when I came back from Vietnam, I just had the greatest brainwashing that anybody can get when you go over to Vietnam. Not only by the generals, but also by the diplomatic corps over there, and they do a very thorough job."

It was a throwaway line, but the national media noticed—as did everyone else. Romney, now painted as a naïf wandering in international thickets, also was accused of slandering two great Americans: the U.S. commander in Vietnam, General William Westmoreland, and Ambassador Henry Cabot Lodge, who was back for a second tour in Saigon.

Like Goldwater, Romney simply could not walk away from the topic du jour. He would make some statement that had not been thought out beforehand, and then defend it wherever he went. He tried to recover his footing with another visit to Vietnam, which was roundly denounced as a shallow campaign trip, a desperate attempt to vault into office over the backs of dying men. In a private poll we commissioned before the New Hampshire primary, Nixon had the edge over Romney 5 to 1. Romney's campaign sputtered along for a few more weeks.

Dick Nixon opened his New Hampshire campaign on February 2, 1968; the uptight Nixon of 1960 had bloomed into a relaxed, jovial master of the press conference. When a newsman asked why he wanted to be president, Nixon parried, asking why anyone would want to be a reporter. "I think," Nixon added, "covering a Presidential campaign is worse than running one."

Nixon's strategy was to take on LBJ from the start and not run against the Republican contenders. He won New Hampshire with more votes than all the other candidates—Democrats, Republicans, and write-ins—combined, more votes, in fact, than any other candidate in any New Hampshire primary ever.

In the middle of the New Hampshire campaign, Vietnam became an acute factor: The Tet offensive demonstrated that the enemy still had considerable force despite years of American efforts and pronouncements to the contrary. Tet was a military defeat for the North. The enemy did not achieve its objectives and did not—despite the myth to the contrary—"capture" the U.S. Embassy. But aided and abetted by a media that convinced the nation that it was a Communist victory, Tet was a morale-buster of major proportions and would drive Lyndon Johnson out of office. On March 31, 1968, he announced to the nation: "I shall not seek and I will not accept the nomination of my party for another term as your president."

Some influential Republicans—the higher-society crowd, of which Richard Nixon could never be a member—launched a Draft Rockefeller movement. Just a month earlier, when Romney had folded, some reporters had made inquiry of Rockefeller, and he had reiterated that he would not be a candidate "directly or indirectly." Now, Rockefeller was persuaded to announce an active candidacy. He tried to get started, but he seemed to have lost his rudder. At a meeting of editors and reporters, according to a friend of mine who was there, Rockefeller fell flat on his face. He read a speech that seemed to be put together by committee, and the audience was bored. He entered some primaries but was basically ignored. Rockefeller did try to convert some Nixon delegates. Perhaps he thought he could force a second ballot, then go head-to-head with whoever was still standing.

Although I had dropped back from playing a public role in the Nixon primary campaigns—in deference to my official position with the RNC, which mandated fair and equal treatment for all candidates—I nonetheless kept my options open as a potential convention delegate from Connecticut. A local poll taken in December had Rockefeller squeaking past LBJ with 20,000 votes, but Nixon losing by more than 200,000. By the end of April, with Nixon winning primaries and LBJ out of the picture, Rockefeller still seemed to have the edge in Connecticut. I sat down with State Republican Chairman Howard Haussmann to try a bit of horse trading. I said, "Nixon's out in front nationally, and I'd hate to have Connecticut holding out for a sentimental but possibly un-electable favorite."

Howard grunted, then countered: "I have 177 people running for the state legislature, and if I become convinced that the majority would win with X candidate and only 10 percent with candidate Y, no matter what might happen nationally, I have no choice."

There was another latecomer to the race: Ronald Reagan. Just after the 1966 landslide in which he had been elected governor of California, Clif White had been brought aboard to plan a 1968 presidential run for him. It didn't work out, through no fault of Clif's. In the summer of 1967, one of the governor's aides was unmasked as a homosexual; by itself, this was not so harmful, politically, but he had been putting his buddies on the staff. Serious presidential campaigning was put on hold, until the assassination of Bobby Kennedy in June 1968 put Reagan back in the game. He took a page from the Rockefeller playbook: Siphon off just enough Nixon supporters to bring on a first-ballot deadlock. And Clif White was back in the saddle, counting delegates.

The months leading up to the 1968 Republican Convention were crowded with great events, all of which were significant, but most are outside the scope of this memoir. Suffice to say that agitation over Vietnam and the assassinations of Martin Luther King, Jr., and Bobby Kennedy spurred a brawl within the Democratic Party that spilled out into the streets; thus the Democratic National Convention in Chicago became a sad marker in American political history.

In July, RNC staffer Ray Underwood and I met with the campaign managers for the two leading Republican contenders. The meeting with the Rockefeller group came first; his team included, notably, Len Hall, who had been cut adrift by the end of the Romney campaign. Nixon's team included John Mitchell, Maury Stans, Jerry Milbank, Peter Flanagan, and Dick Kleindienst. We suggested to each that the RNC stood ready to help if their man was nominated, and asked how we might be of service. The Rockefeller meeting was dominated by Len Hall's reminiscing about the 1952 campaign. The only useful but unsurprising bit of information we learned from him was that if Rockefeller got the nomination, the campaign would be run out of New York.

We spent about ninety minutes with the Nixon team. This group was a great deal more interested in budgeting and particularly keen to review data from the 1964 campaign. We suggested that the RNC Finance Committee was well equipped to handle campaign services on their behalf, including income, cash accounting, coordination with various committees, and so forth, just as we had in 1964.

I briefed Ray Bliss on our conversations, but he immediately shot me down. He wouldn't allow the RNC to be the "checkwriter" when someone else was controlling the expenditures. To my mind, it was a matter of budgeting and then holding everyone to the budget. But Ray thought that we would have to take the blame for any problems, even though we wouldn't have any control over the spending. "Christ's sake," he said, "you can't operate that way. If Cordiner hadn't locked horns around here in the Goldwater campaign, I would have started out $2 to $3 million in the red, and you know it. He was a tough customer, but he kept the committee in the black." He paused, then said, "What put you in the black was Reagan's speech."

I was losing the argument before it began. I did not, however, try to explain that Cordiner's rules got in the way of the campaign and that it was Goldwater, not Cordiner, who had preserved a positive balance.

"If I were a candidate," Ray added, "I'd buy your idea in two minutes. I spend the money and the National Committee is obligated to pay."

I wasn't ready to quit. "I was thinking only of the mechanics, of how the money is dispensed, under solid accounting principles," I said.

"Who would have the authority?" he countered.

"The budget committee."

"Well, the hell with the budget committee," Ray said. "I've dealt with so many so GD long they make me tired. . . . I can tell you right now they will want to control the expenditures and they won't let us write the checks. They decide they want to buy $3 million on spot announcements up in New York in their headquarters and I'm sitting down here, responsible for keeping the GD place in the black. . . . What will happen if they go out and spend $15 million and only raise $10 million, and the National Committee now has a $5 million deficit?"

I apologized for apparently stepping out of line. Ray was quick to back off a bit. "No, I don't mind your exploring it," he said. "And, of course, if they come along and name their own chairman, as they might, well then they will have complete control. Their man will be responsible for the deficit, not Ray Bliss."

About a month later, Nixon's campaign team did indeed appoint a chairman: Maurice Stans. He told the RNC Finance Committee that he was taking responsibility for a $20 million campaign and would leave the committee in good shape. And he did. As promised, we (the RNC) provided the main comptroller function of the national campaign, paying bills, preparing financial reports, and maintaining records of account. There was no deficit.

Toward the end of July, with the convention a week away, the Republican committee chairman for Washington, D.C., Carl Shipley, and I called on selected members of the Congress. Gerald Ford said that Nixon was "stuck at 90 percent" of the needed delegate votes "because of the Rockefeller advertising blitz, favorite-son candidates holding firm in Michigan, Ohio, and California, bottling up any pro-Nixon delegates, and the rapid rise of Ronald Reagan." I said, "Gerry, I think if you were the VP candidate, Michigan would go Nixon in a flash." "Oh, no," he said, with a wink: "I'm not a candidate for vice president. I just want to be Speaker of the House."

John Tower predicted that Texas would split between Reagan and Nixon. John Rhodes liked the idea of a Rocky-Reagan or a Nixon-Lindsay ticket, but not a Nixon-Reagan ticket. John Ashbrook would support Nixon on the first ballot, though his lines remained open to Clif White and Reagan. But he warned that any breakdown in the Nixon camp might throw the whole thing to Rockefeller. George Murphy favored a Nixon-Reagan ticket and was opposed to putting Lindsay on any ticket. If Nixon faltered on the first ballot, he said, we should consider a shift to Reagan.

I called Peter O'Donnell, and we developed a working strategy for the delegates whom we could influence: If Nixon started to fade—we would not go for Rockefeller, nor for Lindsay except in the second spot. Our fallback would be Reagan. And with the convention underway and only forty-eight hours to go before the balloting, Reagan announced, "As of this moment, I am a candidate." It may have been the shortest formal candidacy on record, but Ron milked it for all it was worth, attending thirty-five caucuses.

I had managed to be reelected as a delegate from Connecticut. Soon after I arrived in Miami for the convention, Clif White invited me to a meeting with Reagan. I knew that Nixon was paranoid about any of his people seeing Reagan, but I went anyway. The reason for the meeting was obvious, and a relaxed, charming, self-effacing Reagan made a strong but friendly pitch. He asked if I would shift my vote and bring along as many of my friends as possible. I had to say no, that it was too late in the game, and that although I truly considered Reagan the ideological successor to Goldwater, I was honorbound to stick to my commitment to Nixon.

At the convention-eve Republican Gala I sat at a table with Ray Bliss; among other personalities who stopped by was John Wayne, whom I had met during the Goldwater campaign. He was going from table to table, warning, "Look fellows, if you don't vote for Nixon, I'll break all your heads open."

I guess they were listening: Nixon won with 692 votes. Rockefeller got 287, and Reagan 182. *Newsweek* for August 19, 1968, said that Nixon "owed his stunning comeback victory . . . to his own brilliantly meticulous planning and his rivals' failures of nerve and political judgment. . . . Even his straightforward ambition proved winning, as against Nelson Rockefeller's in-again, out-again vacillation and Reagan's transparent noncandidacy."

I could not help but recall David Broder's 1966 comments in the *New York Times,* when he said that no one was "going to 'lock up' the 1968 Republican nomination by advance work, as F. Clifton White and his colleagues did for Barry Goldwater in 1964. . . . Nixon is trying to take the remnants of the Goldwater team and give it some responsibility but it won't work." But that is exactly what he did, and the grass roots—along with other "remnants of the Goldwater team"— were behind Nixon all the way. Along the way, in every poll that had been taken of Republican local officials and potential delegates, no matter which candidate was the supposed "front-runner" against LBJ, and then Humphrey, Nixon came out ahead. He had earned that support.

Here's a small footnote to political history: Jerry Milbank and I had decided early on to push George "Poppy" Bush for VP. We thought he could run well with any of the three leading candidates, no matter which one got the nomination. Granted, he was a first-termer in

Congress and not well known, but his personality was a natural for television and he would quickly make his mark. Points in his favor included: his youth, his mix of East Coast sophistication and Texas determination, which could balance Nixon's California background, and a politically well-connected father to facilitate fund-raising.

We worked the convention, lining up what was probably a sufficient number of votes for him to win the VP nomination. We obtained letters of support from delegations from seven states. As reported in the August 5, 1968, *San Antonio Light:* "Houston Congressman George (Poppy) Bush's vice presidential stock went up this weekend, with the national Republican treasurer pushing his candidacy for the GOP No. 2 spot."

I was not pushing for Bush in my official RNC capacity, however, but as a friend and member of the Connecticut delegation. I had a banner made up that said, "Bush for VP," and hung it in the lobby of his hotel. I spoke at a press conference to encourage support for him. I think Poppy was taken by surprise when he saw the number of reporters who met his plane upon his arrival in Miami a few hours later.

The morning after Nixon had the nomination, Milbank and I went to make our pitch. He was still in bed, but reading a newspaper. "Mr. President, we'd like to put forward the name of George Bush for vice president." We assured Nixon that we had the votes.

"Oh, gosh, fellows," he said. "Gee, that's too bad. We're not going that way. I've already decided to put Agnew on the ticket." Spiro T. Agnew, governor of Maryland, was an avid supporter of fellow-governor Rockefeller and hardly known to the rest of the country, but that didn't seem to matter to Nixon. "Agnew," Nixon explained, "will unite the party with Rockefeller, and besides, he made a terrific nominating speech on my behalf."

I think we both blurted out, "Who?" We tried to talk about it, but Nixon was adamant. "This is my man! My man! Sorry fellows, you've really done great work, but Agnew's my man!"

Campaign headquarters was divided between two locations: the main office at New York's Waldorf-Astoria, and Citizens for Nixon-Agnew, headed by John Warner, at the Willard Hotel in Washington, D.C., which had been basically vacant before we moved in. My role in the campaign was less exciting than it had been with the Goldwater campaign because it was more confined to the traditional tasks of a treasurer: This time, I wasn't called upon to handle celebrity scheduling or speechwriting, just solid grunt work and financial coordination.

The night of the election, Nixon's secretary, Rosemary Woods, called and said that Nixon wanted a few of us—Strom Thurmond, Fred LaRue, Jerry Milbank, and a couple of others—to come over to the hotel. We were asked to wait out in the hall by the elevators outside Nixon's suite, with some chairs and a TV set. Every now and then, Rosemary would come out of the suite to assure us that Nixon wanted to thank us for our great support; we were "his team" and he wanted our recommendations for important appointments. This was, I must admit, our primary goal in supporting Nixon: We did want to ensure that conservatives would occupy significant positions in the new administration.

We waited. Shortly after midnight, an elevator door opened and Bill Rodgers, Herbert Brownell, and some other Rockefeller types stepped out of the elevators. They went past us to Nixon's suite; the door opened, they went in, the door shut. Perhaps an hour or so later, the door opened, they came out, got back into the elevator, and went down. I don't remember if they said anything to us, going or coming.

At about 2:00 A.M., Rosemary came out and apologized—the boss had gone to bed, she said, and would have to see us in the morning. I later found out that Nixon actually didn't go to bed until about 8 A.M. and that, as soon as we had left, he had called in Bob Haldeman and they had begun working the phones. Then he brought in the rest of the immediate campaign staff for an impromptu celebration that went on for several hours. Gratitude, some people have said, is the most fleeting of human emotions. I decided that if Nixon ever really wanted to thank us, he knew how to find us.

Some years later I was giving a talk at the Breakers Hotel in Palm Beach. It was a conference of high-level corporate CEOs, and Brownell was there. It was the first time I'd seen him since that night, I think, and I asked him what had happened. "Don't blame me," he said. "I got a call from Nixon, and he asked me to get together with some other members of the Rockefeller team, draw up our suggestions for the Cabinet, and bring them over immediately. We presented our list; he accepted some, not others."

I find it sad to note that few of the Rockefeller types would give Nixon the time of day until he was elected—and then he was courting them. Some might think this was a brilliant move and argue that Nixon was holding out a hand of friendship to the opposition. I think it was more of an example of Nixon's insecurity, a need to be liked. He tended to ignore those who were loyal to him, but those who fought him, or stood up to him, would find him seeking their friendship.

It's not surprising, however, that Nixon was up all night; the election was in doubt until well into the morning. I don't think the TV pundits were calling it for Nixon until breakfast time, and Humphrey didn't concede until 11:30 A.M. The final numbers were interesting: Nixon 31,770,237; Humphrey, 31,270,533; Alabama Governor George Wallace, 9,906,141. Nixon actually had 2 million fewer votes than in 1960, even though the total number of votes was higher than in 1960 by some 4 million. In his *Making of the President 1968*, Teddy White wrote, "The election of 1968 was the first landslide of its kind in American history, a negative landslide. Americans turned against the Democratic policy and leadership, but didn't know where they wanted to go." I have to give credit where credit is due, to those folks at Gallup and Harris; they had warned that a "race involving Nixon, Humphrey and Wallace would be virtual dead heat, with Wallace perhaps holding the balance."

But a win is a win. "Close" counts in more games than just horseshoes.

CHAPTER 21

Epilogue

PETER FLANAGAN WAS COORDINATING Nixon's presidential appointments. He asked, "Bill, if you were to come work in Washington, what would you like to do?" I told him there was one position that interested me—secretary of the Navy. I knew that I was the only person ever to seek the post who actually had a degree in naval science. Well, word came back that Mr. Nixon would be pleased to have me in that post. However, a few weeks later, I got another call from Flanagan. "The Boss sends his apologies, but he feels that he has to give the Navy job to John Chafee." Chafee had been governor of Rhode Island but was now out of a job. He was not a Nixon loyalist— far from it—but Nixon wanted to reach out to the Rockefeller camp, and Chafee wanted the navy job. "Would you mind," Flanagan asked, "stepping aside for the time being?" I would be next in line, he said, but in the meantime, would I mind picking some other post? Anything I wanted.

I was disappointed, but not surprised. By now I could have predicted that although we'd been told that some of Nixon's supporters were to be brought on board, some of his more fervent detractors were at the head of the line.

I asked Peter for a day or two to think it over, but selecting another post wasn't difficult: I asked to serve as ambassador to the Netherlands. I had been close to the Netherlands for many years—in fact,

Austen Colgate and I owned the Van Waverin Tulip Bulb Company. It was the second-largest tulip company in Holland and, dating from Rembrandt's time, one of the oldest in the world. Thus, I already knew a fair number of businessmen and community leaders there. (I did have some competition for the post, I would later learn: Shirley Temple. She eventually was appointed as a delegate to the United Nations General Assembly.)

My father was incensed: Why would I give up a seven-figure Wall Street income for a government job paying $40,000 a year? Well, perhaps because I'd already learned how to make money, and now I wanted to learn how to make contributions of a different sort. I stayed in the Netherlands—for four years—because I loved it, and I loved making progress on behalf of the United States. I became bitten by the bug called "public service," a disease which would overwhelm my immune system off and on over the next eighteen years. My father, who like so many in the investment community had almost been destroyed in the Depression but managed to come back, simply didn't understand.

I had a good tour in the Netherlands. I had been well prepared by more than 125 meetings with officials at the State Department, the Treasury Department, the Commerce Department, the CIA, and the U.S. Information Agency (USIA) and with scores of senior officials at the White House and other government agencies as well as leaders of such major international businesses as IBM, Chase Bank, Citibank, and Chemical Bank. One of those White House officials was the national security adviser, Henry Kissinger, who said, Bill, stay close to me. Bill, he said, the president and I would like to have you communicate directly with us on the major issues, such as NATO, passing by the State Department intermediaries in such cases.

Ah, Henry. As I quickly learned, it is impossible to operate an embassy on the receiving end of thirty or forty telegrams a day, some of great magnitude, and on every issue imaginable—agriculture, trade, business, military affairs—without the support of a very competent desk officer and others at the State Department. There is no way in the world that any ambassador could channel his communications through a White House official with barely any support staff at all. In truth, though, Henry's primary foci—Russia, China, and Vietnam— demanded most of his attention, and he didn't have much to do with issues concerning the Netherlands. Once in the job, I dealt more often with Henry's deputy, Helmut Sonnenfeldt, than with Henry himself, but only within the established chain of command.

Thanks to the intensive briefings, I got to know almost everyone I needed to know at the State Department before I went overseas. Or, more important, they got to know me. I was not a faceless bureaucrat at the other end of the communications chain. When I had a request or needed support, I got it. In fact, during my first couple of years, I think I made fourteen trips back to the states to meet with various agencies to present and discuss the embassy's needs. All but one of these trips, I would add, were at my own expense. State Department rules for expenditure of travel funds were, in my judgment, counter-productive. They may have saved a few bucks, but they certainly got in the way of getting the job done.

In May 1972, the Nixon team invited me to come back home to serve as treasurer for the next campaign, which was conducted under the banner of what must have been the strangest acronym ever given a campaign: CREEP ("Committee to Re-Elect the President"). But I had started a program to encourage increased trade and investment be-tween Holland and the United States and wanted to finish that work, so I elected to remain at my post. (As with my decision not to join the John Reed Society back at Harvard, I had escaped another bullet. Had I become treasurer, my name would have been on a lot of checks that ended up in Watergate-tainted hands.) My resolve to stay was validated from another source: the December 16, 1972, *Business Week* suggested that, because of my business background and this focus on trade issues, I was one of the more effective ambassadors in Europe.

After Nixon won the election, however, my Netherlands tour ended anyway. I went back to Middendorf, Colgate for a while. It was financially rewarding, of course, but the business was running on automatic. I gladly accepted an appointment as undersecretary of the Navy in 1973 and soon was promoted to secretary—so my turn had come after all. By then, it was the last days of the Nixon administration. (The discovery of personal income-tax fraud forced Nixon's man Spiro T. Agnew to resign as vice president in 1973; Gerald Ford, who had only wanted to be speaker of the house, was appointed to fill his term, and then became president upon the Watergate-driven resignation of Dick Nixon in 1974.) I continued in my post with the Navy until Ford left office in 1977.

But something strange happened on the way to my promotion. Nixon was so preoccupied with keeping his own job that he was little concerned with employment issues at the Pentagon. James Schlesinger, the secretary of defense, had his own candidate for the Navy Department, a man in the shipping business. Some of my friends learned of this—Schlesinger certainly never told me so himself—and I quickly mounted a small counteroffensive. Having been treasurer of the Republican Party for so many years, I'd made a lot of friends on the Hill, and I called some people who would be supportive: Bob Wilson in the House, and Barry Goldwater, John Tower, and John Stennis in the Senate. I didn't play sore loser—complaining that "I was promised"—but let them all know that I was very much interested in the job, if they might be pleased to speak on my behalf. A few days later, a group from Congress sent a petition over to the president, urging him to appoint me as secretary.

Nixon may not have been paying much attention before, but he certainly noticed this petition. He was having problems with the Congress—and was likely to have a lot more, if talk of impeachment moved beyond the talking stage. The president clearly had decided that, if it would make some people on the Hill happy to see me as secretary of the Navy, then I would be secretary of the Navy. With Richard Nixon, years of support, loyalty, and service seemed to count for little or nothing.

Nixon later told me that Barry Goldwater was not one of the people who supported my candidacy, which I found hard to believe. According to Nixon, when my name finally came to his attention, he called Goldwater: "Your guy is up for secretary of the Navy. Should I push it or let it go?" And, according to Nixon, Barry said, "Oh, Bill's had two top jobs—that's enough." That doesn't coordinate with Barry's warm support for me when the Senate Armed Services Committee held my confirmation hearing—which, according to Barry, may have been, measured in minutes, the shortest on record.

Barry Goldwater was returned to the Senate in 1968. He served for three more terms, retiring in 1987. In the meantime, the conservative movement, anchored by the Draft Goldwater veterans and a host of new volunteers, continued to grow, gaining sufficient influence to bring a true conservative, Ronald Reagan, to the presidency in the election of 1980.

The list of young men and women who were inspired by *The Conscience of a Conservative* to begin or enhance political careers with the Goldwater campaign reads as a "who's who" of Republican leaders of the last third of the twentieth century. They included, of course, George H.W. Bush and Ronald Reagan, many of the people already mentioned in this memoir, and also such later standouts as Senators Howard Baker, James Buckley, Phil Gramm, Paul Laxalt, Trent Lott, Fred Thompson, and Governors Tim Babcock, James Edwards, and Don Samuelson. William Rehnquist offered legal advice to the campaign in 1964, and his 1952 Stanford Law School classmate (he was first in the class of 102, she was third) Sandra Day O'Connor stuffed envelopes for Barry's 1958 Senate campaign. 1968*

Edwin J. Feulner, who was a grad student in 1964, was also inspired by Barry. He is now head of the Heritage Foundation, by far the nation's largest conservative organization. Patrick Buchanan, then an editorial writer for a St. Louis newspaper, was later a Nixon aide and, still later, a 1992 candidate for the Republican presidential nomination. Upon

Barry's passing in 1998, Pat said, "He was the Moses of the conservative movement. He led us to the promised land but didn't make it himself." Morton Blackwell—at twenty-three the youngest Goldwater delegate in 1964—went on to establish the nonpartisan Leadership Institute in 1979, which to date has trained more than 40,000 conservatives interested in serving in politics, government, and the news media. And I would be remiss if I didn't mention high-school senior Hillary Rodham, a Goldwater Girl in 1964 who went on to head the Young Republicans at Wellesley. Her political preferences later took another direction.

Of the Goldwater campaign's more senior figures, many went on to significant achievements. Bill Buckley—our philosophical guru, the man who, more than any other, set the conservative movement in motion—ran a quixotic race against the more-or-less renegade Republican John F. Lindsay for mayor of New York in 1965 as a candidate of a newly formed Conservative Party. He didn't expect to win (when asked, "What will you do if you win?" he replied, "Demand a recount!") and finished third behind Lindsay and runner-up Democrat Abraham Beame. However, Bill launched the long-running TV show *Firing Line* in 1966, was a delegate to the United Nations in 1973, and received the Presidential Medal of Freedom from President George H.W. Bush in 1991.

John Ashbrook continued to serve in the Congress, had some policy disagreements with Nixon, and launched a run for the Senate in 1982, but died early in the year. The Ashbrook Center for Public Affairs, at Ashland University, was established to house his personal papers and carry on his legacy.

Clif White worked on the successful 1970 senatorial election of Bill Buckley's brother, James, and on the Reagan election in 1980. He became director of the Ashbrook Center in 1983. When James Buckley was elected, he was also supported by my brother Harry, who was then leading the Conservative Party in Manhattan. William Rusher retired as publisher of *National Review* in 1988 but continues to write a syndicated weekly newspaper column.

Peter O'Donnell—our Cincinnatus, who did so much for the conservative movement and who could have had almost any job in any Republican administration—returned home to Dallas. Jerry Milbank continued running the family foundation and doing some behind-the-scenes politicking. Stets Coleman continued as an entrepreneur and philanthropist; the Coleman Foundation, established by Stets and his wife, specializes in support of cancer care, entrepreneurial education, and services for the disabled. Dean Burch was Barry's 1968 senatorial campaign manager and later served as head of the FCC, counselor to both Presidents Nixon and Ford, and chief of staff for the George H.W. Bush vice-presidential campaign of 1980.

Dick Kleindienst became attorney general in the Nixon administration but fell victim to the Watergate probe in 1973 (although he was not directly implicated). Fred LaRue and Bob Mardian ran the Watergate cover-up for Nixon; LaRue was the first conspirator to plead guilty and served about six months in prison. Mardian was convicted, but his conviction was overturned. Each was for some time suspected of being "Deep Throat" of Bob Woodward and Carl Bernstein fame. John Grenier ran for the Senate in 1966 against the Alabama powerhouse John Sparkman; he lost, but at 39 percent, his vote was the highest ever registered against Sparkman. Chuck Lichtenstein became Jeanne Kirkpatrick's UN deputy during the Reagan administration.

Congressman Bill Brock—a member of the December 2 "band of brothers"—moved up to the Senate in 1971, was later chairman of the RNC, and then served as U.S. trade representative and secretary of labor in the Reagan administration.

Lee Edwards went from Goldwater PR work to the world of higher letters, earning a Ph.D. from the Catholic University of America in Washington, D.C., and doing advanced studies at the Sorbonne in Paris; he was the founding director of the Institute on Political Journalism at Georgetown University and a Fellow at the Institute of Politics at the John F. Kennedy School of Government, Harvard. He is the

Distinguished Fellow in Conservative Thought at the Heritage Foundation. Lee is the author of sixteen books about the leading individuals and institutions of American conservatism.

Bo Callaway became secretary of the Army in 1973 and for a time was chairman of the 1976 election committee for President Ford. Frank Shakespeare, president of CBS Television Services during the 1964 campaign, later served as director of the U.S. Information Agency, head of Radio Free Europe, vice president of Westinghouse, vice chairman of RKO General, and ambassador to Portugal (1985–1986) and the Vatican (1986–1989).

George H.W. Bush became a two-term congressman (1966–1970), ambassador to the United Nations, special envoy to China, chairman of RNC, director of the CIA, and, of course, Ronald Reagan's vice president through two terms and then president of the United States for one (1988–1992). At some point along the way, he confessed to me that he didn't much like his boyhood nickname, "Poppy." However, I have retained its use on occasion in this memoir as a point of historical accuracy.

I had long thought of Nelson Rockefeller as a devious plotter, sitting in his castle on the river thinking of ways to spend his vast fortune in support of liberal causes. Among many New Yorkers he was a long-running joke: They called him "Old BOMFOG" because in almost every speech he gave, he invoked "the Brotherhood of Man, the Fatherhood of God."

But then I got to know him.

I'd had some tangential contact with him over the years—his brother David, the banker, was a good friend of mine, his nephew-in-law George O'Neill had been an usher at my wedding, and I did actually contribute to Nelson's first gubernatorial campaign. But my opinion of him had been soured—permanently, I thought—by his treatment of Barry Goldwater.

When Vice President Ford became president in 1974, he chose to fill the vice presidential slot with, of all people, Nelson Rockefeller.

One day, when I was lobbying the Congress for our shipbuilding program, Nelson and I—literally—bumped into each other in the Senate cloakroom. To my surprise, he was a most engaging fellow, very outgoing, who seemed genuinely interested in my efforts to boost the Navy. He said, "Bill, I'm somewhat underemployed here as vice president and I'm looking for a mission. I love the Navy. How can I help?" And I said, "Welcome aboard!"

With Nelson's tireless assistance, our program to build 156 new ships for the Navy was approved and signed into law in 1976. Sadly, one of Jimmy Carter's first acts as president was to cut the program in half. Our hard work, vital (in our reasoned judgment) to the national security, gone in the blink of a political eyeball. Welcome to Washington, where nothing is permanent. Some say this is the genius of American democracy. I demur: This case, at least, bears witness to the witless exercise of partisanship. But that's another story for another time.

Just after the 1964 election, I set down my immediate observations about campaigns and the political process. Some may be dated, some are certainly naive, but some are just as relevant today as they were then. Here, uncorrupted by hindsight (and unadjusted for the sometimes seismic changes in what is called "conservatism," in both economic and social matters) is my 1964 Goldwater Postmortem:

1. The liberals seem to campaign twelve months of the year—year after year. We conservatives tend to come out every four years. Success at the polls: the sum total of energy and judgment of every worker—at the local, state, and national level.
2. We must deal openly and fairly with the working press, and not treat them as an alien species. The press wants news, not PR. There is a difference, and we need to know what it is.
3. Raise enough cash, early in the campaign, to finance victory. Early money is worth at least ten times as much as cash that comes in on election eve. Election eve cash—like a bank loan—

only comes when you don't really need it. Also, be wary of people who say "go ahead and start and we'll take care of your
needs." Make sure you have some money in the bank first.

4. Beware the impractical, even if ideologically correct, candidate.
    Or the candidate motivated only by ideology. Either one will be
    trouble-prone, will embarrass you, and will not survive. Above
    all, have a candidate who understands the concept, "make sure
    brain is engaged before putting mouth in gear."

5. Keep smiling under every attack, never engage in personal at-
    tacks yourself. Ignore attacks by the opposition unless they
    move on the wires. If facing an incumbent, try to get your op-
    ponent into debate. If you are the incumbent, avoid debate.

6. Some "experts" say that, the higher the office, the more the
    candidate must be in charge of all details of the race. I dis-
    agree. Beware of candidates who write all of their speeches,
    plan their own tours. There isn't enough time in the day or wis-
    dom in anyone.

7. Seize on those few great moments when you have the whole au-
    dience. You're only looking for the "undecideds," but you had
    better know in advance who they are. And if you lose—don't
    just go on TV and lick your wounds but send a positive message
    to your supporters. You will need them again.

8. Concentrate on two or three gut issues and don't try to reshape
    the world with twenty issues at every campaign stop. And try to
    have one, at the most two, truly memorable phrases. Churchill,
    Roosevelt, Kennedy always had something pungent; but few
    honest men can remember anything useful from any speech
    Ike, Nixon or Truman ever made. LBJ had a great line, which
    he used over and over: "I am the president of all the people." I
    think he varied it once, "I am your only president." Barry did
    have one infinitely memorable line—"Extremism in the de-
    fense of liberty." Unfortunately, it was the wrong line.

9. The public likes a winner—act like one. Many people had a visceral aversion to Kennedy, but he acted like a winner. He had class.

10. As a movement conservative, I hold dearly the inspiration of our Founding Fathers, love of country (and, of course, the economic principles of Von Mises and the warnings of Hayek). However, in a political campaign where the opportunities to educate or explain are so brief, we must be wary of invoking the standard old conservative notions: They have the effect of telling persons without Revolutionary War forebears that they can never hope for success. A man whose father came from Poland in 1910 may be turned off by talk of "the values that made this country great." Or, a man who himself may have come from anywhere else. In any given year—yea, since the beginnings of the nation—about 10 percent of the population is foreign born.

11. By the same token, the typical "old" conservative is viewed by the average liberal as a person of the old WASP stock, probably running a small to moderate-sized business, granted thereby some level of power that he inherited, but of which he is no more deserving than anyone else.

12. Be wary of calls to "patriotism." All Americans are patriotic. To many of our ethnic minorities, notably black citizens, "patriotism" is associated with the actions of a white Anglo-Saxon plurality. Especially in the South, much of which has been ever ready to wrap itself in a Confederate flag.

13. We lost the battle of semantics. "In your heart you know he's right" was catchy, but no threat to the running Democratic promises: Roosevelt offered the "New Deal," Truman, the "Fair Deal"—who wants to be unfair? With "New Frontier," Kennedy added the power of myth. And Johnson capped them all with a call to a "Great Society" for everyone. What

did we Conservatives offer in return? Research teams, professors, position papers, brain trusts, millions of words. But few of them the right words. The Democrats had long since learned that most voters knew little, and cared less, about issues much larger than a stoplight. The Democrats appealed to emotion. To those of us who came into politics to spread the conservative economic gospel of Von Mises and Hayek, it was all a distraction, divisive of our goal to build a conservative movement. We appealed to logic. We lost.

CHAPTER 22

Coda

THE OPENING LINES FROM "The Framing Wars," by Matt Bai, in the *New York Times Magazine* on Sunday, July 17, 2005, said this:

> After last November's defeat, Democrats were like aviation investigators sifting through twisted metal in a cornfield, struggling to posit theories about the disaster all around them. Some put the onus on John Kerry, saying he had never found an easily discernible message. Others, including Kerry himself, wrote off the defeat to the unshakable realities of wartime, when voters were supposedly less inclined to jettison a sitting president. Liberal activists blamed mushy centrists. Mushy centrists blamed Michael Moore. As the weeks passed, however, at Washington dinner parties and in public postmortems, one explanation took hold not just among Washington insiders but among far-flung contributors, activists and bloggers too: the problem wasn't the substance of the party's agenda or its messenger as much as it was the Democrats' inability to communicate coherently. They had allowed the Republicans to control the language of the debate, and that had been their undoing.

If, indeed, the Republicans were able "to control the language of the debate" in 2004, I guess that means that we have finally figured it out. And that the Democrats have forgotten how.

Appendix:
Members of Draft Goldwater

Original members of the Draft Goldwater movement, meeting October 8, 1961:

John Ashbrook, Ohio, member of Congress

Charles Barr, Illinois, lobbyist for Standard Oil of Indiana

James Boyce, Louisiana, a nominal Democrat who was a volunteer for Nixon in 1960

Donald C. Bruce, Indiana, member of Congress

Robert F. Chapman, South Carolina, soon to be chairman of the Republican state committee

Ned Cushing, Kansas, banker and Republican state finance chairman

Samuel Hay, Wisconsin, businessman and chairman, Milwaukee County Republican Committee

Robert E. Hughes, Indiana, state treasurer

Robert Matthews, Indiana, former chairman of the Republican state committee

Gerrish Milliken, Connecticut, one of the owners of the textile firm Deering Milliken

Roger Milliken, South Carolina, brother of Gerrish and chairman of Deering Milliken

Roger Allan Moore, Massachusetts, attorney, counsel to the Republican state committee, and chairman of the board of the *National Review*

Robert Morris, Texas, president of the University of Dallas

David Nichols, Maine, chairman of the Republican state committee

Leonard Pasek, Wisconsin, businessman

Speed Reavis, Jr., Arkansas, a volunteer for Nixon

John Keith Rehmann, Iowa, businessman and Republican activist

William Rusher, New York, publisher, *National Review*

Gregg Shorey, South Carolina, chairman of the Republican state committee

Charles Thone, Nebraska, Republican National Committee member
Frank Whetstone, Montana, newspaper publisher
F. Clifton White, New York, public relations executive

Members added for the December 10, 1961, meeting (four of whom had been invited to the first meeting but were unable to attend):

Sam Barnes, California, former Republican county chairman
Sullivan Barnes, South Dakota, executive in the American Football League, former national chairman of the Young Republican National Federation
Edward O. Ethell, Colorado, public relations executive, former Republican county chairman, administrative assistant to U.S. Senator Gordon Allot
Albert E. Fay, Texas, Republican National Committee member
John M. Lupton, Connecticut, state senator and former public relations executive
William G. McFadzean, Minnesota, businessman
Donald Nutter, Montana, governor
Tad Smith, Texas, chairman of the Republican state committee
John Tope, Alabama, steel company executive, former national chairman, Young Republican National Federation

Members added at the December 2, 1962, "secret" meeting:

Hazel Barger, Virginia, Republican National Committee member
William Brock, Tennessee, member of Congress
Robert Carter, Colorado, airline executive, former assistant to Republican National Committee chairman Len Hall
J. Stetson Coleman, Illinois and Florida, philanthropist
John Grenier, Alabama, Republican state committee chairman
Ione Harrington, Indiana, Republican National Committee member
Patricia Hutar, New York, cochair of the Young Republican National Federation
Ed Lynch, New York
James Martin, Alabama, recent (defeated) candidate for the U.S. Senate
John McClatchey, Pennsylvania
J. William Middendorf II, Connecticut and New York, investment banker
Jeremiah Milbank, Jr., Connecticut and New York, philanthropist
Peter O'Donnell, Texas, Republican state committee chairman
Wesley Phillips, Oregon
Randy Richardson, New York and Georgia
Hayes Robertson, Illinois, chairman, Cook County (Chicago) Republican Committee

John Tyler, Oklahoma, cochair of the Young Republican National Federation
Wirt Yeager, Mississippi, Republican state committee chairman
Jack Whittaker, Ohio

Source: This information was assembled from F. Clifton White, with William Gill, *Suite 3505: The Story of the Draft Goldwater Movement* (New Rochelle, N.Y.: Arlington House, 1967).

Notes

CHAPTER 1

1, 5 *Goldwater, in some imperceptible investiture: Time,* August 8, 1960.

6 *In recent weeks, an organization:* Editorial, *New York Sunday News,* March 5, 1961.

7 *With tickets priced: New York Times,* March 8, 1962; Edwards 1995, 159.

12 *If we held a meeting:* White 1967.

13 *They determined to move forward:* Ibid., 23–25.

13 *One of the most remarkable clandestine operations:* Novak 1965, 119.

13 *A secret decision: Harvard Crimson,* July 11, 1967; that writer, Boisfeuillet Jones, is today the publisher of the *Washington Post.*

13 *Carefully selected friends:* See Appendix.

CHAPTER 2

19 *Senator Cotton won on the merits: New York Times,* October 11, 1962.

20 *A cooperative arrangement: New York Herald Tribune,* November 16, 1962.

22 *The President's Inner Circle: Human Events,* undated, 1962.

22 *First Family feared Goldwater:* Rusher, *National Review,* February 12, 1963.

22 *Better than 2 to 1 said: Congressional Quarterly,* April 3, 1963.

23 *I still haven't made up my mind:* Shadegg 1965, 54.

23 *Within the realm of reasonable possibility:* Edwards 1995, 165–166.

24 *Gallup poll on Republican "presidential possibilities": Time,* December 14, 1962.

24 *Well, we thought we might:* White 1967, 105.

25 *There's Dirksen with his fuzzy hair: Time,* March 16, 1962.

25 *The image is wrong now: Business Week,* January 19, 1963.

CHAPTER 3

28 *Thank you very much:* Letter, Barry M. Goldwater to J. William Middendorf II, January 25, 1963.

28 *Tea-leaf readers:* Rusher, *National Review,* February 12, 1963.

29 *At no time have I committed:* White 1967, 108.

33 *To convince these people:* Jack Bell, *Boston Sunday Herald,* March 3, 1963.

34 *Could do irreparable harm:* White 1967, 158.

37 *I am greatly flattered:* Letter, Barry M. Goldwater to J. William Middendorf II, April 9, 1963.

37 *I'm not taking any position:* White 1967, 121.

37 *I don't want the nomination: New York Times,* April 15, 1963.

38 *Come home, George: Detroit News,* May 3, 1963.

38 *Have we come to the point:* Transcript of speech, personal files.

39 *Goldwater is now way out in front:* Letter, J.D. Stetson Coleman to Jeremiah Milbank, Jr., and J. William Middendorf II, May 10, 1963.

CHAPTER 4

42 *Among professional politicians: New York Times,* June 13, 1963.

42 *A surprising number:* Cited in White 1967, 146.

42 *If the Republican national convention: Time,* June 14, 1963.

43 *Friendly to the Rockefeller wing: New York Times,* June 23, 1961.

44 *Hard-faced, implacable young men:* Novak 1965, 197.

CHAPTER 5

46 *Rocky Declares War: New York Journal-American,* July 15, 1963.

46 *Well-publicized personal triumph: Time,* July 26, 1963.

48 *It is my considered judgment:* White 1967, 160.

50 *Electronic memory device:* Shadegg 1965, 72.

51 *Goldwater for President ship: New York Times,* September 16, 1963, 30.

51 *Culprit was Baroody:* Goldwater 1988, 146–147.

CHAPTER 6

55 *People will start asking:* Bradlee 1975.

56 *"Goldwater Tells G.O.P. He's Willing . . . ": New York Times,* October 25, 1963.

57 *The chuckles were heard: Time,* November 1, 1963.

57 *An AP poll:* Goldwater 1988, 148.

61 *There is absolutely no truth:* Undated clip, personal file.

CHAPTER 7

63 *Well, Lyndon, I guess:* Goldwater 1988, 149.

64 *A slip of paper:* Ibid., 149–150.

64 *It became the great cliché:* Novak 1965, 252.

64 *Would involve a lot of innuendo:* Goldwater 1988, 151.

65 *Lose the election:* Ibid., 154.

66 *But Barry's Arizona friends convinced him:* Shadegg 1965, 92.

67 *I have no intention of running: Time,* January 10, 1964.

67 *I will seek the Republican Presidential nomination: New York Times,* January 4, 1964.

69 *As you know, Clif:* Shadegg 1965, 89–90.

69 *When they find you have made me somebody's assistant:* Ibid.

71 *Ready for a divorce:* Ibid., 88–91.

CHAPTER 8

73 *For mismanagement, blundering and sheer naiveté:* White 1965, 103.

75 *How can there be sanity: Time,* January 10, 1964.

81 *I do not believe that the mere fact: New York Times,* January 16, 1964.

81 *We are told:* Cook 1964, 160.

83 *I've never said, "Let's get out":* Edwards 1995, 210.

84 *If some of these colleges: New York Times,* January 23, 1964.

85 *Much of the press coverage virtually ignored:* White 1965, 105–106; *New York Times,* March 6, 1964.

87 *The briefing went so well:* White 1967, 255–256.

88 *I've got it made:* Perlstein 2001, 297.

88 *I'm not one of these baby-kissing:* White 1967, 268.

88 *His campaign strategy was perfectly tuned:* Novak 1965, 317.

89 *The final tally: Time,* March 20, 1964.

89 *Touted as the front runner: Time,* March 20, 1964.

90 *In one way, New Hampshire:* Shadegg 1965, 100.

CHAPTER 9

92 *Strategy session:* Shadegg 1965, 120.

93 *Maybe two and two don't make four: Washington Star,* April 16, 1964.

95   *When challenged about his lapse of manners:* Shadegg 1965, 108–110.

95   *The Eisenhower telegram:* Ibid., 114–115.

96   *Steve Shadegg complained:* Ibid., 111.

96   *I am the only man who cares:* Ibid., 113.

96   *Barry Goldwater ordinarily is an amiable sort: Time,* May 15, 1964.

97   *We had to destroy Barry Goldwater:* Goldberg 1995, 189.

97   *They set to work:* Shadegg 1965, 116.

98   *Goldwater's Plan to Use Viet A-Bomb: San Francisco Examiner,* May 25, 1964.

98   *Goldwater Poses New Asian Tactic: New York Times,* May 25, 1964, 1.

98   *Spencer-Roberts spent $120,000:* Goldberg 1995, 189, 191.

100   *He was not a fan:* Ibid., 194.

100   *In the meantime, an invitation: New York Times,* May 28, 1964.

101   *A fog of reasons was given:* Shadegg 1965, 123–124.

101   *A serious blow: Los Angeles Times,* May 29, 1964.

101   *Read anyone out of the party: New York Times,* June 2, 1964, 25; Edwards 1995, 223.

101   *The efforts of Kleindienst:* Goldberg 1995, 194.

102   *2,150,000 votes:* White 1967, 325.

102   *Ike had encouraged him:* Ibid., 337.

102   *If . . . his views deviate:* Ibid., 339.

103   *Even Rockefeller, speaking with reporters:* Ibid., 340.

103   *Looking at the future of the party:* Ibid., 342.

103   *I fail to understand:* John S. Knight, *Detroit Free Press,* June 21, 1964.

104   *Has no part of the heritage:* White 1965, 160.

104   *All that now was left for Scranton:* Novak 1965, 449.

CHAPTER 10

106   *Could be trusted to bar discriminations: New York Times,* March 29, 1963.

107   *Barry Goldwater is not my candidate:* "Editor's Notebook," *Detroit Free Press,* June 21, 1964.

108   *The people who have suffered: Arizona Magazine, Arizona Republic,* September 17, 1967.

109   *Some 98.5 percent: National Review,* December 1, 1964, 1053.

109   *In scores of Southern cities:* Rusher, *National Review,* February 12, 1963. Emphasis in original.

110   *In the 1962 U.S. Senate race:* Ibid.

110   *Their embrace does not: New York Times,* October 28, 1964.

110   *Since the power of the Democratic Party: Time,* July 26, 1963.

CHAPTER 11

111 *Another name for some ultra-rightist society:* Quotations by Scranton, Rockefeller, Lodge, and Romney from *Time*, July 17, 1964.

114 *The most troublesome plank:* White 1967, 361–362.

115 *Full implementation and faithful execution:* Republican Platform 1964, pamphlet issued by Republican National Committee.

116 *The* New York Times *grabbed the story:* All quotations from the transcript and Scranton's comments appeared in *New York Times*, July 10, 1964.

117 *Be starting his campaign here in Bavaria:* Goldwater 1988, 176.

117 *Senator Goldwater has decided: New York Times*, July 13, 1964, 18.

118 *Guilty of sloppy writing:* Goldwater 1988, 177.

118 *Despite a brilliant record:* Ibid., 180.

118 *In frequent and friendly correspondence: New York Times*, July 15, 1964, 21.

118 *To their credit: New York Times*, July 31, 1964, 10.

CHAPTER 12

121 *This bit of handiwork by an overzealous staffer:* All quotations in this paragraph are cited in Donaldson 2003, 172.

124 *As he taunted them:* White 1965, 201.

CHAPTER 13

131 *Clif White was "stunned":* Edwards 1995, 275–276.

131 *My God, he's going to run:* White 1965, 217.

131 *Senator Keating of New York:* Perlstein 2001, 391–392.

132 *Jumble of high-sounding contradictions:* James Reston, *New York Times*, July 19, 1964.

132 *In counterpoint, editors: National Review*, August 4, 1964.

133 *There's no more extreme action:* Edwards 1995, 277.

133 *The two sentences in question:* Ibid., 278.

133 *We were EXTREMISTS: New York Times*, October 28, 1964.

133 *Barry Goldwater could have recited:* Goldwater 1988, 187.

136 *Most older politicians: Newsweek*, July 27, 1964.

CHAPTER 14

145 *Advertising agencies:* Shadegg 1965, 97.

146 *They had engaged the services:* Ibid., 107–108.

147 *It's a rumor around here:* Transcript of broadcast, *Today Show,* August 24, 1964.

147 *The miscreants: New York Times,* August 27, 1964.

149 *That tastes like piss:* Perlstein 2001, 333.

149 *Most popular:* Edwards 1995, 287.

150 *The purpose of this book:* Howell 1961, 11.

150 *Goldwater—the man, the myth, the menace:* Cook 1964, 161.

151 *Orders from high up: New York Times,* August 19, 1964.

151 *I see no sense: Time,* January 10, 1964.

151 *I cannot believe:* Novak 1965, 318–319.

153 *To take all necessary measures: New York Times,* August 5 and 8, 1964.

153 *Meanwhile, the press was working:* All quotations in this paragraph cited in Shadegg 1965, 181–182, 199.

154 *Not as an equal:* Memo, Jack Valenti to Lyndon Johnson, cited in Schoenwald 2001, 154.

CHAPTER 15

159 *Perhaps 4,000:* Shadegg 1965, 202; Perstein 2001, 409–410; *New York Times,* September 4, 1964.

160 *For nineteen peril-filled years: New York Times,* September 8, 1964.

161 *The White House announced that: New York Times,* September 9, 1964, 31.

162 *Hung the nuclear noose:* Viguerie and Franke 2004, 83.

162 *The press conference held to celebrate the signing of the Code of Fair Campaign Practices:* Transcript of press conference, September 11, 1964.

164 *A Harris poll reported: New York Times,* September 14, 1964.

167 *A statement in which you make clear:* Perlstein 2001, 420.

167 *Should help to strip: New York Times,* October 6, 1964.

169 *The general manager of KTBC-TV didn't want to "disrupt": New York Times,* October 22, 1964.

169 *By September 8:* All quotations in this paragraph are quoted in *New York Times,* September 8, 1964.

170 *The possibility exists that:* Goldwater 1988, 204.

170 *Is manifestly unqualified: Saturday Evening Post,* September 19, 1964.

171 *Barry Goldwater has become the most slandered: Cincinnati Enquirer,* September 29, 1964.

172 *The first was a filmed address:* Shadegg 1965, 247.

174 *"Conversation at Gettysburg" was seen:* Perlstein 2001, 443.

176 *The calls, telegrams, letters:* Shadegg 1965, 245–246.

177 *One of LBJ's boys: New York Times,* October 17, 1964.

CHAPTER 16

179   *Kitchel, Baroody and friends had decided:* Shadegg 1965, 212–213.

181   *But that uncorrected snippet:* Ibid., 232.

182   *Do you want that to continue?* Ibid., 236.

182   *I have no intention of stopping:* New York Times, September 20, 1964.

182   *"Humphrey Charges Goldwater's Policy . . . ":* New York Times, September 20, 1964.

183   *I pledge to you:* Shadegg 1965, 237; New York Times, October 17, 1964.

183   *Audience reaction:* New York Times, September 19, 1964.

183   *Adding insult to injury:* Shadegg 1965, 268.

184   *Goldwater speechwriting:* Ibid., 213.

186   *At a campaign stop in Hammond:* New York Times, October 6, 1964.

187   *It was easier to gain an audience:* Novak 1965, 8.

187   *You go back and tell your crowd:* Edwards 1995,, 298; Shadegg 1965, 241.

187   *Well, we knew what we were getting into:* Hess 1967, 21.

189   *We are not going to send:* Steinberg 1968, 690.

189   *By a thumb on a button:* Public Papers of the Presidents of the United States: Lyndon B. Johnson, 1963–64. Volume 2, entry 648, pp. 1281–1288. Washington, D.C.: Government Printing Office, 1965.

189   *The reporter was still waiting:* Sabato 1991, 44.

190   *LBJ's study:* New York Times, September 4, 1964; Foley 2003, 54.

190   *LBJ had created a sixteen-man panel:* New York Times, September 11, 1964; Shadegg 1965, 215.

190   *Yesterday's race:* New York Times, September 11, 1964.

191   *You don't have to wait:* New York Times, October 6, 1964; Washington Star, October 11, 1964; Perlstein 2001, 437.

191   *Once, during a private meeting:* Shadegg 1965, 238.

191   *You do what the president:* Edwards 1995, 310.

191   *The chief of covert action:* Hunt 1974.

191   *George Reedy confirmed:* Goldwater 1988, 200.

191   *It may have been mere coincidence:* Goldberg 1995, 225.

192   *Deeply shocking and disturbing:* UPI, October 13, 1964.

193   *"A 'Spy' Double-Crosses Party Lines":* New York Times, October 14, 1964, 1; Shadegg 1965.

CHAPTER 17

195   *A concurrent Harris Poll:* New York Times, October 12, 1964.

195   *Dramatic event:* New York Times, October 6, 1964.

196   *Fought like the devil:* Chicago Tribune, October 24, 1964.

198 *Clark Clifford suggested:* Some years later, Clifford's reputation would be
     tarnished by his involvement in the largest banking scandal in history,
     the failure of the Arab-owned Bank of Credit and Commerce Interna-
     tional (BCCI). BCCI, seeking a toehold in the United States and with
     Clifford's assistance, engineered an unfriendly takeover of First Ameri-
     can Bank—a highly successful multistate banking company of which I
     was president and CEO from 1977 until the takeover, 1981. BCCI
     turned out to have been a massive Ponzi scheme, and failed, spectacu-
     larly, in 1991. Clifford was indicted by the federal government, but the
     case was dropped in deference to his age and poor health.

199 *It's a sad state of affairs:* Script, personal files.

199 *It is not so much that the American people:* New York Times, October 24,
     1964.

201 *The moral fiber:* New York Times, October 11, 1964.

202 *Gasped at how fast:* Time, April 10, 1964; the description of the *Choice*
     program draws from *New York Times*, October 21, 1964.

203 *The sickest political program:* New York Times, October 22, 1964.

204 *Johnson turned and grumbled:* Memo, Don Dornan to J. William Midden-
     dorf II, undated.

204 *Golden shower:* New York Times, October 18, 1964.

210 *A program of voter intimidation:* New York Times, October 30, 1964.

211 *Unaccountably, 60 percent:* New York Times, October 29, 1964.

211 *Goldwater is right in most:* New York Daily News, October 30, 1965.

212 *He was welcomed:* New York Times, October 31, 1964.

212 *Compulsory integration:* New York Times, October 31, 1964.

214 *We must crush for all time:* Republican National Committee "Victory Bul-
     letin," November 1–2, 1964.

CHAPTER 18

221 *I am convinced that conservatism:* National Review, December 1, 1964,
     1052.

221 *All of the landslide majority:* Ibid., 1055.

222 *Let me say this:* Notes, personal files, November 5, 1964.

223 *The data from 1962 until the convention:* Fortune, November 1965.

225 *Democratic reluctance:* Herbert E. Alexander, "Financing the 1964 Elec-
     tions," Citizens Research Foundation, 1965.

227 *Shadegg's poll:* Shadegg 1965, 265–268.

228 *You cannot campaign three months:* Republican National Finance Com-
     mittee, minutes of meeting, January 21, 1965.

228   *we know that 92%:* Fulton Lewis III, Newsletter of the Teen Age Republicans, undated [1965].

229   *Seeks to present the examinee:* Newsletter of the Republican Congressional Campaign Committee, September 13, 1965.

CHAPTER 19

231   *In a postelection poll:* Opinion Research presentation to Republican National Committee meeting, January 22–23, 1965.

233   *Dominated by the activists:* Mason 2004, 14.

236   *"Splinter groups" were destructive: New York Times,* August 27, 1965.

236   *How can research into the principles:* Goldwater, syndicated column, *New York Herald Tribune,* July 11, 1965.

236   *All of these ultra-conservative "out" groups: Los Angeles Times,* December 5, 1965.

238   *Mr. Bliss did not support:* Note, P.E. Binzel, Jr., to Treasurer, Republican National Finance Committee, April 11, 1965.

238   *I can understand the losers' strategy:* Letter, Harold N. Simpson to Treasurer, Republican National Finance Committee, April 9, 1965.

238   *Only when the Republican Party unites:* Undated note, Joseph Coors to Treasurer, Republican National Finance Committee.

238   *Eastern me-too Republicans:* Letter, Willard L. Veirs to J. William Middendorf II, April 2, 1965.

238   *I have no intention:* Letter, John Randolph Harrison to J. William Middendorf II, April 3, 1965.

239   *Bombing targets in North Vietnam: New York Times,* May 4, 1965.

239   *Barry Goldwater was talking about this kind of a military campaign: New York Times,* May 14, 1965.

241   *Dick Nixon is wandering:* Undated clip, personal files.

242   *Dick Nixon is in for a terrible shock: New York Times,* February 14, 1966.

245   *"5-minute broadcast" idea: New York Times,* May 14, 1965.

246   *In recent years, the Democrats: Washington Star,* January 23, 1966.

246   *"Congress Is Found Turning to Right," New York Times,* September 5, 1966.

CHAPTER 20

247   *A GOP House candidate: New York Times,* November 27, 1966.

247   *Bobby made a big hit: Chicago Tribune,* undated clip, personal files.

248   *They expressed regret:* Letter, Robert S. Allen to J. William Middendorf II, January 22, 1966.

249 *When you finish boiling down:* Letter, Barry M. Goldwater to J. William
     Middendorf II, December 23, 1966.
251 *Blind faith in the political luck:* Rowland Evans and Robert D. Novak,
     Washington Post, January 11, 1968.
251 *Well, you know when I came back:* Cannon 2003, 256.
252 *"I think," Nixon added:* White 1968, 129.
255 *No, I don't mind:* Transcript of telephone conversation, personal files.
257 *Going to "lock up" the 1968 Republican nomination: New York Times,* Febru-
     ary 14, 1966.

CHAPTER 21

263 Business Week *suggested: Business Week,* December 16, 1972.
266 *He was the Moses: People Weekly,* June 15, 1998.

Selected Bibliography

Much of the material in this book was drawn from memory backed up by an extensive personal archive of notes, memos, letters, recordings, and clippings. But at the outset, I knew that I could not frame an accurate history of our movement without input and corroboration from other sources. These sources are listed below.

Alexander, Herbert E. *Financing the 1964 Election*. Princeton, N.J.: Citizens' Research Foundation, 1966.

Beschloss, Michael, ed. *Reaching for Glory: Lyndon Johnson's Secret White House Tapes, 1964–1965*. New York: Simon and Schuster, 2001.

Bradlee, Ben. *Conversations with Kennedy*. New York: Norton, 1975.

Cannon, Lou. *Governor Reagan: His Rise to Power*. New York: PublicAffairs, 2003.

Cook, Fred J. *Barry Goldwater: Extremist of the Right*. New York: Grove Press, 1964.

Dallek, Matthew. *The Right Moment: Ronald Reagan's First Victory and the Decisive Turning Point in American Politics*. New York: The Free Press, 2000.

Donaldson, Gary. *Liberalism's Last Hurrah*. Armonk, N.Y.: M.E. Sharpe, 2003.

Edwards, Lee. *Goldwater: The Man Who Made a Revolution*. Washington, D.C.: Regnery, 1995.

Foley, Michael S. *Confronting the War Machine—Draft Resistance During the Vietnam War*. Chapel Hill: University of North Carolina Press, 2003.

Goldberg, Robert Alan. *Barry Goldwater*. New Haven, Conn.: Yale University Press, 1995.

Goldwater, Barry M. *The Conscience of a Conservative*. Shepherdsville, Ky.: Victor, 1960.

———. *Why Not Victory?* New York: McFadden Books, 1963.

Goldwater, Barry M., with Jack Casserly. *Goldwater*. Garden City, N.Y.: Doubleday, 1988.

Hayek, Friedrich A. *The Road to Serfdom*. Chicago: University of Chicago Press, 1944.

Hayward, Steven F. *The Age of Reagan: The Fall of the Old Liberal Order, 1964–1980*. Roseville, Calif.: Prima, 2001.

Hess, Karl. *In a Cause That Will Triumph*. Garden City, N.Y.: Doubleday, 1967.

Howell, Millard L. *An Answer to Goldwater*. New York: Vantage Press, 1961.

Hunt, Howard. *Undercover: Memoirs of an American Secret Agent*. New York: Berkley, 1974.

Mason, Robert. *Richard Nixon and the Quest for a New Majority*. Chapel Hill: University of North Carolina Press, 2004.

Mattar, Edward Paul, III. *Barry Goldwater: A Political Indictment*. Riverdale, Md.: Century Twenty-One Limited, 1964.

Micklethwait, John, and Adrian Wooldridge. *The Right Nation: Conservative Power in America*. New York: Penguin, 2004.

Nash, George H. *The Conservative Intellectual Movement in America Since 1945*. Wilmington, Del.: Intercollegiate Studies Institute, 1998.

Novak, Robert D. *The Agony of the G.O.P. 1964*. New York: Macmillan, 1965.

Perlstein, Rick. *Before the Storm: Barry Goldwater and the Unmaking of the American Consensus*. New York: Hill and Wang, 2001.

Rusher, William A. *The Rise of the Right*. New York: William Morrow, 1984.

Sabato, Larry J. *Feeding Frenzy: How Attack Journalism Has Transformed American Politics*. New York: The Free Press, 1991.

Schlafly, Phyllis. *A Choice Not an Echo*. Alton, Ill.: Pere Marquette Press, 1964.

Schoenwald, Jonathan M. *A Time for Choosing: The Rise of Modern American Conservatism*. New York: Oxford University Press, 2001.

Shadegg, Stephen. *What Happened to Goldwater? The Inside Story of the 1964 Republican Campaign*. New York: Holt, Rinehart and Winston, 1965.

Shirley, Craig. *Reagan's Revolution: The Untold Story of the Campaign That Started It All*. Nashville, Tenn.: Nelson Current, 2005.

Steinberg, Alfred. *Sam Johnson's Boy*. New York: Macmillan, 1968.

Viguerie, Richard A., and David Franke. *America's Right Turn: How Conservatives Used New and Alternative Media to Take Over America*. Los Angeles: Bonus Books, 2004.

White, F. Clifton, with William Gill. *Suite 3505: The Story of the Draft Goldwater Movement*. New Rochelle, N.Y.: Arlington House, 1967.

White, Theodore H. *The Making of the President 1964*. New York: Atheneum, 1965.

———. *The Making of the President 1968*. New York: Atheneum, 1969.

Index